DAVID LEWIS

Mind Skills

Giving Your Child a Brighter Future

GRAFTON BOOKS

A Division of the Collins Publishing Group

LONDON GLASGOW
TORONTO SYDNEY AUCKLAND

Grafton Books
A Division of the Collins Publishing Group
8 Grafton Street, London W1X 3LA

Published by Grafton Books 1988

First published in Great Britain by
Souvenir Press Ltd 1987

Copyright © David Lewis 1987

ISBN 0-586-20034-7

Printed and bound in Great Britain by
Collins, Glasgow

Set in Times

This book is warmly dedicated to Dr Sandra Shockley, an able and energetic advocate of the concept of helping all children to achieve their true potential, and to the staff and students of the Social Circle City Schools, Georgia, USA, for their enthusiastic exploration of the ideas underlying this home-training programme.

. . . every man should be wholly educated, rightly formed not only in one single matter or in a few or even in many, but in all things which perfect human nature.

John Amos Comenius, 1632

Do not confine your children to your own learning, for they were born in a different time.

Hebrew proverb

Human history becomes more and more a race between education and catastrophe.

H. G. Wells

Contents

Acknowledgements

I am grateful to the following authors and their publishers for permission to reproduce copyright material:

Fourth Rate Estate by Tom Baistow, published by Comedia.

Technostress by Craig Brod, published by Addison-Wesley Publishing Company.

Listening the Forgotten Skill by Madelyn Burley-Allen, published by John Wiley and Sons, Inc.

The Making of the Micro by Christopher Evans, published by Victor Gollancz.

The Aquarian Conspiracy, by Marilyn Ferguson, published by Routledge & Kegan Paul.

The Inner Game of Tennis by Timothy Galloway, published by Jonathan Cape Ltd.

How Children Fail by John Holt, published by Penguin Books.

Silicon Valley Fever by J.K. Larsen and E.M. Rogers, published by Allen & Unwin.

The Right To Be Intelligent by Luis A. Machado, published by Pergamon Press Ltd.

World Out Of Work by Giles Merritt, published by William Collins and Sons.

'The Pain that Lingers', by Nick Millman, published in the *Times Educational Supplement*, January 1985.

Megatrends by John Naisbitt, published by Macdonald/ Futura.

Crisis in the Classroom: The Remaking of American Education by Charles E. Silberman, published by Random House Inc.

The Psychophysiology of Thinking by Roger Sperry, published by N.Y. Academic Press.

The Wealth of Information by Tom Stonier, published by Methuen Ltd.

Straight and Crooked Thinking by R. Thouless, published by Hodder and Stoughton Educational.

Future Shock by Alvin Toffler, published by The Bodley Head.

A Kick in the Seat of the Pants by Roger Von Oech, published by Harper and Row.

Tools for Thought by C. H. Waddington, published by Jonathan Cape Ltd.

Whole Brain Thinking by J. Wonder and P. Donovan, published by William Morrow and Co. Inc.

I am grateful for permission to quote from an interview with Seymour Papert by R. Schultz, which was published in Vol. 8, No 1 of *Omni* magazine and to Drs Thomas, Chess and Birch, and the publishers of *Scientific American* for permission to quote from their article *The Origin of Personality* which appeared in Vol. 223, No 2, pp 102–109. August 1970.

My special thanks to Dr Bernice McCarthy for permission to quote from her excellent and innovative book *The 4-MAT System: Teaching to Learning Styles with Right/Left Mode Technique* which is obtainable from Excel Inc, 200 W. Station St, Barrington, IL 60010.

I should like to record my thanks to the many teachers and academic researchers who have stimulated my thinking about the nature of mind skills, especially those attending the 1984 Tarrytown conference, *The Coming Education Explosion*; Don Campbell; Dee Dickinson, of New Horizons for Learning; Dr Betty Edwards; Dr Reuven Feuerstein; Dr Howard Gardner; Jeff Haller; Dr Jean Houston; Dr Mel Kaushansky; Dr Luis Machado; Dr Bernice McCarthy; and Bob Samples. And also to the administrators, teachers and presenters at the 18th Fellows Program of the Institute for the Development of Educational Activities, 1985, for their stimulating comments and valuable insights. Also to Richard Armstrong for the illustrations.

Finally, I am – as ever – tremendously indebted to my associate Shandy Mathias for her tireless organization, inspiration and exertions both on our continuing research programme and in helping prepare this book for publication.

1

Mind Skills that Your Child Must Master

This is a book about your child's brain and how, with your help, it can function more efficiently. I will be describing a wide variety of easily applied, practical procedures for improving all aspects of thinking, from learning and problem-solving to decision-making and creativity. By enhancing these mind skills, you will enable your child to flourish, rather than flounder, in a world where brain power has replaced muscle power as an essential passport to success.

During the past decade, mankind has embarked on the most mentally challenging era in human history. In the words of American futurologist John Naisbitt: 'We now mass produce knowledge and this knowledge is the driving force of our economy.'

The computer revolution, which has so drastically reduced the demand for unskilled and semi-skilled workers, has no less dramatically increased employment opportunities for those using their heads rather than their hands. Never have brain workers been so much in demand or so richly rewarded. Never have the penalties for impoverished intellectual performance proved so severe. Already a gulf exists between those who can understand and use the new technologies and those unable to comprehend or cope with their challenges. By the year 2000, at a time when your own child may be leaving school in search of work or starting to carve out a career, that gulf will have widened into a yawning chasm.

Many social forecasters now predict the creation of a sharply divided workforce among all the developed nations. On one side, secure and prospering, will be an intellectual élite, possessors of the mind skills necessary for exploiting the opportunities of a brain-intensive environment; on the other, the second-class citizens of the silicon chip society, condemned by inadequate knowledge, obsolete skills or redundant expertise to dead-end jobs or a lifetime without employment.

Over the next ten years, in Europe alone, some twenty million young people will leave school in search of a job. Currently it is predicted that only one in three will be successful. In 1982, US unemployment figures were at their highest for forty-two years, with eleven million Americans seeking work, and an additional 1.6 million so demoralized by their lack of success that they had given up job-hunting. Although the number has fallen significantly since then, the underlying trends give cause for serious concern. Financial writer Giles Merritt, in his book *World Out of Work*, comments:

It is a cruel irony that the tens of millions of young Europeans destined to search fruitlessly for work . . . were born into an age of unparalleled prosperity and optimism. Their birthright was to have been greater economic wealth and sounder social progress than that achieved by their parents. Instead, most stand to inherit uncertainty and distress.

However much we may deplore the emergence of alpha and epsilon workers, foreshadowed half a century ago by Aldous Huxley in his totalitarian nightmare, *Brave New World*, there is virtually no possibility of halting the computer revolution. What one can do, however, is to avert its anticipated consequences by helping to ensure that today's children are given the best possible chance of succeeding in tomorrow's dauntingly demanding employment climate.

The challenge facing parents is, therefore, both serious

and urgent. The fact that you have been sufficiently interested to start reading this book suggests that you share this sense of importance and urgency. Tragically, this is not the view of many parents, who fail to appreciate the extent of the social changes wrought by machines with the power to manipulate and magnify the processes of human thought. Dr George Tressel, of America's National Science Foundation, warns:

Parents do not seem to understand that their children will live in a world where listening, talking, thinking machines are everywhere. The pressing problem is to give our children enough technological literacy so that they will be able to compete on this exciting new frontier. Otherwise they are destined to become second-class citizens of the new society.

One reason for the widespread reluctance adequately to prepare children to face these challenges lies in their unfamiliarity. 'Our thinking, our attitudes, and consequently our decision-making have not caught up with the reality of things,' suggests John Naisbitt. 'The level of change involved is so fundamental yet so subtle that we tend not to see it or, if we see it, we dismiss it as overly simplistic and then we ignore it.'

A second barrier to a more active parental involvement lies in the widely held misconception that teaching mind skills is a task so complex that it can only be undertaken by professional teachers, and that there is no role for untrained, albeit loving, mothers and fathers. Nothing could be further from the truth. Your help is not an optional extra, a useful addition to a basically sound system of formal education. In many cases it may be a child's best hope. For our schools are failing not just the unfortunate few, but the great majority of students. Far from producing trained minds, they are making bright, lively, energetic and enthusiastic youngsters dull, dispirited and apathetic.

For every child who discovers enjoyment in learning and attainment behind a desk, three others are intellectually and emotionally handicapped by their 15,000 or more hours of education. The failure of formal education is an important topic, and one to which I will return later in this book. Here let us just note that in many schools the methods used to prepare the workforce of the future remain deeply rooted in the educational traditions and social expectations of some forty years ago. The authors of a recent report on American schools have commented:

At all levels of schooling, a very few teaching procedures – explaining or lecturing, monitoring classwork and quizzing – accounted for most of those activities we observed in our sample of 1,016 classrooms. Teachers varied in the quality of their lecturing, but 'teacher talk' was by far the dominant classroom activity. Teachers rarely encouraged student-to-student dialogue or provided opportunities for students to work collaboratively or to plan, set goals . . . and the like.

In other words, the emphasis in too many classrooms is on *teaching* rather than on *learning*, with knowing 'what' being seen as more important than understanding 'how'. I am not, of course, suggesting that all schools fail to an equal extent, or that every teacher is blind to the urgent need for radical changes in educational attitudes and procedures. But the sad truth is that most young people leave full-time education utterly ill-prepared to face the challenges of a society where constant change has become the only certainty.

The third assumption many parents make is that a child's mental ability depends primarily on genetic inheritance, with the result that intellectual failures are attributed far more to inadequate nature than to ineffective nurture. This, too, is a fallacy – perhaps the most pervasive and damaging of them all.

Consider the belief in this light. Over the past 40,000 years mankind has undergone few, if any, evolutionary changes. The time span is just too short. This means that the same sort of brains one might have found in the skulls of Upper Palaeolithic hunters and farmers are contained in the heads of twentieth-century space pilots, neurosurgeons, computer programmers, writers, painters, genetic engineers, theoretical physicists, specialists in quantum mechanics, mathematicians, and managers of multinational companies. Yet nobody could dispute that, at least in most of these men and women, the brain's reasoning and creative powers are superior to those of our ancient ancestors by a factor of many hundreds! The explanation for such ever-increasing intellectual sophistication lies not in progressively superior genes, but in the brain's remarkable capacity for matching the changing demands of an ever more complex environment. Venezuela's first Minister of State for the Development of Human Intelligence, Luis Alberto Machado, has pointed out: 'With the same brain, the number and quality of creative men have been increasing constantly . . . The reason for the change is not biological. Education is the key. What has changed, and in turn caused change, is not the brain; it is education.'

In my book *You Can Teach Your Child Intelligence*, I remarked that every child is born gifted – gifted by nature with a brain of virtually unlimited intellectual abilities, and endowed by millions of years of evolution with the ability to grasp complex ideas readily and solve intricate problems effortlessly. Whether or not that tremendous innate promise is fully realized, however, depends on the lessons learned during childhood. It depends on you.

HELPING YOUR CHILD TO THINK SUCCESSFULLY

Fortunately, the mind skills your child fails to learn in class can be learned, with your assistance, at home. In the training programme described in this book, you will discover how to teach your child not what to think but how to think, not what to learn but how to learn. You are not going to teach facts and figures, which, as we shall see in chapter 2, could already be out of date, but to explain ways of retaining and recalling all kinds of information more rapidly and accurately. You will be showing your child how to solve problems more easily and more creatively, and how to make decisions more effectively, especially when working under pressure. You will learn how to improve the poor student's attitude towards schoolwork, how to motivate the under-achieving child and enhance the self-confidence of one who has come to doubt his or her intellectual ability.

Helping your child to develop and enhance vital mind skills requires neither professional qualifications nor previous teaching experience. Mostly you will be doing just what you would want to do anyway: playing games, talking and listening. You will be asking questions, but now in a special way; and you will be providing answers – again, in a manner which helps to expand brain power rather than simply satisfying curiosity. Already many hundreds of families have successfully used these teaching procedures, motivated by the knowledge that as parents they are in a unique and privileged position to set their children on the road to attainment.

THE SECRET OF SUCCESSFUL LEARNING

While your child is capable of learning virtually anything in the world, attempts to impose knowledge or skills through rote learning, tedious drill and constant repetition, even when successful, will have extremely limited applications. For instance, children can fairly easily be schooled, as they frequently are, to chant their times tables with mechanical precision. Yet their understanding of what they are saying, and why it is being said, remains minimal and they often prove incapable of generalizing that knowledge, of going beyond the information given to find answers to real-life problems. Furthermore, the boredom created by this strategy can strait-jacket the mind to such an extent that it becomes less and less capable of attempting, and increasingly unwilling to undertake, intellectually demanding tasks.

Successful teaching consists not so much of imparting new knowledge as of providing access to it, while at the same time stimulating and nourishing an individual's natural desire to learn.

You can demonstrate the truth of this statement for yourself by a simple thought experiment. Imagine that you decide to write down everything you have ever learned from the moment you were born to the present time. Your biography will include every single scrap of knowledge, item of information, experience and memory stored away in your brain during an entire lifetime. This has to remain an experiment of the mind since, in practice, the task would prove impossible. As new information is constantly being generated, only your death would bring the story to a conclusion, and, even then, with millions of thoughts left unrecorded. (It has been estimated that an adult's brain holds more information than is contained in all the British Library's more than nine million volumes.)

Before you had proceeded very far with the task, one thing would have become abundantly clear: the information gained in school, during those years of formal instruction, constitutes only a tiny fraction of all the things you know. What is more, most of that school-won knowledge serves little or no practical purpose. In fact, virtually everything useful that you know was acquired with little or no direct teaching, and many of the most vital lessons were learned before the age of five. During those first five years you learned, among many thousands of other skills, to walk, talk, dress yourself, find your way around, play with toys, make friends, paint, draw, manipulate building blocks, and operate a wide variety of grown-up gadgets; you discovered the difference between pain and pleasure, hard and soft, sweet and sour, up and down; you learned to name and coordinate the different parts of your body, mastered a whole host of intricate social rules regulating your behaviour, and maybe even found out how to calculate, read books and write your name.

Adults, especially your parents, played a vital role in this early learning. Yet it is most unlikely that they sat you down for formal lessons or tried directly to teach all those skills you mastered. So how did they help you to learn?

First, they demonstrated what was wanted and how it could be done. They walked and talked, cut up food and ate it off plates, drank out of cups or glasses, got dressed and tied their shoe laces. You looked and you learned. Now and then they slowed down their movements, repeated certain actions over and over again so that you could follow every stage of a task. Much of the time, however, they merely went about their normal lives, while you observed them and imitated them and practised again and again – first until you got it right, and then until the skill became so automatic that your brain could do it without a second thought. You absorbed this new knowledge easily and eagerly because, like all young children, you possessed an insatiable appetite for learning. Your intense curiosity about the world, combined with a powerful desire for mastery and control over, first, your own body, and then your surroundings, encouraged exploration and experimentation. You learned because your brain was highly receptive to new knowledge and eager to acquire fresh skills. And mastering this knowledge and acquiring these skills fine-tuned your intellectual powers even further.

Your parents helped by correcting or pointing out mistakes, while offering the encouragement and support essential to overcome setbacks and learning from your failures. By doing so they provided the three ingredients on which all successful learning depends:

1   Information – in the widest possible sense
2   Motivation – through encouragement and example
3   Security – safe surroundings in which to learn.

You teach mind skills in exactly the same way: by encouraging learning rather than imposing teaching. And while helping your child to think more successfully, you will also be discovering how to make even better use of your own brain. In doing so, you offer a model for your child to observe and follow.

If your child is going to develop an interest in solving novel problems, learn to persist despite frustrations, to communicate clearly, act confidently and think logically, you must learn to do the same – not just occasionally, but consistently, until these high-level mind skills come as second nature to both of you. Under these circumstances, children learn easily and joyfully, not because they are being brilliantly taught but because they are being allowed to use their inborn ability for brilliant learning. By making discoveries for themselves, through their own effort and ability, rather than having answers handed to them on a plate, they find these insights both meaningful and thrilling.

Seymour Papert, a pioneer of computer education and the creator of a unique learning language called Logo, describes this joy of self-discovery in a little girl who was using Logo to control the movements of a symbol, called a 'turtle', on the monitor screen. When she gave it a speed of 100 the turtle travelled rapidly. At speed 0 it stopped. After playing for a while, the ten-year-old had a sudden flash of insight. In one blinding moment of intellectual truth she solved, all by herself, a mystery which baffled mathematicians for millennia. She discovered what zero means. Papert recalls:

The girl became very excited about that. She realized that standing still was moving with a certain speed, namely zero. This means that zero is a number, as ten, one hundred, and negative ten are numbers. Greek mathematicians did not know about zero. Hindu mathematicians discovered it sometime later.

What does it mean to discover zero? The experience of this girl shows there was something deeper than using a symbolic circle to represent it.

Children with a desire to learn are active explorers of their environments. They exercise their curiosity, search for solutions and revel in making connections. Their learning is direct and personally meaningful. In short, they are developing, expanding and enhancing those mind skills which have taken mankind from the Bronze Age to the space age.

To help your child master the mind skills essential for future success, therefore, you need do nothing more complicated or demanding than you did during those early years of maximum learning. Namely, put into practice the ABC of effective teaching by:

1 Acting as an information resource
2 Building on the child's natural desire to learn
3 Creating secure surroundings in which to practise and perfect his or her mind skills.

If your child is aged between five and ten, now is an ideal time to start enhancing mind skills. He or she will, we hope, be eager to learn and highly receptive to the procedures I describe. If your child is older, and perhaps having problems at school or developing a negative attitude towards intellectually demanding tasks, do not despair. Much can still be achieved. It is never too late to bring about significant improvements in thinking, by making better use of the brain.

2
The Challenges Facing Your Child

Before considering the practical ways in which you can help your child to develop and perfect essential mind skills, let us take a more detailed look at what these skills are and why they will assume increasing importance in the years ahead. By understanding more fully the demands and opportunities of an information-based society, you will better appreciate the role that these skills will play in personal and professional attainment.

The challenges facing your child come under four main headings. All are related to the exponential growth in knowledge resulting from the computer's ability to manipulate, store, generate and transmit information.

CHALLENGE 1: THE CHANGING WORLD OF WORK

At the turn of the century, a majority of people in both Europe and the United States worked in agriculture. Whether sowing crops, raising livestock, felling timber, hunting or fishing, the pace of their lives followed the seasons and their lifestyle changed little from one generation to the next. Today, only 10 per cent of Europeans, and fewer than 3 per cent of American workers, earn their living from the land or the sea. In fact, more Americans are currently employed by universities than work in farming!

During the late eighteenth and early nineteenth centuries, the Industrial Revolution transformed both landscape and labour, with factories replacing farms as the main source of employment. Pastures and meadows disappeared beneath the urban sprawl of manufacturing plants, mills and mines. Small towns, unchanged since Roman times, grew into cities, while cities spread beyond their ancient boundaries into the surrounding countryside. One observer of these changes noted in 1785:

Coalbrook Dale itself is a very romantic spot. Indeed, too beautiful to be much in unison with that variety of horrors art has spread at the bottom: the noise of the forges, mills, etc., with all their vast machinery, the flames bursting from the furnaces with the burning of the coal and the smoke of the lime kilns.

Within the span of a single lifetime agricultural produce gave way to manufactured products as the basis of economic prosperity. Directly or indirectly, the Industrial Revolution affected the life of every individual, transforming social attitudes, religious beliefs and political aspirations. Increased affluence created greater personal expectations, and the need for a literate and numerate labour force led to the rapid expansion of education. It changed family life, the friends people made, the clothes they wore, the food they ate, the entertainments they enjoyed, the hazards they faced and the way they could die. Once under way, the revolution proved so powerful that no force was capable of resisting its self-generating dynamism. Social reformers like Charles Dickens protested at industrialization's inhuman consequences. The Luddites attempted to slow its momentum through intimidation and the destruction of machine plant. But the irresistible force of the revolution swept it remorselessly onwards, with no regard for either the protests of the intellectuals or the violence of the mob.

This revolution was characterized by one further significant feature: those living through it were, for the most part, unable to foresee just how profound and permanent was the transformation being wrought.

The same characteristics of rapid, radical, unstoppable change are present in the twentieth century's computer revolution. 'As with the Industrial Revolution, it will have an overwhelming and comprehensive impact, affecting every human being on earth and every aspect of his or her life,' writes computer expert Christopher Evans. 'Again, paralleling its predecessor, the Computer Revolution will run at a gallop, though its time course will be shorter.'

The computer revolution also possesses a driving force against which, as with the nineteenth-century revolution, neither protest nor anger can prevail. Like the Luddites, some of those working with computers have become sufficiently stressed to try to stem the electronic tide by violence. In 1978 a distraught postal inspector in the southern French city of Montpellier fired five bullets into the main post office computer, and a similar fate overtook an American computer which was 'gunned down' by an irate policeman. Other disgruntled employees have attacked them with hammers, axes and even fists, while more subtle sabotage has involved pouring coffee or soft drinks into the works.

Others warn that by relying too much on computers we devalue human ability, comparing our own brains unfavourably with the tireless speed and accuracy of the microchip. American psychotherapist Craig Brod cautions: 'As we grow more and more impatient with human imperfection and variation, we move further and further away from the very essence of our own humanity.' But despite widespread apprehension and anxiety, as well as the anger of its opponents, the second Industrial Revolution has proved as irresistible a force as the first. In 1980 a total of just over 700,000 personal computers were marketed by twenty-four companies. Three years later one company alone, Apple, sold more than one million. It has been predicted that by 1988 60 per cent of the American workforce will be linked to a computer, while already, in the world's financial centres, five times as many computers as humans are talking to one another at any given moment.

As office work increasingly replaces factory work, small and medium-sized service companies are taking over from major manufacturing concerns as major employers. 'Between 1980 and 1983,' says MIT's Professor David Birch, 'corporations with less than 500 employees raised their employment by 2.7 million.' In manufacturing, employment either was static or showed a decline. Out of twenty million new jobs created in the United States during the 1970s – the most at any period in America's history – only 5 per cent were in manufacturing and only 11 per cent in the goods-producing sector as a whole; 90 per cent of the total came from organizations which either provide services or create knowledge. Professor Tom Stonier warned a recent conference of company directors in London:

We are now seeing the rapid disappearance of the industrial workforce. It is probably correct to say that within 20 to 25 years it will take no more than 10 per cent of the workforce for all materials production. That 10 per cent will largely be people with advanced engineering degrees in factories and, as we already see in the United States, farmers with university degrees.

With the brain-driven sector of the economy now accounting for more than half their gross national product, the developed nations are seeing a rapid increase in the demand for the intellectually accomplished, combined with a sharp decline in employment opportunities for those lacking such mind skills. Where nineteenth-century machines amplified muscle power, silicon chip technology amplifies mind power. 'We are working ourselves out of the manufacturing business and into the thinking business,' says David Birch. A recent analysis of vacancies in the *Los Angeles Times* lends support to this view. Of 5,000 job offers, more than 75 per cent were for knowledge workers.

In the UK, the number of manufacturing jobs has declined by a quarter over the past decade, while the service sector, including banking, finance, insurance, medicine, teaching and the law, now provides employment for more than half the workforce. Such statistics are signposts in the shifting sands of social change. They point both to how far we have come and to the direction we are set to travel in, as new technology creates employment opportunities which, even five years ago, simply could not have existed. At the same time we are witnessing the gradual, but inexorable, extinction of skills once vital to industrial and commercial success.

According to a recent report compiled from data gathered by US government agencies, the doomed occupations include spot-welders, office typists, clerks and farm workers, all of whom are destined to 'go the way of the steam boat pilot and the blacksmith'.

CHALLENGE 2: KNOWLEDGE MACHINES

Most of the world's resources are finite. One day the last coal mine will close, the last oil well run dry. We will be out of natural gas, copper, nickel and tin. Knowledge, on the other hand, has the unique property of being endlessly renewable. Facts beget further facts. Information breeds fresh information. Computer technology provides the means by which this endless production of data may be elaborated, extended and exchanged most rapidly and efficiently. 'The production of knowledge has already become the key to productivity, competitive strength, and economic achievement,' comments management expert Peter Drucker. 'Knowledge has already become the primary industry, the industry that supplies the economy with the essential and central resources of production.'

The extent of this knowledge growth may be illustrated by considering the amount of information available at different periods during the last nine hundred years. When, in 1066, William the Conqueror stepped ashore on Pevensey beach, the sum total of mankind's carefully gathered knowledge could probably have been contained in a few thousand bulky volumes. These would have included information on agriculture, boat-building, metal-working, religion and making war. Over the next six centuries the production of new knowledge was so slow that not until 1665 were sufficient numbers of scientific papers being written to justify the publication of the world's first academic journals, *The Philosophical Transactions of the Royal Society of London* and, in Paris, the *Journal des Scavans*.

Between dawn and dusk today, as on every day of the year, academics and other experts will have put the finishing touches to some 7,000 scientific articles. But by next year this figure will be out of date. The number of papers is currently growing by around 13 per cent each year – a doubling of new information every five and a half years. Before the end of this century the number is expected to increase by 40 per cent, resulting in a doubling of knowledge every twenty months. This is partly due to the increasing number of scientists and technical experts – more are alive today than have lived in the whole of human history – and partly to the speed with which knowledge can be processed and communicated via computers.

The quantity of information now being dealt with as a matter of routine is well illustrated by a legal dispute between the computer giant IBM and a company called CDC during the 1970s. In submissions to a Minneapolis Court, IBM's lawyers asked CDC for some eighty million documents, later rising to 120 million, while CDC responded with a request for thirty million documents. When IBM complied and sent over the first seventeen million, they weighed 87 tons and needed 6,300 boxes to hold them!

Within the next decade it is expected that more than one trillion items of data will be on file in the offices of major corporations – 90 per cent on computers – and that simply storing other people's information will have become one of the world's most important businesses.

Biological limitations place an upper value of about one thousand items per minute on the nervous system's capacity for perceiving and processing information. Furthermore, we can only discriminate between as few as seven or eight pieces of incoming data simultaneously. When the demands being made on the brain outstrip its capabilities, we experience overload and our performance declines. You may have noticed, for example, that while it is easy to chat to a passenger when motoring in light traffic, you find it stressfully distracting to carry on the same conversation when attempting to reverse into a narrow parking space against the flow of rush-hour traffic. Since a single video disc is capable of holding the contents of the *Encyclopaedia Britannica*, and computers can deliver this information at a rate of more than a million items per minute, problem-solvers, decision-makers, planners and forecasters will have to become extremely skilled at rapidly evaluating and analysing data.

CHALLENGE 3: KNOWLEDGE ROT

Even after employment had moved from farms to factories, traditional skills remained sufficiently valuable to be worth handing down from father to son or from craftsman to apprentice. A few years' primary education was sufficient to meet the demands of factories and offices, while public schools included Latin and Greek to prepare the sons of gentlemen for Church, medicine or the army. Whether the pupil was aristocrat or commoner, however, the same assumption applied: an individual's education, completed in a decade or so, could provide enough knowledge to last a lifetime. Today knowledge and skills are highly perishable commodities. 'One of the most important effects of the rapid increase in the volume of information is that information is very rapidly rendered obsolete by the discovery of new facts,' comments Professor Conrad Waddington.

Let us see what this would mean to the career prospects of an imaginary student, whom we will call Jim Jones.

Jim was bright in class and went on to study chemistry at university. A freshman in 1970, he proudly mounted the graduation platform four years later to shake hands with the chancellor and collect his degree. He then got a job and began putting his knowledge to work. The years passed, and Jim married and raised a family. He also developed many outside interests, played squash, watched TV and went away on frequent trips with his wife and children. As a result, he had no time to keep up to date in his speciality. He never read a book on chemistry, subscribed to a technical journal, attended a conference or took evening classes. His firm was not interested in employee-training, and offered no incentives or free time for further education. So what sort of shape is Jim's knowledge in by 1980?

The answer depends on how fast new information accumulates in his subject. We will suppose that it is not an area where fresh discoveries occur every day, and that it takes a decade for the amount of knowledge to double.

If we let X be equal to the total knowledge available when Jim was attending his first lecture, then by 1980 it will have become 2X. The American researcher Dr De Solla Price uses the term *coefficient of immediacy* to describe the growth of knowledge over a specified period. In Jim's case, the coefficient is $\frac{x}{2x}$ or ½. Let us put it another way. Half of all the relevant information in his area of expertise did not even exist when he started his university career. So Jim Jones has experienced 50 per cent knowledge rot. Unless he goes back into education and works at updating his information, by the time he is middle-aged around 80 per cent of his knowledge of chemistry will have rotted away. He will be struggling along on obsolete expertise.

And, compared with many, Jim is fortunate. If he had chosen a faster-developing field such as computing or genetic engineering, the period over which knowledge doubles could be as little as two years rather than ten. Now Jim would find himself suffering knowledge rot from the moment he was handed his degree. Without constant re-education, Jim would celebrate his fortieth birthday with the knowledge that 90 per cent of his specialist knowledge was about as obsolete as a Model-T Ford.

Jim is fiction. But there are hundreds of thousands of men and women like him currently struggling to hold down jobs, while hard-won knowledge rots steadily inside their skulls. 'Five years out of college, 50 per cent of an engineer's knowledge is obsolete,' explains Judith Larsen and Everett Rogers in their study of California's Silicon Valley. 'Working engineers must be recycled. There has been a call for universities to provide off-campus, part-time graduate programs for engineers, and for industry to encourage engineers to spend up to 10 per cent of their time in graduate-level classes.' As Professor Waddington points out, 'The figures are pretty alarming to anyone who thinks all you have to do is to learn a certain number of facts at university and they will last you the rest of your life.'

CHALLENGE 4: THE HIGH SPEED OF HIGH TECH

On Sunday 18 June 1815, by a pioneering piece of information technology, the Rothschilds, with the help of some carrier pigeons, laid the foundations of their family's vast fortunes. At 11.30 that morning, the first shots were fired in the Battle of Waterloo. By dusk it was all over, troops commanded by the Duke of Wellington having defeated the forces of Napoleon I. England had to wait several hours for news of the victory to be conveyed by despatch riders and cross-Channel packet. Thanks to their pigeons, the Rothschilds were the first to know. They also knew that the stock-market would skyrocket when the news was announced. By investing heavily they turned a little knowledge into a great deal of hard cash.

Today, if a tourist uses her American Express card in a Brussels store, details of the transaction are sent from Belgium to Amex headquarters at Brighton. From there, the information travels via satellite and landline to Phoenix, Arizona, where computers check that the card has not been stolen and that the client's credit is good. Despite having to travel a distance of some 46,000 miles, the whole operation, including checking time, takes less than seven seconds. The customer leaves the store without ever realizing the remarkable technical achievement her purchase represents.

By the 1990s, at least 50 per cent of all American workers will be using electronic terminals as a matter of routine, and within offices, between offices and from one

nation to another, most information will travel electroni-
cally. Only private mail and special items will still be
physically transported by post. The changes brought
about by the speed with which knowledge is communicated will be just as far-reaching as those produced by the
quantity and quality of the data generated. 'Man's thinking will be transformed by the rate at which electronic
technology transmits information,' warned Marshall
McLuhan during the sixties; 'Speed is the root of our
problems today.' His prediction has proved only too
accurate. Not only has increased organization resulted in
an ever-accelerating growth in information, but the speed
with which that knowledge can be transmitted around the
world has transformed traditional notions of time and
space.

The printed word has many advantages. Books and
magazines provide the most private, direct and involving
form of communication between the minds of author and
reader. Because printing offers random access to information, enabling you to select items at will, move backwards or forwards through the text, check facts and
achieve high levels of comprehension by rereading
especially tricky passages, it remains the most effective
method for presenting complex ideas. The disadvantage –
and it is a big one – lies in the delay. Publications have to
be written, edited, typeset, printed, bound and distrib-
uted. Inevitably, some of the information they contain
may be out of date before it reaches the readers,
especially when the subject is a highly technical one. Even
in the early nineteenth century the French poet Alphonse
de Lamartine was complaining that 'the book arrives too
late'.

Today many people are either unwilling or unable to
wait. As a result, books in electronic form, read via a
computer terminal, and even pocket-TV-style 'news-

papers', seem likely to have replaced many forms of publishing by the year 2000. But the price of speed may be excessive simplification. I remember being briefed, on one occasion, by a TV interviewer before an item about my research into children's intellectual development:

I'd like you to explain your findings in some detail, tell the viewers why some children fail whilst others do so well in class, explain the link between anxiety and performance in school, talk briefly about the differences between left- and right-brain function and offer practical advice on ways our viewers can help their own children do better. We've got three minutes!

Many politicians now have their speeches structured in such a way as to include many short, self-contained comments known as 'speechbytes'. These are written to last from twenty to thirty seconds, complete with background, build-up and punch line. That way they may be easily edited into TV news bulletins. Similarly, commercials are designed to pack a maximum punch into a minimum space. The brief for the producers of even serious TV programmes is not to go above the heads of an averagely bright fourteen-year-old. For most programmes the intellectual pitch has to be even lower. 'We are all besieged and blitzed by fragments of imagery, contradictory or unrelated, that shake up our old ideas,' says Alvin Toffler.

The danger is that information provided in this way leads to a shallow, dangerously simplistic understanding of important but complex issues. Tom Baistow, a former Fleet Street editor, points out that the typical tabloid presentation of news, with a huge picture and 'massive monosyllabic headlines', can occupy so much of the available space that the story must be told in a 'blip'-sized chunk of less than eight hundred words. Front-page stories often have fewer than two hundred words. 'It is,' he remarks, 'a format which demands a degree of over-simplification perfectly suited to the dramatization of the trivial and the sordid into the sensational.'

To make matters worse, the high-speed transmission of fragmented facts, superficially presented and often absurdly dramatized, greatly reduces a person's powers of concentration. Many teachers have told me that the attention span among some students is so poor that it is impossible for teachers to talk on any one topic for more than a couple of minutes. If they try to do so, they learn the hard way that the children get bored and inattentive. They start complaining, grumbling and talking among themselves. 'After five minutes the murmurs of annoyance get even louder,' reported one Californian science teacher, 'and after fifteen the lecture collapses into a shambles.'

THE MIND SKILLS THAT THESE CHALLENGES DEMAND

As one might expect, these include such fundamental skills as retaining and recalling information, logical thinking, efficient problem-solving and effective decision-making. We have considered many of these while exploring the four great silicon chip challenges. But there are, in addition, other mental abilities which, although central to successful thinking, are seldom recognized as having a vital role to play in intellectual attainment.

To see what these are and why they have such importance, consider the three roles that your child will have to play to perfection in order to succeed.

1 The adventurer
Consider the qualities that have distinguished the great explorers, pioneers and adventurers down the centuries.

What does it take to venture into unknown territory? Self-confidence, an independent spirit, and a flexible mind able to adapt to strange and rapidly changing circumstances. When voyaging into the uncharted terrain of career-building in the year 2000, your child will need all these skills in good measure – and more besides. To provide the driving force to embark on intellectual adventures in the first place, he or she must have a strong need for achievement, a will to win, and the desire to establish goals and to strive to accomplish them. And this means not just material goals, of course, but also those concerned with personal growth and spiritual fulfilment. This holds true even when the goals finally attained are very different from those which inspired the adventure in the first place. Columbus set off for the New World expecting to discover India; Alexander Graham Bell tried to invent a hearing-aid and ended up with a telephone. The Russian physiologist Pavlov studied digestion in dogs and discovered the famous reflex.

'I find that a great part of the information I have was acquired by looking up something and finding something else on the way,' says science writer Franklin Adams, echoing an experience shared by many. How many times have you, too, started out on one course, but found yourself ending up doing or discovering something completely different? The important point is, of course, that like all adventurers you took that essential first step on your journey.

With so many of today's facts becoming tomorrow's fallacies, children must also learn how to learn, instead of being taught what to learn. It is far more essential for them to understand and apply general concepts, than to spend their time memorizing information of dubious accuracy and little relevance. 'Children must be taught how to seek out knowledge and use it – not merely to regurgitate facts,' says Professor Malcolm Fraser, Dean of Chemistry at the University of East Anglia. 'Knowing where and how to find out is more important than knowledge itself which, in any case, will soon become out of date.' Carl Rogers, the eminent American psychologist, considers that 'the man who is educated is the man who has learned how to learn; to adapt to change; so that the process of seeking knowledge gives a basis for security.'

To summarize – your child, like a successful adventurer, must develop self-confidence, independence, flexibility and a strong desire for achievement. He or she must be motivated by an intense curiosity to seek out knowledge and gain first-hand experience of the world. And in order to master the knowledge necessary for these voyages of intellectual discovery, the mind skills of rapid retention and accurate recall must be practised and perfected. Once the landing has been made and a stake to the territory claimed, however, a different set of skills have to be brought into play in order to exploit the discoveries. Now your child must don the garb of the artist.

2 The artist

A great artist turns raw materials into works of truth and beauty. He or she looks at a block of marble and sees the finely sculptured head concealed within. Tubes of paint and stretched canvas are transformed into landscapes, portraits, compelling abstracts. Metal, wood, paper, clay . . . what exists is, for the artist, less important than what might be brought into existence. Intellectual adventuring provides the raw materials in the form of facts and figures, concepts, themes, visions, hunches, ideas and associations. Intellectual artistry takes these intangibles and creates something real: a building, a theory about the way nature works, a drug, a drama, a business plan or the patent for self-lighting cigars.

Here imagination and intuition, the ability to see beyond the boundaries of what *is* to discern what *might be*, are the keys to achievement. With so many careers demanding increasing specialization, the specialists who can also think like generalists and look beyond their individual areas of expertise will become increasingly valued. Such men and women will serve as the blenders, mixers and synthesizers of knowledge, teasing out and then drawing together strands of discovery from a variety of sources in their search for fresh meanings and original creations.

With an idea conceived, your child must have the creative energy and enthusiasm to take it out into the world and persuade others to share his or her vision. To do so he or she must doff the beret and step into running shoes. For the skills needed now are those of the athlete.

3   The athlete
Just as the world's most superbly developed physique only proves its worth when strength, stamina and agility are put to the test, so must the most inspired ideas be transformed by action before they can acquire utility. To convince others of the soundness of new ideas, to instil the enthusiasm and conviction needed in order to over-come obstacles to attainment, your child will need powers of persuasion and clarity of expression. In order to enjoy the cooperation and confidence of others, he should be emotionally warm and empathic. He should also develop the sports champion's determination, self-discipline and desire for perfection, so that he is constantly driven to stretch and extend the limits of his mind. For, as with the muscles of the body, the cells of our brains perform best when exercised regularly and worked hard.

*   *   *

Adventurer, artist, athlete – these are the three activities which best characterize the mind skills your child must master in order to survive and prosper in the year 2000.

It is, you will agree, a formidable list of accomplishments. Yet by the end of this century, these skills are likely to have become commonplace in the high achievers capable of finding success and fulfilment in challenging occupations. The good news is that, because all these skills can be learned, every child has the chance to acquire them and every parent can assist in their mastery. They are created when the inquiring mind of the child comes into contact with an environment that stimulates and stretches it. However, as with all complex and demanding skills, the right kind of help is needed if children are to get the best from their brains. And since there are no short cuts to successful thinking, the earlier these mind skills are learned the more effortlessly and effectively they will be employed.

3

How Your Child's Brain Works Best

If you were to slice off the top of a human skull and examine the pinkish-grey matter of the brain, you would find that it consisted of two partially separated hemispheres, linked by a broad band of connective tissue called the *corpus callosum*. Containing some 200 million nerve fibres, it functions like a vastly complex telephone exchange, not merely passing millions of messages between the left and right hemispheres, but also making decisions about which signals can be allowed through.

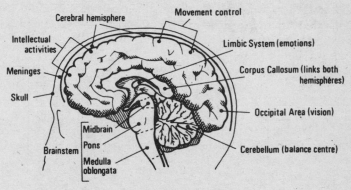

Fig. 1   The functions of the brain

As early as the nineteenth century, neurologists recognized that different areas of the brain were designed to perform specific functions (see figure 1). During the 1860s, for instance, a French surgeon named Paul Broca discovered that our powers of speech are usually controlled by the left side of the brain. Later, Carl Wernicke,

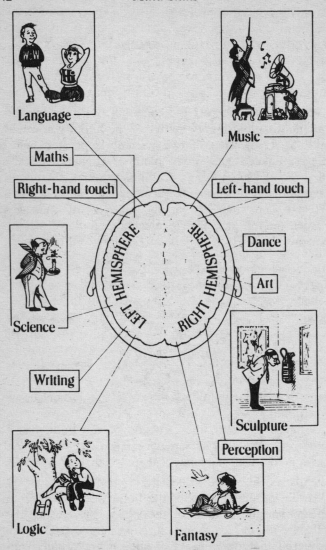

Fig. 2 The right and left sides of the brain

a twenty-six-year-old professor at the University of Bres-lau, identified a second area, also on the left side of the brain, responsible for making sense of the spoken word. Findings like these suggested that the left and right hemispheres were likely to perform rather different tasks. But it was not until the present century that the full extent of these differences was recognized, as a result of studies on patients whose corpus callosum had been severed during operations to prevent violent epileptic seizures. The result was that all communication between left and right hemispheres ceased, leaving the patients with what were essentially two independently operating brains con-tained within the same skull.

Although obviously drastic, this surgery put an end to the seizures which had defied all other methods of treat-ment, and appeared to have no significant side effects. Patients seemed able to function perfectly well with their split brains. It was only during the 1960s, when their intellectual performance was subjected to detailed exami-nation by Dr Roger Sperry and his co-workers at the University of Chicago and the California Institute of Technology, that remarkable differences came to light. In Dr Sperry's own words, their research 'suggested new concepts and new lines of thought and . . . opened up a wealth of new possibilities for investigating the mysteries of the mind'.

As figure 2 shows, the left side of the brain has a primary responsibility for language, and tasks requiring a logical, methodical and analytical approach, such as maths problems. The left brain keeps track of time and operates rationally. Its mode of operation is linear – that is, it proceeds by linking one idea to the next so as to arrive at a conclusion.

The right hemisphere, by comparison, is non-verbal and non-rational. It deals in images and intuitions, bringing together disconnected ideas and creating fresh unities. Its special talents include music, painting, sculpture, movement and dance. We are using the right side when we have hunches or gut reactions to a situation, when we suspend judgement and come to a conclusion that apparently flies in the face of the facts.

The right brain is good at seeing the forests but bad at spotting individual trees; the left brain excels at finding the trees but, in doing so, sometimes overlooks the forest. While the left brain requires hard facts before reaching a conclusion, the right is happier dealing with uncertainties and elusive knowledge. It favours open-ended questions, problems for which there are many answers rather than a single, correct solution. The left is most responsive to sights and sounds, the right to touch, taste and movement. The left specializes in precise descriptions and exact explanations; the right enjoys analogies, similes and metaphors. The left demands structure and certainty; the right thrives on spontaneity and ambiguity. The left is good at remembering names; the right is better at recalling faces. The left thinks with language and logic; the right reasons using images.

What the left brain does best	*What the right brain does best*
Explaining with words	Explaining visually
Remembering using language	Remembering using images
Step-by-step thinking	Holistic thinking
Controlling emotions	Expressing emotions
Taking life seriously	Approaching life playfully
Working with facts	Working with pictures
Analysis	Synthesis
Logical reasoning	Intuitive understanding
Practical tasks	Abstract tasks
Structured activities	Fluid, open activities
Organization	Improvisation

In her fascinating book *Drawing on the Right Side of the Brain*, American psychologist Dr Betty Edwards summarizes the differences like this:

We now know that despite our normal feeling that we are one person – a single being – our brains are double, each half with its own way of knowing, its own way of perceiving external reality. In a manner of speaking, each of us has two minds, two consciousnesses, mediated and integrated by the connecting cable of nerve fibers between the hemispheres.

She also offers an intriguing demonstration of left-brain/right-brain differences that you may like to try.

Take a line drawing with plenty of detail in it and make a copy (not a tracing), with the illustration the right way up. Now set it aside for a while, and then repeat the task, only on this occasion turn the illustration *upside down* before making your copy. This time, of course, the copy will also be upside down, but you must make no attempt to reverse it while drawing. Start at the top and fit the parts together like a jig-saw puzzle. If you come across parts which might be named – a face, a house, a tree and so on – refrain from doing so. Do not verbalize, just draw. When you have finished, compare the two copies. Unless you are already a skilled artist, you will probably find that the upside-down copy is superior to the right-way-up version. You may also notice that making the inverted copy is far easier and more enjoyable. Why? Betty Edwards believes a plausible explanation is that the left brain declines the task of processing the inverted illustration: 'Confused and blocked by the unfamiliar image and unable to name or symbolize as usual, (the left hemisphere) turned off, and the job passed over to the right hemisphere. Perfect! *The right brain is the hemisphere appropriate for the task of drawing*. Because it is specialized for the task, the right brain finds drawing easy and enjoyable.'

So long as the corpus callosum remains intact, there is a considerable overlap between the functions of each hemisphere. Most people, for example, possess some language ability in the right hemisphere, so that should an accident destroy their major left-hemisphere speech centres they often recover limited powers of conversation by switching to the right side of the brain.

Because the left hemisphere controls the right side of the body, while the right is responsible for controlling the left, an injury to the right hemisphere could produce paralysis in the left arm or leg. This means that left-handed people are more likely to be right-brain-dominant (although this is not invariably the case). It may be that many right-handed, right-brained people are natural left-handers who adapted early on in life. Some evidence for this can be seen from the fact that whereas in the early 1930s there were an estimated 2 per cent of left-handed people in the USA, today this proportion has risen to around 15 per cent – an increase probably due to parents and teachers no longer compelling left-handed children to use their right hands. It is, however, hazardous to base decisions about left- or right-brain dominance on handedness, because there are probably many natural left-handers who, as children, chose to use their right hands rather than appear different from their companions.

There are also developmental trends in brain preference, with the left hemisphere exerting increasing influence from early childhood onwards, both as a result of the greater use of language and because our society strongly favours left-brain thinkers. Scientists and technologists, for example, are usually more highly regarded and rewarded than painters, dancers and musicians. Furthermore, as Jacquelyn Wonder and Priscilla Donovan point out in their book *Whole Brain Thinking*, 'Cultures that prefer mystical, involved, intangible, and artistic values are not politically or socially powerful . . . American Indian, black and Hispanic groups generally have right-brain values.'

In order to succeed, therefore, members of these minority groups must adopt left-brain thinking. So, too, must children when they start going to school.

SCHOOLWORK AND BRAIN WORK

In class, students are expected to acquire knowledge one step at a time, adding methodically to their storehouse of facts until they have sufficient to pass an examination. This demands left-brain skills. The problems students are given to solve more often demand an analytical than an intuitive approach. This, too, as we have noted, is a task for the left hemisphere. Written work, by which ability is chiefly evaluated, must be organized, well argued and logically structured. As we have seen, writing, organization and sequencing are all left-brain skills.

The students considered most intelligent and successful are those who strive after academic goals, can control their emotions in class, follow instructions, do not ask awkward questions, are punctual and hand in class assignments on time. Goal-setting, emotional restraint, time-keeping and matching your behaviour to other people's expectations are all left-brain skills. Children are meant to learn by listening, keeping notes and reading books. All these, too, of course, are tasks in which the left hemisphere specializes.

No wonder, therefore, that children who are natural left-brain thinkers will regard school studies as far easier and much more enjoyable than will those who favour the right side of their brains. The former will be advantaged,

Mind Skills

the latter disadvantaged, by the way in which information is prepared and presented during most lessons in the vast majority of classrooms. 'Our educational system, as well as science in general, tends to neglect the non-verbal form of intellect,' comments the pioneer of split-brain studies, Dr Roger Sperry. 'What it comes down to is that modern society discriminates against the right hemisphere.'

And he is not describing a small number of children unfortunate enough to form a minority of right-brain thinkers in a left-brain-dominant world. Research in both the UK and the USA suggests that a significant proportion of students remain right-brain thinkers all the way through their school careers. These findings, based on a study of more than 600 students aged between eleven and sixteen, are shown in table 1.

Table 1   Brain preference

	Left-brain-dominant (percentages)	Right-brain-dominant (percentages)	Both hemispheres used equally (percentages)
Boys	34	51	15
Girls	23	44	33

What this means is that in an average mixed-sex class with thirty children, one might expect to find nearly half of them handicapped, not by lack of intelligence but because the way they are being taught conflicts with the way their brains work best. 'The over-emphasis on left-brain thinking operations continues even though we know that the greater achievements of the human mind require the integrated functioning of both hemispheres of the brain,' comments American educationalist Bob Eberle. 'If our goal is to develop healthy personalities, if we desire to cultivate creativity to the fullest, then it becomes necessary to teach for hemispheric harmony.'

HOW YOUR CHILD'S BRAIN WORKS BEST

It is likely that you already have a shrewd idea of how your child prefers to use his or her brain. For instance, a very neat, methodical child who likes maths more than music, and is better at writing than drawing, is more likely to be left- than right-hemisphere-dominant. Equally, a dreamy, intuitive, emotional child who loves art but is hopeless at science, who paints and draws with flair but finds it hard to express ideas verbally, will almost certainly have a more active right hemisphere.

Knowing whether your child is left-brain-dominant or right-brain-dominant, or has a more integrated brain, is an important first step in teaching mind skills. By analysing the extent of any dominance, using the easily administered questionnaire below, you can gain a far clearer understanding of his or her intellectual strengths and weaknesses. These insights may then be used to improve motivation, increase self-confidence and transform mentally demanding tasks from chores into exciting challenges. By exploring your own brain preferences, you will be able to discover whether these complement those of your child, or conflict in a way that could lead to mutual misunderstandings.

Carry out the assessments that follow at a time when neither you nor your child feels stressed or pressured. Not surprisingly, children are sometimes wary when asked to complete this sort of test, out of concern that the results will somehow be used to make them appear stupid or inadequate. This makes them reluctant to answer, and anxious while doing so. They may also try to provide the responses they believe adults want to see – a form of bias called 'faking good'. The best way of preventing this problem is by ensuring a pleasant, reassuring atmosphere in which to complete the assessment. Do this by:

1 Making it clear that it is *not* an IQ test, or other measure of intellectual ability. He or she is not going to be evaluated on the outcome.

2 Never putting pressure on your child to complete the assessment. If he or she is not willing to answer the questions, respect that decision. Either complete the form yourself, or try again in a few days' time.

3 Allowing your child to select the time and place for completing the assessment. That way you will avoid a clash with favourite TV programmes, playing games with friends and so on.

4 Discussing the results and using them as the basis for an exploration of the meaning of different mind styles and ways of looking at life.

Your child should complete the assessment below by ticking, or noting on a separate sheet of paper, his or her chosen answers to each of the ten questions. In question 6, time how long the child takes to come up with an answer. If no answer has been given within ten seconds, tell her or him to move to the next question, but when doing so do not imply by your tone that he or she has failed. Remember there are *no* right or wrong responses in this assessment.

Assessment 1 – for your child to complete

1 Which of these three subjects do you most enjoy?
   (a) Art?   (b) English?   (c) Arithmetic?
2 Do you like taking part in contests and competitions:
   (a) Seldom or never?   (b) Occasionally?
   (c) Most of the time?

3 The TV has broken down and there is half an hour before you go to bed. Would you sooner pass the time by:

    (a) Painting or drawing?   (b) Reading a book?

    (c) Playing with a construction toy, such as Lego?

4 Glance quickly at figure 3. Is the face

    (a) smiling or   (b) frowning?

Fig. 3

5 In an English class, you have to do one of three writing assignments. Would you sooner:

    (a) Invent a fantasy story?

    (b) Describe something that you did during the holiday?

    (c) Explain how to build or make something?

6 What do you think the figure shows?

Fig. 4

7 Which drawing illustrates the way you hold your pen or pencil when writing or drawing?

   (a) 5a?   (b) 5b?   (c) 5c?   (d) 5d?

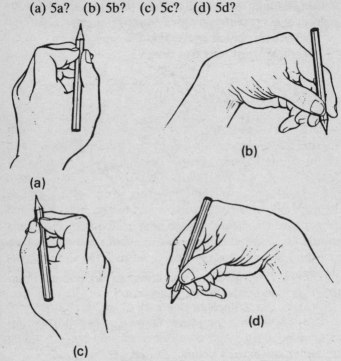

Fig. 5   The four ways of holding a pencil

8 Which of these would you sooner be?
   (a) Musician or painter?
   (b) Writer or photographer?
   (c) Scientist or engineer?
9 After hearing a song a few times, can you remember:
   (a) The music more easily than the words?
   (b) Both words and music?
   (c) The words better than the tune?

10   Hold a pencil upright, at arm's length, and line it up with a door or window frame. Now shut your left eye and notice whether the pencil moves. Repeat, closing your right eye. Did the pencil move *least*:

    (a) With your left eye closed?

    (b) With your right eye closed?

Scoring the assessment

Award 5 points for every (a) response ticked, 3 for each (b) and 0 for every (c), for all except questions 4, 6, 7 and 10. In question 4, answer (a), smiling, scores 5 points but (b), frowning, gets no points. Question 6 depicted a man on a horse. If your child saw this within five seconds, award 5 points; between five and ten seconds, 3 points; longer than ten seconds, or no answer, 0 points. No points should be awarded for any wrong answer, no matter how fast the response. In question 7, score 5 for an (a) or (d) response and 0 for (b) or (c). In question 10, award 5 points for (a) and 0 for (b).

Before I explain why some of these questions were selected, and what the scores signify, you may be interested in analysing your own brain function by responding to the ten statements below.

Assessment 2 – for you to complete

1   Do you have vivid dreams which you recall easily on waking:

    (a) Frequently?   (b) Occasionally?

    (c) Rarely or never?

2   When given directions to an unfamiliar address, do you usually:

    (a) Visualize the route being described and take no notes?

(b) Sketch a map?

(c) Rely mainly on written notes?

3 While writing, do you print your letters:

(a) Frequently?   (b) Occasionally?

(c) Rarely or never?

4 When talking to people, do you emphasize your points with gestures:

(a) Almost always?   (b) Occasionally?

(c) Seldom or never?

5 If you guess the time, after not having looked at a watch or clock for several hours, are you usually:

(a) Out by more than 15 minutes?

(b) Accurate to within 15 minutes?

(c) Accurate to within 5 minutes?

6 As in question 10 of Assessment 1, hold a pencil upright, at arm's length, and line it up with some vertical feature, such as a door or window frame. Close your left eye, and notice whether the pencil moves. Now close your right eye. Did the pencil move *least*:

(a) With your left eye closed?

(b) With your right eye closed?

7 Sit in a relaxed position and clasp your hands in your lap. Now look at your thumbs. Are they resting so that:

(a) The right thumb is on top?

(b) They are side by side?

(c) The left thumb is on top?

8 After meeting people for the first time, can you usually:

(a) Remember faces better than names?

(b) Recall both names and faces with equal ease?

(c) Bring names to mind more easily than faces?

9 Would you sooner work in a job where:

(a) There is little or no routine?

(b) There is a mixture of routine activities and new challenges?

(c) Work follows a familiar routine with few surprises?

10   Do you rely on intuition and follow your hunches:
   (a) Frequently?   (b) Now and then?
   (c) Seldom or never?

Scoring your assessment

Award yourself 5 points for each (a) response ticked, 3 for every (b) and 0 for each (c), except on question 6, where you score 5 points if you ticked (a) but no points for (b). As with Assessment 1, this gives a possible maximum of 50 and a minimum score of zero.

As you will be referring to these scores a little later in the book, it will be helpful to make a note of them, using table 2 – to avoid marking the book, you can copy the table onto a separate piece of paper.

Table 2   Scores on assessments 1 and 2

Assessment	Myself	Partner	Child	Child	Child
1	—	—			
2			—	—	—

The reasoning behind most of the questions and statements in these two assessments should be apparent from the description of how the two hemispheres of the brain specialize in different tasks. As we saw, right-brain-dominant children prefer art and music to maths and science. Remembering names is a left-brain skill, while recalling faces involves the right side of the brain to a greater extent. Right-brain-dominant adults enjoy having more variety in their working life, while left-brain dominants cope better with routine. Keeping track of the time is more a left- than a right-hemisphere skill. The reasons for choosing some of the other questions are, however, rather less obvious. Here is how they help to assess brain dominance.

Assessment 1
Question 2 'Do you like taking part in contests and competitions?' Studies suggest that children who are strongly left-brain-dominant are more likely to be competitive than those whose right brain dominates. The latter prefer to compete with themselves and seek their rewards within the activity itself, rather than needing to win approval and admiration from others.

Question 4 When glancing briefly at the drawing of the face with an ambiguous expression, a left-brain-dominant child tends to focus on the turned-down side of the mouth, and so concludes that the face is frowning. A child with right-brain dominance, by comparison, first notices the upturned side of the mouth and so sees a smiling expression.

Question 6 Finding meaning in such a pattern is more easily accomplished by the right side of the brain. The more quickly and accurately this task is accomplished, the greater the right-hemisphere dominance is likely to prove.

Question 7 The way a child or an adult holds his or her writing implement depends on the location of his or her brain's main language centre. As we have seen, this is usually found in the left hemisphere, although it can also be located on the right side of the brain. Studies by University of Chicago neurologist Jerre Levy, a pioneer researcher of left-brain/right-brain differences, show that when a right-handed person holds a pen or pencil as shown in illustration (c) or a left-hander as depicted in (b)

– a writing style used by 60 per cent of left-handed people – their language centre will be located on the left side of the brain. If the pen or pencil is held as in (d) by a right-handed person, or as in (a) by a left-handed person, then language is primarily a right-hemisphere function. This suggests that their right brain is more likely to dominate.

Question 10 (Also question 6 of Assessment 2) The pencil test is based on the fact that most people make one of their eyes work harder than the other. When the pencil is viewed through the dominant eye, the smallest movements are observed. Because of contralateral brain control, favouring the right eye indicates left-hemisphere dominance and vice versa. If the pencil moves least when viewed with the left eye, therefore, it indicates right-hemisphere dominance, and if it moves least when viewed through the right eye, left-brain dominance is suggested.

Assessment 2
Question 7 Studies have shown that people whose right hemisphere is more dominant are more likely to rest the right thumb on top of the left when clasping their hands in this way. The left thumb on top therefore shows left-brain dominance, while thumbs placed side by side reveal a more integrated brain. This test is used by hypnotists to assess the suggestibility of subjects, since right-dominated people enter a trance state more readily.

What your scores reveal

There is no sharp cut-off point between the function of the two hemispheres. Rather, it is a continuum, as shown in table 3, with the dominance of one side passing through a stage of integrated functioning before moving into dominance by the other side of the brain. Scores on the two assessments will place you and your child at some point along this continuum. The lower the score the greater the dominance by the left side of the brain; the higher the score the greater the influence of the right hemisphere.

Table 3   The scores

0	5	10	15	20	25	30	35	40	45	50
Left dominant				Integration				Right dominant		

Compare your position on the line with your child's. If the two are very close, it indicates similar brain function. The closeness of the match can be seen in table 4. What really matters is the relationship between your brain preference and that of your child. As the table shows, there are nine possible interactions, of which two are likely to produce conflicting views of the world.

Table 4   The relationship between your brain preference and your child's

Your child's score

Your score	0–15	16–34	35–50
0–15	Good	Fair	Conflicting
16–34	Fair	Good	Fair
35–50	Conflicting	Fair	Good

Starting at the left side of table 4, we see that low scores on the two assessments suggest that you are both primarily left-brain-dominated and therefore likely to share such mental attributes as being logical, analytical, organized and word- rather than image-orientated. This makes it more probable that your child does well at school, and enjoys subjects such as science, maths and languages. Because you both think along similar lines, it is not likely that there will be much disagreement between you about the best way of approaching studying or solving problems.

Agreement is also probable where your score, although higher than that of your child, lies in the integrating-brain function range of 16–34 points, suggesting that you have the ability to switch between the two ways of thinking. This allows you to appreciate the value of both logical reasoning and intuitive understanding. A conflict may occur, however, when your strong right-brain dominance makes it harder for you to appreciate the value of a less creative, more logical and unemotional approach. Equally, a left-brain child may have difficulty in relating to your spontaneous, emotional and intuitive way of thinking about things.

Examining the table's middle column, we see that reasonable understanding normally prevails between children who are able to employ both right- and left-brain thinking with equal ease, and parents with both left- and right-hemisphere dominance. When both parent and child are equally comfortable when thinking in a right- or in a left-brain manner, then not only is the match very healthy, but the child can approach mental challenges with maximum flexibility.

Moving to the final column, we see that conflict can arise between a strongly right-brain-dominant child and a left-brain adult. This occurs for exactly the same reasons, given above, that cause the clash between right-brain-dominant parents and left-brain-dominant children. Now, however, it is the parent's turn to be confused and irritated by the child's way of thinking. Whilst the adult is methodical and logical, the child may appear disorganized, unpunctual and haphazard. When faced with a

problem which, according to the grown-up's way of thinking, should be approached calmly, objectively and logically, the child will become agitated, emotional and
intuitive. Where the parent favours reasoned argument,
the child indulges in wild, free-wheeling bursts of creative
fantasy.

In many households the age-old conflict between the
relative merits of art and science, intellect and intuition,
find regular and often tumultuous expression. Unfortunately such clashes are nearly always won by adults, to
the detriment of the child. When the world is viewed from
such very different perspectives agreement is rare, and
mutual understanding often rarer still.

A right-brain match between parent and child avoids
conflicts; both favour the same intuitive, emotional, creative outlook on life. But it can spell trouble for the child
during formal education. At home you encourage right-
brain thinking. Then your child goes to school and finds
that few subjects are taught in this way, and even fewer
teachers think like this. So clashes occur between child
and school, and perhaps between parent and school as
well.

None of this need happen, so long as the value of both
ways of using the brain is properly appreciated. The world
needs the skills of left-brain thinkers, for many problems
are solved most rapidly and efficiently through logical
deduction. There will be many occasions in your child's
life when achievement depends on remaining emotionally
controlled, or on being punctual, articulate, methodical
or analytical. But there will also be times when making
the right choice or arriving at the most effective answer
will demand intuition, imagination, and the creativity of
the right hemisphere. As I shall explain in a later chapter,
the powerful visual ability of the right brain has a vitally
important role to play in enhancing all kinds of intellectual

activity, from solving problems to acquiring vast amounts of new knowledge more efficiently and effortlessly.

In developing friendships and cooperating with others, the emotional warmth of the right brain provides a better foundation for effective social relationships than does the tightly controlled, objective thinking of the left hemisphere. Yet in order to explain and persuade, the skilled use of language – whether written or spoken – is essential, and this, as we have seen, is usually a left-brain ability. As Jerre Levy comments, 'Normal brains are built to be challenged. They operate at optimal levels only when cognitive processing requirements are of sufficient complexity to activate both sides of the brain.'

It is clear that left-hemisphere thinking is neither better nor worse than right-hemisphere thinking. Both ways of using the brain are of equal importance. 'The dichotomy between the two modes of learning has gone on long enough in education,' says American researcher Dr Bernice McCarthy. 'It is a false dichotomy. It is time to teach both traditionally and humanistically. It is time to teach the "whole brain", intellectual and involved, mind and heart, content centered and student centered.' The ideal is for your child to develop the ability to employ both hemispheres with equal ease and efficiency, for only by doing so can his or her brain's true potential be realized – a major goal when teaching mind skills.

4

Mind Skills and Mind Styles

The old saying about great minds thinking alike could not be more wrong. There *are* important differences in the way people think, and you need to understand what these are in your child's case before attempting to teach mind skills.

Let us look at the way four children in my research study approach mentally demanding tasks. John would sooner use intuition than intellect. Mary favours logical analysis and methodical reasoning. Paul does best when solving practical problems. Kieran has a strong curiosity and vivid imagination but is over-impulsive and easily frustrated, and often makes careless errors. The differences in the ways each of these children thinks, and the varying degrees of success they enjoy in school, are a reflection of the ways their minds prefer to function. They indicate not different levels of intelligence, but differing *mind styles*.

THE TWO STAGES OF THINKING

Imagine you have been driving in an unfamiliar part of the country, have got lost and now want to find your way home. Fortunately you have a road map in the glove compartment, but before this can be of any use you must, of course, determine your exact position. This involves searching the surrounding countryside for landmarks shown on the map, such as road numbers, the names of towns or villages, railway lines, rivers and so on. By locating these you will be able to find out where you are and how best to complete your journey home. Your task, therefore, involves two steps: first, to obtain relevant information from your environment and, second, to organize it in such a way as to plan your return trip. These tasks require two different types of mind skill, as shown in table 5:

Table 5   Finding your way home: the mind skills needed

Step	Activity	Mind skill involved
1	Finding *relevant* facts	Perception
2	Organizing those facts	Processing

Notice the emphasis on *relevant* facts, since both the surrounding countryside and your map will contain vast amounts of information that has no bearing on your immediate task. So the perception stage includes separating what matters from what is irrelevant to the task in hand.

The second, *processing*, step comprises all those activities that we usually refer to as thinking. With any task requiring serious thought, the processing involves the use of many complex mind skills, such as creating mental models of the external world, going beyond the information given by drawing inferences and making deductions, adding to the knowledge acquired through direct perception by drawing on memories, creating analogies, making comparisons, noticing differences or similarities, and so forth.

Now consider a child studying a science text in preparation for an exam. Just like the lost traveller, she or he must first extract relevant facts and figures from the printed pages and then organize them in a meaningful way so as to be able to understand the subject, answer questions and build further knowledge on what has already been learned.

We find that this also requires a perception followed by a processing stage. Research has shown that there are *two* main modes of perception and *two* main ways in which the information obtained may then be processed by the brain, thus creating the possibility of *four* differing styles of thought. Each of these mind styles has its strengths and weaknesses; each is equally valid. Each is not, as we shall shortly see, equally effective when it comes to school studies. In fact, out of these four styles only *one* provides an almost certain passport to school success. Because of the way subjects are structured and taught, the sad truth is that a majority of students are significantly disadvantaged. They fail to enjoy the same level of progress and attainment as their companions not because their brains are any less able, but because the style of thinking they favour conflicts with the teaching they are given.

The four ways of thinking

One of the first to recognize these differences in the way people think was the eminent Swiss psychoanalyst, Carl Jung. He observed that some intellectuals think best when handling abstract concepts, while others prefer dealing more directly with their senses, staying close to impressions of sight and sound, touching, tasting and smelling. Then there are intuitive thinkers who rely on hunches more than abstract reasoning; artists of all kinds are often found in this category. Finally we find those for whom emotions are more important than logic – once again a characteristic more likely to be found in the arts than in the sciences.

Jung's ideas are summarized in table 6, together with

examples of the sorts of careers in which the different styles of thinking might prove most effective.

Table 6   The four ways of thinking

Mind style	Works best with	Helpful for
Using intellect	Abstract concepts	Scientists
Sensing	Sensations	Farmers
Using intuition	Hunches	Artists
Feeling	Emotions	Therapists

In practice, few people think exclusively in any one of these four styles, with most of us employing a variety of styles, depending on the circumstances. You might, for example, use abstract reasoning at your work, but depend on your feelings or intuition in personal relationships. It is still likely, however, that one style of thinking will feel more natural and be used more effortlessly than the others. Since Jung, many psychologists have explored this idea of mind styles and developed more involved theories to try and explain the differences in the way people think.

Step 1 – Perception
Some of the most interesting research has been undertaken by an American psychologist, Dr David Kolb. His studies have led him to define two main ways in which events may be perceived:

1   Through abstraction
2   Through direct experience.

Those who favour the first method he terms *abstractors*, while people who rely more on direct experience he calls *feelers*. 'Those who sense and feel tend more to the actual experience itself,' comments Dr Bernice McCarthy. 'They perceive through their senses. They are involved.' By contrast, abstractors perceive at one step removed from their direct, sensory experience. Having taken in relevant information from their surroundings, they create a highly abstract model in their minds, and this, rather than the real world, then becomes the focus of their perceptions.

As figure 6 shows, David Kolb's view of mind function places three of Jung's categories at one end of a straight line, and his fourth at the opposing pole.

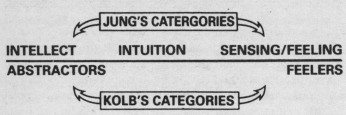

Fig. 6   Kolb's view of mind function

The term I favour for describing those children and adults who perceive through the direct physical experience of the environment, is *absorbers*. They absorb their surroundings and remain closely in touch with their senses. They trust the evidence of their eyes and ears, their experience of taste, touch and smell. This contrasts with the analytical, objective, rational abstractors, whose abstract model of the surrounding world replaces reality as the primary focus of their perceptions.

The differences between these perceptual styles become clearer if we explore the ways in which absorbers and abstractors might perceive a major human tragedy such as a famine. For absorbers, the chief perception is likely to be the direct and immediate physical suffering of the victims. They will become deeply and emotionally involved in the plight of the starving. Abstractors, while no less moved to pity, will be less emotionally and directly involved. Their abstract conception of the tragedy allows them to approach it in a more analytical manner. While the absorber focuses on the feelings of individual victims, the abstractor tends to take a more general view of the disaster and hopes to find more general solutions, such as improving agriculture or transporting supplies to disaster areas more efficiently.

These differences in perception may lead absorbers to condemn abstractors as over-detached and cold-blooded, while abstractors may consider absorbers over-involved and lacking in longer-term vision.

But perceptions change as children grow older. Infants are almost 100 per cent absorbers, allowing only their direct sensory experience – hunger, thirst, discomfort and so on – to dictate their behaviour. As they grow older, more abstract mental models are introduced, and the potency of immediate physical sensations declines. However, the extent to which they continue to dominate the perceptions of older children, and adults, varies greatly. We can represent these different ways of perceiving as the opposite poles on a straight line. As with Jung's four ways of thinking, it is rare to find people who are exclusively either absorbers or abstractors. The majority of children and adults come somewhere between the two extremes, although generally favouring one method of perception more than the other.

Step 2 – Processing
Now let us consider the second step in thinking, during which information is acted on by the brain. Here one can draw a distinction between people who *respond* and those who *reflect*. Give a group of children a task which involves

creating designs by manipulating wooden blocks (this problem forms part of the widely used Wechsler Intelligence Test), and you will notice that some immediately start moving the blocks about, seeking solutions by trial and error. Their style of processing information means that they feel more comfortable when discovering by doing rather than by careful reflection.

Other children, given the same task, will pause for thought, perhaps resting their chins on their hands as they study the problem with all the intensity of a prize-fighter sizing up an opponent. Instead of rolling up their sleeves for immediate action, they move the blocks around in their minds, reflecting on the outcome of each imagined transformation before deciding on an appropriate course of action. When they make their move, the problem has usually been solved and only needs translating from thought into deed.

I call the first group *responders*, because they respond rapidly to changing situations, seldom pausing to consider their best course of action. Those who pause for thought before acting, I term *reflectors*. They carefully weigh up the pros and cons of each action before it is performed; they consider a range of options and consequences, rarely leaping before they have had a long, hard look. As with absorbers and abstractors, one can represent these two distinct modes of thinking as the opposite poles of a straight line. And, once again, it is obvious from our everyday experience that most people can vary their behaviour to some extent according to circumstances, and so would be placed somewhere along the line, rather than at either extreme.

By bringing these two dimensions of thinking – perception and processing – together in a single diagram, it becomes possible to identify the four mind styles that I

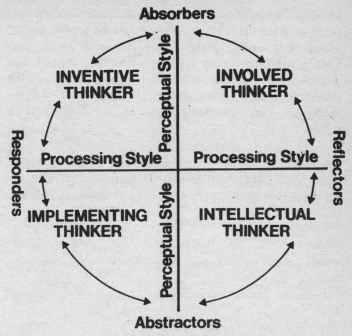

Fig.7 The mind styles created by the interplay of perceptual and processing styles

mentioned earlier. The result, together with the four mind styles that are created, is shown in figure 7.

Starting in the top right-hand section of the diagram, you can see that the child who perceives by absorbing and who processes information reflectively has the mind style of an *involved thinker*. I will explain what this, and the other three terms relating to mind styles, mean in a moment. For now, let us continue our journey in a clockwise direction to consider the second combination. Here reflective processing combines with abstracted perception to create the mind style of an *intellectual thinker*.

The same form of abstract perception, when linked to a preference for the active experimentation of a responder, produces the mind style of an *implementing thinker*. Finally, the 'discovering by doing' tactics of the responder combine with the perceptions of an absorber to create the mind style of an *inventive thinker*. Table 7 summarizes the perception and processing styles of the four thinking styles.

Table 7   The perception and processing styles of the four thinking styles

Thinking style	Perception style	Processing style
Involved	Absorber	Reflector
Intellectual	Abstractor	Reflector
Implementing	Abstractor	Responder
Inventive	Absorber	Responder

THE INFLUENCE OF MIND STYLES

To see how mind styles influence every aspect of a child's approach to school, studying and intellectual challenge, we will return to the four children, John, Mary, Paul and Kieran, whose different ways of thinking were briefly described at the start of this chapter. I have selected these from the many children who have participated in the research on which *Mind Skills* is based, because they best typify the four major styles of thinking. When you read these descriptions, you may well find that one of them describes your own child more accurately than the rest, although there are also likely to be a number of differences between his or her way of thinking about, and responding to, life and those detailed here. Every child is, of course, a unique individual whose intellectual processes are shaped by personal experiences as well as by personality traits, attitudes and anxieties – factors in a child's mental development that we will be considering in more detail in later chapters.

John – An involved thinker

As you will recall, involved thinking is the mind style of people who perceive by absorbing and emotionally colouring information, on which they then carefully reflect before proceeding. Involved thinkers search for meanings in the world around them, and are most interested in seeking answers to questions which start with '*Why* . . .?' – 'Why did you do that?' 'Why are you sad?' 'Why are people cruel to animals?' They are sociable, cooperative individuals who get deeply involved in anything which catches their attention, and are far more interested in people than in either theories or things.

How John thinks best John is a highly imaginative twelve-year-old, full of bright ideas which he likes to discuss and share with others. He makes friends easily, both with his own age group and with older people, enjoys the company of others, and spends part of each holiday doing voluntary work at an old people's home. He is very intuitive, making rapid but generally accurate judgements about people and events, on the basis of hunches and 'gut' feelings. His hero is the late Martin Luther King. John wants to be a teacher or social worker when he leaves school. Most of his questions start with 'Why . . .?' – 'Why can't more money be spent on feeding the starving?' 'Why not let old people come into school to talk about their lives?'

Mary – An intellectual thinker

Children and adults favouring this mind style perceive abstractly and process reflectively. They are objective, rational, logical and factual. Often assertive and emotionally controlled, they seek recognition from others – especially authority figures, for whom they often have a somewhat excessive respect.

How Mary thinks best   Mary, aged eleven, is in the top groups for all her school subjects and recently made a good start at learning German. Her favourite lessons are maths and science, but she has more trouble with creative writing and does poorly at art, which she dislikes. Mary works hard, and diligently searches out and checks her facts. However, she seldom takes an independent stand, preferring to learn what her teachers' or parents' view is before venturing an opinion. She needs to be seen by adults as clever and capable, and becomes very upset when she fails in any intellectually demanding task. She is more interested in theories than in people, and has ambitions to become either an astronomer or a physicist. She asks a great many questions, most of which begin with '*What* . . .?' – 'What do we know about the planet Jupiter?' 'What happens when you mix these chemicals together?'

Paul – An implementing thinker

Children with this mind style combine abstract perceptions with the active processing of information. They are energetic doers rather than deep thinkers, preferring immediate action to lengthy introspection. Their thinking is characterized by an urge to put ideas into practice as swiftly as possible. So far as they are concerned, the best theory in the world is valueless unless it has immediate practical applications.

Rarely very impressed by authority figures, implementing thinkers are prepared to ignore rules and flout regulations when these stand in their way. They dislike being handed answers on a plate and think most successfully when able to get hands-on experience.

How Paul thinks best   Thirteen-year-old Paul's favourite lessons are metalwork and science practicals, although he is weak on the theory side of these subjects. At home, he enjoys discovering how things work. Even when very young, he rapidly took new toys to pieces to examine their mechanisms, and even managed to put them back together again! At the age of four he was able to assemble complicated Lego designs after only a brief study of the plans. Today he is skilled at repairing things, and his parents happily hand over anything from a broken alarm clock to a faulty radio for him to fix.

Paul solves problems best when he can build models or represent abstract concepts in some physical way. He despises what he calls 'useless' ideas, which usually means any which fail to lead to some immediately practical result. Talk to him about aerodynamic theory, and his eyes glaze over. Give him balsa wood and glue, and Paul can construct a flying machine which obeys all the laws he finds it so difficult to make sense of from the blackboard.

Paul loves practical problems and hates being told something that he was on the point of finding out for himself. He has wanted since the age of six to become an engineer when he leaves school. His questions usually begin with '*How* . . .?' – 'How does a computer work?' 'How can I build a transistor radio?'

Kieran – An inventive thinker
Like involved thinkers, children with this mind style perceive by absorbing, and so remain in close touch with their physical sensations. Unlike them, however, they process by responding rather than through reflection,

reacting to intellectual challenges with more speed than thought. They adore change and variety, and are very willing to take risks. Parents and teachers often consider them over-impulsive and insufficiently thoughtful. In fact, of all four mind styles, inventive thinkers usually fare worst in formal education, and are the least popular with their teachers, especially those teaching academic subjects. Such children are flexible, practical, intuitive thinkers who like to learn by trial and error, and are fascinated by experimenting and inventing. Give an inventive thinker a clock, and she or he will probably try to turn it into something completely different.

How Kieran thinks best   Although ten-year-old Kieran gets dismal school reports and is not considered very intelligent by his teachers, he has a vivid imagination and is always finding things out for himself. He plunges straight into any task that catches his interest, and then pursues it with a single-minded intensity, until something new attracts him. He enjoys sport, but shows little scholastic aptitude or interest. His worst subjects are those which demand abstract, reflective thinking, such as maths and science. Most of his questions are about things – how they work, and, especially, how they might be adapted to work in different ways. He dislikes intellectual challenges, and seldom takes time to reflect on the best way of organizing his work. Given a plastic model for his tenth birthday, he did not bother to read the instructions, but immediately tried pushing the parts together in order to learn from experience which parts might fit. He finished up with a creation that satisfied his inventive mind, although it looked nothing like the picture on the lid. Kieran's career choices have included explorer, footballer and jet pilot.

MIND STYLES AND SCHOOL SUCCESS

Studies among students aged from nine to eighteen, in both the UK and the USA, suggest that intellectual thinkers, those most favoured by formal education, may make up less than a quarter of the total. The full results are shown in table 8:

Table 8   Percentages of the four mind styles among students

Mind style	% of students
Involved thinkers	34
Intellectual thinkers	23
Implementing thinkers	17
Inventive thinkers	26

As I have already mentioned, classrooms are kindest to children who are primarily intellectual thinkers, because abstraction and reflection are essential to school achievement. Children who mainly think in this way like learning, achieve good grades and excellent examination results, are praised by their teachers, please their parents, and have a powerful self-image and strong motivation to work hard. 'When somebody is teaching us in our most comfortable style, we learn,' comments Bernice McCarthy. 'But more importantly, we feel good about ourselves.'

This is fine for 25 per cent of students, but very unfortunate for the remaining 75 per cent whose mind styles make them uncomfortable with the way knowledge is presented and teaching structured. As a result, they become discouraged about many aspects of learning, frequently do poorly in such prestigious subjects as science and maths – which are typically taught as abstract/

reflective subjects – seldom enjoy praise from teachers, and soon come to look on school studies as irrelevant.

Their failures are not, however, due to their being less capable or, initially, less enthusiastic about their studies. But, because they are forced to use a thinking style which is alien to them, it is not long before they lose motivation and self-confidence.

The way education has long been organized can be likened to an athletics meeting at which the only sport allowed is the sprint. In this bizarre contest, every competitor, no matter what his or her aptitudes, body build or physical skills, is obliged to run a hundred yards. Those who do well are rewarded, and those who do not are penalized and made to feel utter failures, despite the fact that it is the rules of the game, rather than their own inadequacy, which are responsible for that result. It is very unlikely, of course, that public outrage would allow such a contest to be held more than once, or that anybody would take the outcome seriously. Sadly, intellectual discrimination, which is no less absurd and unjustifiable, has long been educational practice, and many people do take the results very seriously indeed. The myth persists that only children who get right answers in class have any right to be regarded as bright. And, as John Holt points out in his book *Teach Your Own*, so long as schools remain essentially 'round peg for round hole factories', the situation has little chance of changing. Dr Seymour Papert, the pioneer of computer education, notes:

One of the worst things about school is that it forces you to do things in one particular way. It's like taking left-handed people and making them write with the right hand. It's not just that you don't do it very well but that it does lots of harm to you. Schools also wrongly separate the aesthetic from the conceptual and so destroy this driving force of inner motivation.

It is important to realize that all mind styles are equally valid and, given the right teaching and encouragement, children can learn to become flexible thinkers, perceiving and processing information in a way best suited to each circumstance.

MIND STYLES AND BRAIN DOMINANCE

People may be more left- or more right-brain-dominant irrespective of their favoured mind style, although certain styles of thinking are more likely to occur when a particular hemisphere dominates. Table 9 shows the percentage of left-, right- or integrated-brain subjects in each of the four styles, based on a study of some five hundred children aged between eleven and sixteen.

Table 9   Percentages of left-, right- and integrated-brain subjects in the four mind styles

Mind style	Brain preference (percentages)		
	Right	Left	Integrated
Involved	45	31	24
Intellectual	12	65	23
Implementing	48	20	32
Inventive	49	32	19

As might be expected, involved, implementing and inventive thinkers are more likely to be right- than left-brain-dominant, while left-brain dominance is more common among intellectual thinkers. These findings are not so surprising if one remembers how the hemispheres are specialized – the left for language and logic, the right for imagery and intuition.

Once again, we find that formal education disadvantages the great majority of children, since only around 15 per cent of all those studied have been found to be left-brain-dominant, intellectual thinkers – the kind of students most likely to enjoy their studies and get good examination grades. Those students who are right-brain-dominant and favour involved, implementing or inventive mind styles will run a serious risk of being at an intellectual disadvantage in class.

Although, as noted above when considering mind styles alone, we find that some 77 per cent of children are at risk of being handicapped by a mismatch between the way they think most easily and the way subjects are taught in school, when brain dominance is also taken into account the proportion of those more likely to find failure than fulfilment in the classroom rises ever higher.

One reason why children who are successful in primary education, with its greater emphasis on doing things, on being inventive and on developing social skills, start falling behind when they start secondary education, is because its more intellectual, university-oriented teaching conflicts with the way they think most efficiently. Not all children whose mind styles and brain preferences fail to match up to the demands of their surroundings will be harmed to the same extent, however, and many will succeed as well as the more favoured left-brain intellectual thinkers, because so many other factors can increase their chances of achievement. Remember that neither mind-style preferences nor left-brain/right-brain dominance constitute sharply defined categories with precisely delineated boundaries between them. As we have seen, all the differences we have considered lie along a continuum, with most children being found between the extremes.

This means that understanding teachers, a flexible

school curriculum, supportive parents, early successes and a chance to think in ways which come most easily, will significantly improve a child's prospects of attainment. And even when a child has failed miserably in class, all is by no means lost. Once they are liberated from the strait-jacket of formal education, many young people surprise everyone by the ability they reveal. Perhaps the most famous example of the late developer was Albert Einstein, who was regarded as only averagely bright by his teachers, and rarely attended lectures at the Zurich poly-technic because he preferred to spend time studying the subjects that really interested him.

MIND STYLES IN ACTION

Children usually try hard, and sometimes with consider-able success, to adapt their ways of thinking to the demands of schoolwork. Just as some left-handed children can learn to use their right hands when forced to do so, and not be traumatized by the experience, so can many children learn to use mind styles with which they feel less comfortable.

An impulsive, trial-and-error inventive thinker may learn, for instance, that neither of his approaches proves satisfactory in class. So he becomes more reflective and less concrete, and starts to depend on logic more than intuition and to use abstraction in place of direct sense perception. But unless these shifts of mind style are brought about in the right way, the price paid by the child may be considerable. Such children often feel themselves under considerable pressure, not fully understanding les-sons and struggling to keep up with companions who seem to learn so effortlessly.

Even when the mind styles of children and parents are very different, conflicts need not occur at home so long as adults are willing to respect their children's right to think differently, while at the same time offering encouragement and opportunities to explore other ways of using their brains. A major goal of any mind-skills training programme should be to develop all four styles of thinking, rather than favouring one at the expense of the rest. You should then help them expand their intellectual potential so that:

1 Involved thinkers start using logic and reason, or become involved with trial-and-error experimenting, when these will prove the most effective strategies.

2 Intellectual thinkers feel comfortable when depending on intuition.

3 Implementing thinkers can be more reflective when the need arises.

4 Inventive thinkers appreciate the importance of reflecting before they act, to avoid squandering time and energy.

You will find it helpful to evaluate your own, and your child's, preferred way of thinking. This can be done using the mind-style analysis in the next chapter. I suggest that you assess both your own and your child's styles before proceeding further. This will not only allow you to discover the most appropriate ways of providing help, but will also identify any barriers to a proper understanding of his or her intellectual and emotional needs.

5

Analysing Your Family's Mind Styles

The guidelines which I gave in chapter 3 for analysing brain dominance also apply to the mind style assessment below. Never pressure your child into completing it, avoid times when he or she would much sooner be doing something else, and – if you feel this is appropriate – discuss both sets of results with your child, exploring the ways in which various members of the family think alike or differently. Remember that although school success depends more on developing an intellectual style of thinking, this does not mean that it is better than the other three, all of which possess great strengths and have a key role to play in successful thinking.

Assessment 1 – for your child to complete
Tick, or make a note of, any statements with which you *strongly* agree:
 1 I become very involved in anything that interests me.
 2 I come near the top of my class in most subjects.
 3 I prefer solving problems by trial and error.
 4 I would rather make a model than play a game of chess.
 5 I enjoy finding out how things work.
 6 I don't like playing on my own.
 7 I prefer, knowing a teacher's views to be true, saying what I think.
 8 I'd sooner work out a problem for myself than be given the answer.
 9 I check my homework carefully before handing it in.
10 I like social studies better than science.

11   I am soon bored by routine.
12   I get irritated by people with silly ideas.
13   I am good at inventing stories.
14   I enjoy trying anything new.
15   I like repairing things.
16   I get upset when things don't go my way.
17   I get impatient when something takes longer than expected.
18   I enjoy lessons where you make something.
19   I like solving brain teasers.
20   I find it difficult to work on my own.
21   I have a hero (or heroine) whose life I greatly admire.
22   I would sooner paint a picture than make a kit model.
23   I always want teachers to be pleased with me.
24   I like to be sure of my facts before giving my views.
25   I am very impatient.
26   I dislike being told what to do.
27   I often blurt things out by mistake.
28   I don't mind taking risks.
29   I have a vivid imagination.
30   I want people to think I am very clever.
31   I get cross with people who can't make up their minds.
32   I enjoy persuading people to do what I want.
33   I become annoyed when I can't learn things quickly.
34   I am good at making models.
35   I like listening to people's problems and trying to help.
36   I like being taught theories about the way things work.
37   I usually see somebody else's point of view.
38   I enjoy going to school.
39   I'd much sooner build a model than paint a picture.
40   I enjoy it when many different things are happening.

Assessment 2 – for you to complete

As with the previous assessment, complete this by ticking, or noting the number of, any statements with which you *strongly* agree:

1 When a task really interests me I lose all track of time.
2 I can view my personal problems objectively.
3 I solve problems more by trial and error than by logic.
4 I enjoy DIY.
5 I like finding out how things work.
6 I enjoy discussing my ideas with others.
7 I prefer knowing what the experts think before reaching an opinion.
8 I hate being spoon-fed answers.
9 I solve problems logically.
10 I would sooner work with people than things.
11 I dislike routine.
12 I am annoyed by impractical ideas.
13 I have a very vivid imagination.
14 I enjoy a hobby where one is always learning something new.
15 I get a kick out of mending things.
16 I am more assertive than most.
17 I often act on my hunches.
18 I am good at solving practical problems.
19 I analyse all the facts carefully before reaching a decision.
20 I am rarely at a loss for new ideas.
21 I try to model myself on those I respect.
22 I enjoy problems which demand creative thinking.
23 I respect the opinions of experts.
24 I like to know all I can before expressing my views.
25 I am not afraid of flouting regulations to get things done.

26 I make long-term plans to give my life purpose.
27 I often say things that I later regret.
28 I enjoy taking risks.
29 I like finding out what makes people tick.
30 I want to be regarded as highly intelligent.
31 I am irritated by woolly thinking.
32 I like being able to control events.
33 I prefer short-term to long-term projects.
34 I solve problems more easily if able to make a drawing or model.
35 I enjoy helping people solve personal problems.
36 I am very interested in theoretical explanations.
37 I am usually able to see the other person's point of view.
38 I look back on my schooldays with pleasure.
39 I solve many problems by applying common sense.
40 I prefer to have lots of variety in my life.

Scoring the assessments

Both assessments are scored by noting the number of statements ticked against each of the mind styles, as shown in table 10.

Table 10   Scoring the assessments

Mind style	Statements ticked
Involved thinker	1,6,10,13,20,21,22,29,35,37
Intellectual thinker	2,7,9,14,19,23,24,30,36,38
Implementing thinker	3,8,12,15,18,25,26,31,34,39
Inventive thinker	4,5,11,16,17,27,28,32,33,40

I suggest that for future reference you keep a record of your results, either on table 11 or on a separate sheet of paper (to avoid marking the book).

Table 11   Assessment scores

Assessment	Myself	Number of statements ticked			
		Partner	Child	Child	Child
Involved					
Intellectual					
Implementing					
Inventive					

The mind style with the greatest number of statements ticked indicates the way of thinking that comes most easily and feels most natural. Where scores on two or more mind styles are either equal or within one point of each other, an ability to adapt one's way of thinking to meet different intellectual demands is indicated.

The amount of influence exerted by a particular style can be assessed from the total number of statements ticked, as shown in table 12.

Table 12   The influence exerted by a particular mind style

Number of statements ticked	Amount of influence
8–10	Very strong
6–7	Fairly strong
4–5	Moderate
1–3	Slight

Where the influence of one style is very strong and that of the others moderate or slight, it suggests that this way of thinking is dominant, and you or your child may feel unhappy if obliged to think in any other way. Moderate or slight scores for all four mind styles suggest that no one way of thinking is favoured and that your child may still be experimenting with different styles. A score of between five and eight on all four styles indicates an extremely flexible thinker. If this is combined with a left-/right-hemisphere preference score that reveals an integrated use of the brain, then few intellectual challenges should defeat you.

FAMILY MIND STYLES – CONFLICTING OR COMPLEMENTING?

The interplay between your own mind style and that of your child is of considerable importance, since, as table 13 shows, family mind styles can either conflict with or complement one another.

Table 13   The interplay of mind styles

Your child's mind style	Your mind style			
	Involved	Intellectual	Implementing	Inventive
Involved	Perfect	Fair	Poor	Fair
Intellectual	Fair	Perfect	Fair	Poor
Implementing	Poor	Fair	Perfect	Fair
Inventive	Fair	Poor	Fair	Perfect

To use this table, start with the mind style on which you, and your child, obtained the highest scores. Having determined whether these styles conflict with, or complement, one another, consider any other styles where there was a score of five or more statements ticked. If you or your child scored more or less equally on each of the four styles, then there is unlikely to be any conflict. For example, where both parents and child are involved thinkers, the match will be perfect, but if one is an involved thinker and the other an implementing thinker, then the match is a poor one and clashes may occur. Conflicts might also occur between intellectual and inventive thinkers.

When a child's thinking style is very different, his or her ways of perceiving and responding may be so beyond an adult's understanding that he or she runs the risk of being regarded as either muddle-headed or empty-headed. But by trying to think in the way adults expect, children run the risk of failing, because that is not the way their minds work most efficiently.

Yet if they persist in trying to use the mind style that feels most natural, adults may dismiss them as dullards. Avoid this risk, when creating a mind-skill programme for your own child, by appreciating the nature of any conflicts which may arise as a result of different styles of thinking. Build on the strengths of your child's preferred way of perceiving and processing information, while at the same time gently encouraging other styles of thinking.

If your own thinking is dominated by a particular mind style, practise using other approaches. If the assessment showed you to be primarily an intellectual thinker, for example, you should experiment with acting on hunches, relying more on intuition, exercising less emotional control, solving problems by trial and error, and undertaking tasks which demand a practical approach. By constantly changing mental gear in this way you will greatly improve your own thinking skills, becoming more confident and intellectually agile. You will also find it far easier to create a learning world which matches your child's personal learning needs. How this may be done I shall explain in the next chapter.

6
Creating Your Child's Learning World

Children learn most easily when involved, interested and free from distracting anxieties. They learn most willingly from those they love and trust, in surroundings which make them feel emotionally secure. This means that of all the many adults your child will listen to and learn from, you alone are best placed to enhance his or her mind skills.

This can be done by making your home into a world of learning – not, of course, by filling it with blackboards and desks or, I hasten to add, by approaching every conversation as though it was a period of instruction, and every game as a teaching exercise. The kind of learning world I am talking about is created by matching your child's surroundings to the way he or she thinks most easily and naturally. As we have seen, this means taking into account your child's right- and left-brain preferences as well as his or her mind style.

The child's scores on the earlier assessments determine which procedures will prove most effective when creating his or her learning world. By following the simple plan described below, you will be able to develop a programme of mental enhancement which takes account of your child's individual needs.

PLANNING YOUR ENHANCEMENT PROGRAMME

Use table 14 to identify the approaches to follow, based on the mind-style scores from Assessment 1 in chapter 5.

Table 14   Programme planner

If your child is an:	Start with Approach:
Involved thinker	1
Intellectual thinker	2
Implementing thinker	3
Inventive thinker	4

Step 1

Start with the approach indicated by the mind style on which your child obtained the highest score in Assessment 1, chapter 5. This will ensure that the procedures used are the most natural and, therefore, the easiest to work with. Within this approach you will find procedures suitable for children who are either left- or right-brain-dominant. This tends to be more significant in the case of involved and intellectual thinkers than with either implementing or inventive thinkers. At first, use those procedures which match their right- or left-brain dominance. After working with these for a while, begin introducing some of the ideas suggested for the opposite brain preference.

Suppose, for example, that the assessment in chapter 3 had shown your child to favour the right side of the brain, while the assessment in chapter 5 identified him or her as an involved thinker. This combination of scores would lead you to start by using the procedures for right-brain-dominant children that will be described in Approach 1. After working with these for a few weeks, or until positive progress has been achieved, you could try out some of the procedures which have been shown to work well with left-brain-dominant involved thinkers. In this way you would help your child to use the favoured mind style in a more flexible and efficient manner. As a result, his or her brain's potential would be more fully realized.

Where the results of the assessment in chapter 3 indicated an integrated brain, you can start with procedures for either left- or right-brain dominance, but you should work through them all before moving to Step 2.

If your child scored equally highly on more than one mind style, start by working with one on which your own score was the highest, since this makes the programme easier for you to implement. If, for example, your child had similar scores on intuitive and intellectual thinking, but your score for intuitive thinking was higher than for intellectual thinking, it would make sense to start with Approach 1, since you complement one another in this style of thinking. Once you have gained confidence and worked with procedures that stimulate both the dominant and non-dominant sides of the brain, you would move to Approach 2, which contains procedures most suited to enhancing the mind skills of intellectual thinkers.

Step 2
After working for a few weeks with the approach identified by the mind style receiving the highest score, move to the approach indicated by the style on which your child achieved the next highest score. As before, use all the procedures described so as to stimulate both sides of the brain, once again starting with those intended for the dominant hemisphere.

Step 3
After using these procedures for a while, move to the mind style which was ranked third in the assessment, before completing your enhancement programme by fol-

lowing procedures described under the remaining approaches.

To see how this works in practice, let us look at the way the parents of twelve-year-old John, the involved thinker I mentioned at the start of chapter 4, planned their child's mind-skills enhancement programme.

How John's learning world was created

John's scores on the mind-style assessment were as follows:

Involved thinker – 8
Intellectual thinker – 4
Implementing thinker – 2
Inventive thinker – 2

His score in the assessment in chapter 3 showed a strong left-brain dominance. His parents, therefore, started by using procedures described in Approach 1, beginning with those designed for left-brain thinkers. After working with them for some weeks, they introduced procedures for stimulating the right side of the brain. By doing so they helped John to become a more flexible thinker. Two months later, they started working with the procedures described in Approach 2, so as to encourage their son to employ intellectual thinking when the situation demanded it. They worked with the procedures for left-brain dominance for some weeks, before changing to those for right-brain-dominant children.

When he had been helped to employ total brain power using both intuitive and intellectual thinking, his parents went on to consider the remaining two mind styles on which John had obtained low, but equal, scores. This meant that they might have continued with either

Approach 3 (implementing thinking) or Approach 4 (inventive thinking). Since they had both scored higher on inventive than implementing thinking, however, they decided on Approach 4. The final stage of their mind-skills training programme involved working with procedures described in Approach 3.

John's mother, a doctor, was a right-brain-dominant involved thinker, which meant that she found it fairly easy to understand his way of looking at life. His father, a university mathematics lecturer, was a strongly left-brain intellectual thinker. Before completing the assessments, he had often found himself irritated by John's intuitive approach to problems. Once he understood the influence of brain preference and mind styles, however, he appreciated why the boy thought as he did, and worked to increase his own facility with different mind styles.

The parents reported that John gained in confidence and enthusiasm, both at school and at home. Although he had previously disliked maths and science, he became much more interested in both. His parents, too, found their thinking ability enhanced, as they started to approach problems with far greater flexibility. Their lives, they felt, were enriched as they became more open to different modes of thought and new ways of responding.

What you can achieve
Your goal is to enhance both left- and right-brain thinking in all four styles. It is not a process to be rushed; working through all the different procedures typically takes several months. By constructing the training programme in this way, you precisely tailor the help you offer to your child's preferred way of thinking. This builds on his or her strengths instead of exposing weaknesses, and so increases self-esteem, improves motivation and reduces anxiety.

I suggest that you read through each of the approaches

in order to appreciate the similarities and differences between them, before starting work with the approach suited to your child's major mind style. While creating the learning world, keep in mind your own brain preference and mind style. Make an effort to understand how your child's mind works best, in order to complement and not conflict with his or her preferred ways of thinking.

APPROACH 1

You will adopt this approach at the start of your enhancement programme if your child's primary mind style is that of an involved thinker. If your child also favours the left side of the brain:

Enhance learning by presenting information in a logical, structured manner, using the 'basement-up' method described on page 107. Remember that left-brain-dominant intuitive thinkers are fascinated to discover *why* things happen. The questions you ask and the answers you give should take this need fully into account. Always reply honestly to factual queries; if you do not know the answer, then say so rather than making a guess. The logical, left-brain-dominant mind of these children makes it extremely likely that they will spot errors or inaccuracies and so come to mistrust you as a source of information.

If your child favours the right side of the brain:

Enhance learning by free-wheeling, open-ended, loosely structured, wide-ranging discussions. Present information using the 'top-down' method described on page 107. Use imagery, fantasy, simile, metaphor and analogy to exploit your child's right brain's strong visual abilities.

Your role Involved thinkers, whether left- or right-brain-dominant, need regular and constructive feedback in order to monitor their performance and evaluate the direction they are taking. Because they are close to their senses, emotions may divert them from their goals or distract them from the task in hand. Providing constructive feedback means listening carefully, observing objectively and then reflecting back their experiences and discoveries in a positive, performance-enhancing way. (See chapter 7 for a full explanation of talking and listening skills.)

Avoid giving undeserved praise, which either devalues your feedback in the child's eyes or gives an unrealistic impression of what it takes to succeed in life. Avoid frequent or over-critical judgements, no matter how deserved you consider these comments to be, since this reduces self-confidence while increasing anxiety. If, for instance, your child had written a highly imaginative story about the sort of society that might flourish on a remote tropical island, it would be as unhelpful to offer overfulsome praise along the lines of 'That's the most wonderful story I've ever read', as to make sniping criticisms, like 'The story was interesting enough, but your handwriting is terrible.'

Effective feedback would be along the lines of: 'I enjoyed finding out about . . .' 'I think your ideas on . . . were interesting' 'I'm not sure I agree with you about . . .' 'Why did that happen?' Comments like this not only confirm that you have taken your child's work seriously enough to read it thoughtfully, but also draw attention to what you regard as positive and worthwhile ideas. Those you viewed less favourably are not dismissed as irrelevant or ridiculous but, rather, used as the basis for a discussion which expands your child's understanding while providing practice in communicating ideas persuasively.

Even if you are worried by illegible writing or poor spelling, a discussion of content is not an appropriate time to raise these concerns. Nor should you turn an enjoyable exercise in imaginative writing into a punishing experience by making the child write it all out again – 'and neatly this time' – or list incorrectly spelled words.

Provide a warm, emotionally secure home environment in which your child is willing to talk about and explore emotions and to describe a wide range of feelings – his or her own as well as those of other people. He or she may become deeply involved in the lives of others, even of fictional characters, and a sad film is more likely to bring tears to the eyes of an involved thinker than to any other. Do not worry about these intense associations, or seek to prevent your child from feeling involved with others. It helps him or her to make sense of new ideas and unfamiliar experiences.

If you are a very logical or practical person (an intellectual or implementing thinker), your child's flights of fancy and tendency to act on hunches may cause irritation. Recognize, however, that this is a perfectly valid way of thinking, involving valuable mind skills which should be encouraged in this rapidly changing world.

APPROACH 2

You will adopt this approach at the start of your enhancement programme if your child's primary mind style is that of an intellectual thinker. If your child also favours the left side of the brain:

Enhance learning by formal instruction. Children with this mind style and brain preference learn most easily when information is presented in a logical, carefully structured way using the 'basement-up' method described on page 107.

If your child favours the right side of the brain:

Enhance learning by informal lessons. A carefully structured approach is generally less effective here, and you
should present information using the 'top-down' method
described on page 107.

Your role   Provide the necessary instruction, and guide
the child towards extracting information from other
sources. Remember that a major motive for these children
is finding answers to *what* makes things happen.

The strength of this style, especially when associated
with strong left-brain dominance, is that it is most suited
to the learning world of the classroom, and excels when
tackling problems that can be solved by logical analysis.
But you should allow such children to build their storehouse of knowledge at their chosen pace, never forcing
them to leave a topic until they have understood it to
their own satisfaction. Act as an information resource,
providing access to knowledge and, even more importantly, to ways of finding things out from books, libraries,
museums and so on.

Avoid talking down to intellectual thinkers, since they
take learning seriously and, even at an early age, expect
adults to do the same. Never patronize them by such
comments as 'You're much too little to understand.'
Remarks like this create negative attitudes in any child,
but intellectual thinkers, because of the importance they
attach to their mental abilities, are especially vulnerable
to insensitive assaults. The best method is to direct them
towards suitable reference sources, instruct them on how
information can be looked up, then leave them to gather
the facts they need to answer questions that intrigue
them.

Intellectual thinkers develop their mind skills most fully
and efficiently when left alone to solve problems and work
things out by themselves. Do not be tempted to rush

them, or insist on their responding rapidly to information or ideas. Because they process information reflectively, before proceeding they need time to consider all the aspects and explore all the implications of an unfamiliar topic. You are more likely to be able to do this if you share their style of thinking. It may prove harder if you are an implementing or inventive thinker, since, for you, knowledge is a raw material to be processed by rapid action and trial-and-error experience, rather than by abstract theorizing.

There is a risk that younger intellectual thinkers will become over-dependent on the opinions of others, especially adults with authority (teachers, youth club leaders and so on), for whom they often have a somewhat excessive respect. Their tendency to adapt readily to intellectual demands, combined with an often present anxiety over being seen as nonconformist, acts as a barrier to their challenging received views and establishing a personal viewpoint.

As a result, they may fail to reflect on the wider implications of their actions. With their abstract, some-times unemotional, attitude towards problems, and their intense desire to find answers to technical questions, they may ignore social or personal consequences. The unemo-tional scientist, fascinated by the challenge of building ever bigger and more destructive bombs at the bidding of an authority for which he has too much respect, is not entirely a stereotype. The training that intellectual think-ers receive in school and at university often over-empha-sizes the value of solving technical problems, without giving sufficient attention to the humanitarian or ethical implications.

Encourage intellectual thinkers to broaden their views and develop more flexible, creative, problem-solving strategies, by introducing them to what are termed *diver-*

gent problems. These are tasks with several equally valid answers, rather than a single correct solution. I shall describe how to do this in detail in chapter 7.

Because their relationships are often treated to the same objective appraisal, many children with this thinking style tend to have few close friends. In the absence of agreeable companions, the child may prefer his or her own company, spending hours reading books or playing with a computer. The solitary young computer 'hacker', who prefers keyboards to friendships, often lacks social skills and is made anxious by having to meet others and develop close ties or intimate relationships. If you, too, scored high on this mind style, you may well have a strong sympathy for your child's attitude, which probably mirrors your own feelings. However, remember that children who fail to learn how to get on with their peers lack important mind skills, no matter how intellectually able they may be.

Glance back to the list of mind skills which the adventurer, artist and athlete will need to succeed in tomorrow's world, and you will see that getting along with others and being able to present ideas persuasively are of great importance. Employers are not just looking for very bright young people to take into their companies; they want intelligent youngsters who can work in a team, cooperate with others, and communicate their ideas effectively. These social skills, together with insight into their emotional needs, are often poorly developed in intellectual thinkers, especially when strongly left-brain-dominant.

When creating your child's learning world, therefore, you must include ways of improving cooperation and sharing, and nurture a more emotional, less intellectual involvement with others. Your child should be encouraged to broaden his or her range of friends and become more experienced in social situations.

APPROACH 3

You will adopt this approach at the start of your enhancement programme if your child's primary mind style is that of an implementing thinker. If your child also favours the left side of the brain:

Enhance learning by making resources available. Formal instruction is generally of little interest to these children, who typically do poorly in class. Yet when implementing thinkers leave school, where they have often been made to feel intellectually inferior, and get the opportunity of learning through doing, they frequently excel. I have seen training workshops where teenagers dismissed as unteachable at school and condemned to years of uncomprehending boredom at the bottom of the class, reveal themselves to be highly skilled electrical and mechanical engineers, repairing cars, constructing computers, cooking, building their own stereo hi-fi equipment and proving themselves high achievers in scores of activities which are mentally demanding, but in a practical rather than a theoretical sense.

If your child favours the right side of the brain:

Enhance learning by creating as many opportunities as possible for him or her to experiment and explore. Satisfy his or her curiosity by providing resources and offering assistance, where and when needed. Right-brain dominance usually produces a broader interest in finding answers to '*how?*' questions than one finds with strongly left-brain thinkers. Right-brain thinkers' range of experiments may be more diverse and they are frequently criticized for having 'butterfly minds', seldom remaining interested in one thing for any length of time.

Your role Be both guide and friend. Your child is likely to have a powerful curiosity about the way things work, although he or she will probably be more interested in discovering how specific things function than in seeking more general explanations. Given a battery-driven car, for instance, he might want to take it apart to discover what makes it go, but show far less interest in learning the theory behind electric motors.

Help by providing access to physical resources, such as paint, paper, card, timber, string and tools. For older children, junkyard equipment of all kinds, which can be purchased for next to nothing, makes far more exciting and mind-expanding toys than the most expensive toyshop offerings. Implementing thinkers are usually thrilled at being given equipment that they can do what they like with – strip down, tear apart, break up, use as spares, convert, cannibalize, repair or rebuild – without fear of being reprimanded. If space allows, give your child a work area for his or her exclusive use, in which to create, experiment and make a mess without feeling guilty or having to tidy things away at night.

Offer guidance in developing certain skills, especially where these involve such potential hazards as sharp knives or soldering irons. But do not take over the task on the excuse that she or he is too young or inexperienced to cope with it. While both are valid reasons for reducing the risks involved to a minimum, and even for completing minor aspects of the task, they are certainly not reasons for turning the child from a participant into a spectator.

If your child is very impulsive, then early mistakes caused by lack of strength, insufficiently developed hand-eye coordination, or other problems of manual dexterity, may end in an explosion of fury. During such rages, damage may be caused to materials and tools. Never respond by saying, 'Since you can't take proper care of things, you can't use them again.' Not only does such a punishment deny a child important learning experiences, it also prevents much-needed practice in self-control. The child who, in a fit of temper, smashes up a model which took hours to construct, will feel miserable enough once the anger has passed, without any help from adults. Give your child the tools, and let him or her get on with the job. And having made the gift, recognize that you no longer have the right to exercise an owner's control. If the child wants to dismantle a costly radio-controlled aircraft to find out how it works, or breaks it in pieces after failing to make it work, that is his right, and you really have no legitimate reason to criticize, however angry or upset such destructive curiosity makes you feel.

Implementing thinkers often feel happier when dealing with objects than with human relationships. However, as I explained in chapter 2, social skills are essential for success in life and should be acquired and practised within an emotionally secure environment, where cooperation and sharing are regarded more highly than competition and self-interest. Encourage projects which require collaboration as well as practical expertise. A group of older children, for instance, might work together to repair – and perhaps learn how to drive – an old car; construct a tree-house; prepare food for housebound old folk; create an attractive mural for the local library, and so on. The more implementing thinkers are able to use their special skills in situations which involve others, the easier it becomes for them to adapt to working as one of a team on leaving school.

APPROACH 4

You will adopt this approach at the start of your enhancement programme if your child's primary mind style is that of an inventive thinker. If he or she also favours the left side of the brain:

Enhance learning by providing guidance in his or her quest for self-discovery. This often means curbing his more hazardous ideas without reducing his strong desire to find things out for himself. To carry off this challenge successfully requires diplomacy, patience and understanding.

If your child favours the right side of the brain:

Enhance learning by allowing scope for practical experiments. Avoid censure when the idea sounds crazy, even if the results live up to your worst fears. These children are more interested in translating vivid fantasy into reality than in producing anything of great practicality.

The right-brain-dominant child has a greater ability to make less obvious connections and is often far more imaginative in his or her experiments and discoveries. As a result, many of his or her creations may have a surrealistic appearance and may prove quite impracticable.

Your role Offer guidance and provide practical advice. Instead of discouraging or prohibiting experiments, offer sufficient supervision to allow curiosity to be safely satisfied.

These children's strong curiosity and powerful drive to discover *what would happen if* . . . frequently gets them into trouble with adults – and with good reason. The more dramatic examples of this desire to discover reported to me, include pouring ink into the cistern to find out what colour the bath water would turn; seeing what a younger brother would look like bald; setting up a pirate radio station using an ex-army radio transmitter; wondering how high the family cat could fly in a home-made hot-air balloon (she was rescued moments before her maiden flight!). Small wonder that the parents of inventive thinkers often have frayed nerves and neighbours who refuse to talk to them!

But taking one of the examples given above – for example, performing the first experiment with different kinds of dyes – only using bottles of water and rubber tubes instead of a plumbing system, could provide useful practical lessons. Similarly, the illegal radio station, which led to official confiscation of the equipment and considerable embarrassment to the parents, might have been made perfectly legal if the child had been helped to build an intercom or use a CB system. And a child interested and clever enough to construct a workable hot-air balloon from illustrations in a family encyclopaedia deserves encouragement, although the cat clearly cannot be expected to suffer in the cause of self-discovery! Toy animals of different weights, plus a safe location from which to fly the balloon, would have transformed this into a valuable learning experience.

The essential thing is never to damage or diminish the child's curiosity by imposing needlessly severe restrictions on his desire to experiment. So offer support and encouragement. Provide the materials and resources needed, and guide the child without restraining his imagination.

THE TWO WAYS OF LEARNING

Some children learn most easily when their knowledge is built up slowly but surely, one fact being added to the next in a careful, methodical manner. Because this resembles building a house one brick at a time, starting from the foundations, this is called the *basement-up* method: information is mastered by gradually accumulating facts. This is how many textbooks and school courses are structured.

Other children learn best when helped to understand general concepts before being taught specific facts. This enables them to appreciate the way different pieces of information relate to one another and to the subject as a whole. Because this provides, before work begins, an overall view of what the finished construction will look like, this is known as *top-down* learning.

If your child finds a school subject difficult, confusing or dull, a conflict between the teaching style used and his or her preferred way of learning could be responsible. For instance, children who favour a top-down approach can quickly get bored or baffled by the methodical piling-up of facts involved in the basement-up teaching method. Equally, children who favour basement-up learning may become confused by being exposed to the many different aspects of a subject when general concepts are taught before specific facts.

The best way of explaining how to use these two methods is to look at an actual example. Suppose your child is having difficulty in learning history, which is being taught using a basement-up method. This means that he or she is given a great many facts – dates, personalities, battles, places, treaties and so on – but little, if any, overview of the topics. As a result, your child may be finding it hard to integrate and understand the information. Let us also imagine that one of the topics being taught by this method is the discovery of the New World. Here you might widen the child's horizons by discussions of what life might have been like for native American Indians before the white man came, their culture, life-style, methods of hunting, the homes they lived in and so on. The backgrounds of such explorers as Columbus and Cabot, life at sea, navigational methods, the food eaten, the weapons carried, the way early settlements were built – all of these might be made the basis of enjoyable practical activities, involving drawing, painting, model-making, and visits to museums and libraries.

Top-down learning must never become a chore: as long as it remains an interesting game, your child will acquire knowledge through enjoyable first-hand discovery.

Now let us suppose that the same subject is being taught using a top-down rather than a basement-up method – not uncommon in the more progressive schools. Here your child's confusion could be due to his or her need for a carefully structured basement-up approach coming into conflict with the school's teaching methods. So your task is to present the information in a more methodical way, in order to overcome the confusion and allow the child to slot the facts together one at a time. You can do this by encouraging him or her to construct tables listing dates, places, people, the number of ships that sailed on different voyages, how many sailors were involved, what kind of cargoes were shipped home, and so on. By matching the presentation of information to your child's favourite way of learning, you will build both confidence and knowledge.

Strongly left-brain-dominant children usually, but not invariably, favour the basement-up approach, while right-brain-dominants tend to feel more comfortable when learning by the top-down method. Children with inte-grated brains can generally switch from one method to the other without difficulty.

Start by using the learning method suggested in the approach you have followed above. But be ready to change to the alternative strategy if your child appears to find this way of learning confusing or unhelpful.

A plan for basement-up learning

1 Prepare a study schedule which lists the key topics to be covered, and suggest a time period over which the learning must take place – for example, in order to be ready for an exam.

2 Review the schedule every few weeks to make certain that your child feels comfortable with the plan, and is not being compelled to move forward too quickly. Basement-up learners should never move to a new topic before earlier ones are fully understood.

3 Your child must be encouraged to proceed methodically. While nobody enjoys making mistakes, this is especially damaging to basement-up learners, who lose confidence and become more anxious. Reduce this risk by helping to break down complex topics into smaller, simpler items. By steadily building his or her knowledge in this way, your child should be able to double or even treble his or her learning efficiency.

A plan for top-down learning

Here, rather than building one fact on top of another, in a logical step-by-step manner, you should help your child to gain an overall understanding of the subject. Do not be afraid to provide information in fragmented form. Facts and ideas which, while relevant to the topic under discussion, are not directly connected with it, can be offered without fear of creating confusion, since your child will integrate different items into a meaningful whole.

1 Top-down learning should start with a study of general concepts, so that the child has a good grasp of the main issues before getting down to fine detail. The best way is to jump in at the deep end by reading around the subject as much as possible.

2 Create a fairly simple study plan which ensures that the wider issues are all being covered.

3 Although much of what the child reads and learns initially may not make complete sense, a few misunderstandings will not impede the top-down learner's progress as it would that of a child who favours the basement-up approach. In fact, top-down learners are motivated by early failures of comprehension to dig deeper and discover even more. Far from confusing them, this method provides the opportunity for maximum learning efficiency, since it creates mental links between different aspects of the subject.

WORLDS WITHIN WORLDS

People live not in one world but in six, and each influences their thoughts and emotions in different ways and with varying intensity. These worlds within worlds are illustrated in figure 8.

Fig. 8 The World of Learning

The centre circle represents world one, your child's unique, individual world: the personal inner environment created from brain preference and mind style, personality traits and anxieties which, together with experiences, determine how the remaining five worlds are viewed. The results of these perceptions and processes are moods, attitudes, opinions, beliefs, motivations and the sense of self, all of which make the child behave in various ways. His or her behaviour usually makes a strong impact on world two, that of their immediate surroundings, but exerts a rapidly diminishing influence over the remainder.

In this book I suggest many practical ways in which you can help your child to develop world one skills for coping with the challenge of uncertainty and change. Bring about such adjustments of attitude and approach in your own inner world as well, by adopting the same mental procedures and by expanding your own mental abilities through an understanding of brain preference, mind styles, the influence of personality traits and the effects of anxiety on performance.

World two comprises the home and those living there. This, the chief arena for the interplay of ideas, thoughts and emotions among the individual family members, is where parents have the greatest influence and can bring about beneficial changes most easily.

Create a warm, supportive, non-judgemental environment in which your child does not feel afraid to experiment, to explore and to experience. Keep restraints, physical and emotional, to a minimum. Have a small number of sensible rules, and explain them by the power of reason rather than by the strength of your position. Then apply them *consistently*. Fill your home with creative opportunities of all kinds, but do not pressure the child into participating. Creativity can be exposed by opportunity, but never imposed by authority.

World three consists of your child's school. Your opportunities for bringing about changes here will depend both on the attitudes of teachers and on the way you approach them. Very often you need to try and make changes here, especially when the child is anxious about some aspects of school life. Open a constructive dialogue with your child's teachers. Participate as fully as possible in the life of the school. Do not be defensive or aggressive. Listen to what is being said about your child as objectively as possible. The great majority of teachers are on your child's side; they want him or her to succeed, to be happy and fulfilled. They care about the failings of the system under which they are forced to work, and appreciate only too well the stresses it creates for themselves and their students.

Have the confidence to help your child, not in competition with the school, but in cooperation. Research has shown, for example, that the participation of parents has improved ability in both reading and arithmetic, and children making six months' progress in two months is commonplace.

In world four, your neighbourhood and local community, apply pressure on those in authority to take education seriously, and to pay more than public relations lip service to the importance of all children being given the best chance in life. Nursery schooling, for example, can make a significant difference to the rate at which children learn later on. A recent American study suggests that children who get an early start in learning are far more likely to enjoy success throughout their school careers.

Unless one has achieved a position of power in the community, it is harder here to exert much influence on one's own. Groups, of course, can exert far more pressure, and it is always worth finding out if there are other parents with similar problems or interests who might be prepared to cooperate in schemes for helping children with special needs.

As I have suggested, intellectual thinkers might be

helped to acquire better social skills through the forma-
tion of a local club where they could meet and take part
in mentally stimulating activities. By appealing to their
thinking style you are far more likely to interest them in
social activities. The Explorer Clubs, run in Britain by the
National Association for Gifted Children, has been doing
this with great success for many years. In addition to
weekend activities, which cater for a wide range of
interests – for example, astronomy, art, playing musical
instruments, working with microcomputers – they also
run summer camps, and there is no reason why parents
with intellectually able but isolated and, perhaps, socially
anxious children should not do the same in their own
neighbourhood. It is also worthwhile investigating what
facilities are available to enable children with various
thinking styles to find stimulation and entertainment, so
that they can learn through play.

World five comprises the cultural heritage and social
norms of one's country, and world six those of other
nations. While the influence of world five is usually strong
– it determines the type of formal education a child
receives, for example – the power of world six to impose
ideas and views varies considerably. Parents sometimes
seek to reduce their children's knowledge of world six
through acts of censorship, as, of course, do the govern-
ments of many countries. It is far better, however, to help
provide a child with the mind skills of critical analysis,
judgement, taste and discrimination, and then allow unre-
stricted access to any sort of knowledge, than to try to
raise barriers or impose prohibitions. Not only are they
hard to enforce, they also make the forbidden fruit appear
far more appealing than it usually is.

In world five, there are support groups dedicated to
improving and expanding education by providing teachers
with modern facilities and with rates of pay reflecting

their professional training and social responsibilities, and ensuring that children are given the books and equipment necessary to expand their mind skills and realize their brains' true potential. All these can only come about as a result of political will and popular pressure. Education may be costly, but a society always pays a far higher price for ignorance.

Worlds five and six are, of course, those over which individuals can usually exert the least influence, although, here again, pressure groups can often bring about significant changes in attitude, on a national and even a global level.

Society as a whole must also start changing its attitude towards teaching and learning, which is only to say that individuals must come to view education from a different, more generous perspective. More than seventy-five years ago John Dewey, the American philosopher and educator, observed that what was required was the 'improvement of education, not simply by turning out teachers who can do better the things that are now necessary to do, but rather by changing the conception of what constitutes education.'

Putting these procedures into practice

There can never be any hard and fast rules for creating a learning world for your child. But by adopting the approaches suggested above, and by planning a mind-skill enhancement programme which takes into account your child's brain dominance and mind style, you stand a good chance of achieving the best possible match between the way your child thinks most effectively and the manner in which information and experiences are presented. By moving, slowly but surely, from styles with which he or she is familiar to less familiar ways of thinking, you encourage your child to become more fluent and flexible in the use of his or her brain. At the same time your own thinking should improve considerably, as you stimulate and develop a wide range of new mental skills.

How can you tell whether your approach is the right one, or whether it needs to be changed? The answer will be found by asking your child the right questions and listening correctly to her or his replies. While this may seem little more than common sense, the skills involved are actually subtle and complex, and must be employed properly to be fully effective. In chapter 7 I will explain how this can be done.

7
Listening and Talking – The Mind Enhancers

If you think back to your own schooldays, you will probably recall that the most effective teachers were also the best communicators. During their lessons you not only learned a great deal, but you also felt stimulated and excited. You looked forward to their lessons with pleasurable anticipation rather than dread or indifference, and came away feeling you had really learned something worthwhile. Probably you worked even harder for these teachers than for other members of staff, and found that doing well came more easily. These excellent teachers might not always have had as much knowledge or experience as some of their colleagues, but when it came to listening and talking they were in a class of their own. Their eloquence and sensitivity fired your enthusiasm and helped you learn without even realizing it.

Listening and talking, two of the most commonplace and seemingly simple tasks we undertake, are in fact among the most complex and subtle of human activities. They are also the two basic tools for enhancing mind skills. Research has shown that progress by children whose parents are skilled at listening, and know how to ask the right kind of questions, greatly exceeds that of students who, although aided by skilled specialist teachers, were denied a listening ear at home. So let us consider each in turn, to understand how, when used correctly, they can exert such a powerful influence over mental development.

THE THREE LEVELS OF LISTENING

If you want to find out what your child really thinks and feels, stop talking and start listening – not only to what is being said, but, no less importantly, to words left unspoken. Effective listening is not a difficult skill to master, and the rewards, for both you and your child, can prove considerable. You will not only start understanding other people far better, but you will also gain valuable insights into your own attitudes and emotions.

As figure 9 shows, listening is the most important component of communicating.

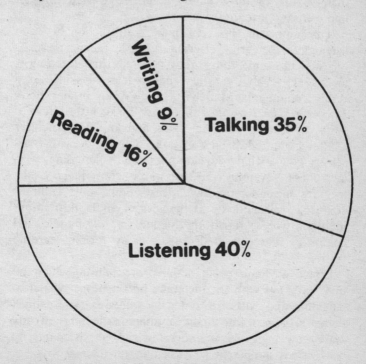

Fig. 9   Four components of communication

The idea that listening is a skill which requires knowledge and practice to use effectively may strike you as surprising. We listen so routinely and effortlessly – the average person spends around 75 per cent of his waking moments in verbal communication – that it seems unlikely there could be much more to learn. Yet research has shown that the average parent or teacher listens with an efficiency of around 25 per cent at best. Translating these figures into classroom situations, and assuming that, out of forty hours of study sessions per week, teachers devote some thirty hours a week to talking, it suggests that more than twenty of those hours could be wasted through impoverished listening.

It is important, first, to make a distinction between listening and hearing. Because people regard these as one and the same thing, they conclude that listening is an instinctive ability rather than a learned skill. 'As a result,' comments Madelyn Burley-Allen in her book *Listening: The Forgotten Skill*, 'we make little effort to learn or develop listening skills and knowingly neglect a vital communication function, thereby denying ourselves educational development and increasing self-awareness.' Among the inevitable consequences she includes misunderstandings, frustrations, hurt feelings, confused instructions and the loss of vital information: in other words, much the same kind of muddle and confusion that one finds in so many formal learning sessions.

Effective listening is an active process during which the mind interacts with the incoming information, evaluates, analyses and visualizes it, and creates associations between the new knowledge and facts or feelings already stored away in the memory. Ineffective listening, by contrast, is a passive process during which words are heard but only superficially attended to.

The American researcher Dr Anthony Alessandra has identified three levels of listening. At level three we find passive listening, paying attention with half an ear, and listening in spurts. During this sort of listening we fake interest and pretend attention, really preparing our replies rather than focusing on what is being said. Level three listening is often easy to identify, with the speaker realizing that he or she is not holding the other person's interest or attention.

During level two listening, the surface meaning of the words is attended to, but little or no effort is made to seek out deeper meanings. This type of listening can be difficult for the speaker to detect, since the listener may appear to be giving his or her full attention. This can lead to misunderstandings and confusions: instructions may not be followed, or the impression gained by the listener may be exactly the opposite of what was intended. 'I don't mind missing the school trip,' a child tells his mother who, listening at level two, jumps to the conclusion that he really does not care about the lost treat. It may be, of course, that level one listening – where attention is paid to underlying feelings as well as to facts – would have conveyed a very different impression.

Mistakes can also arise when the parent or teacher assumes that their explanations must have been understood, since the child showed no obvious signs of inattention. Strongly left-brain-dominant children and adults have a tendency to favour level two listening, because they prefer analysing facts to exploring emotions. Level two listening is also used by adults who are being told something they would sooner not hear. A parent who finds it hard to cope with his or her child's honest feelings – to do with sexuality, for instance – may switch to this level of listening when fearing that some potentially distressing self-disclosures are about to be made. He or she may immediately try to change the subject, jolly the child out of it, or pretend not to hear.

At level one we find active listening. Here the listener is attending both to what is said and to what has been left unspoken. He or she is conveying, by expression, eye contact, posture and other key body signals, that the words being spoken are of deep interest to him or her. Such active listening not only aids understanding, but it also encourages the speaker to keep talking, to elaborate ideas, to risk greater self-disclosure, to expand on beliefs and to dig deeper into his or her memory for information.

At level three one encounters mostly *negative listening*, of the type described below. At level two there is mainly *neutral listening*, while level one involves the most import-ant skill of all – *positive listening*. By listening in this way you stand a much better chance of discovering the true causes of your child's difficulties and distress. (You can also, of course, help to ease anxieties and fears by encouraging him or her to talk about any problems openly and honestly.)

Let us review each of these different ways of listening in turn, to see how they arise and what their consequences are likely to be.

Level 3 – negative listening

When adults listen to children, they often do so negatively because they have adopted a patronizing attitude towards them. Their sense of moral, physical, emotional or intel-lectual superiority leads them to hear most easily anything that appears to justify their preconceptions. Equally, one finds children using the same negative forms of listening because they are upset, frightened, annoyed, frustrated or disappointed by what parents and teachers are trying to tell them.

This happens because the words we hear are not

attended to in an objective way, but perceived through a variety of mental filters. These consist of all our beliefs, assumptions, attitudes, anticipations, experiences and expectations, and they cause us to focus on, and highlight, certain features of what is being said, while overlooking or ignoring others. Mind styles have a part to play here, too. Involved thinkers, for example, are more likely to notice the emotional aspects of speech, and intellectual listeners to fasten on to facts.

While reading through the nine major ways of listening negatively that I am about to list, reflect honestly on the extent to which you have used any of these with your own child over the past few weeks. You should also consider how often, and under what circumstances, your child seems to use negative listening. This can provide helpful insights into feelings, fears and frustrations.

1 Emotional listening Here excitement, anger, envy, frustration, bitterness, jealousy, disappointment or some other powerful emotion colours everything that is heard. Emotional listening is a sort of inner deafness in which the highly aroused brain is virtually incapable of rational thought.

When your child becomes over-excited, or has a temper tantrum or some other outburst, do not fall into the trap of responding with emotional listening. However upset or uptight you feel, try to listen at level one by employing either *diagnostic* or *empathic* listening (see pages 125 and 129). If you become too upset to continue, stop the conversation in order to allow a cooling-off period.

2 Dismissive listening This occurs after the listener has decided that what the speaker has to say will not be worth listening to. Adults listening dismissively to children often betray the fact by the use of such casually contemptuous comments as 'Don't be so silly'; 'I've never heard such nonsense'; 'You're too young to know what you are talking about'.

Not long ago I heard the following exchange between Jane, aged ten, and her mother Mary. Jane wanted the hall light left on while she went to sleep. Mary thought her daughter was behaving like a baby and pointed out that, during the winter, she walked home from school in the dark without feeling afraid. Jane considered this for a moment, and then remarked, 'But darkness always looks more scary indoors.'

It was an interesting and perceptive comment, which Mary might have used as an opportunity for exploring her daughter's fears. The child had tantalizingly half-opened a door on to the normally hidden world of anxieties. Had Mary listened positively, she might have achieved a much deeper understanding of her daughter. Instead, having made up her mind in advance that her request was infantile, she dismissed any remarks the child might make by way of explanation for her request: 'Don't be silly, darling,' she replied briskly as she clicked out the light.

Children listen dismissively to adults when they are being told something they would sooner not hear. 'Unless you are prepared to buckle down and work hard this term, you'll never get the exam grades needed.' 'Yeah, yeah,' says the dismissively listening child, who has no intention of doing anything of the sort.

Dismissive listening in children is often linked to anxieties. By refusing to allow themselves to hear the things they would sooner not hear, they reduce their distress in two ways. First, through avoidance: it is only human nature to prefer not to confront the truth when it upsets us, and to seek to escape from our anxious feelings by dismissing the worry from our minds. Secondly, dismissive listening can reduce anxiety by means of a denial of the reality of a situation. Again, this is a common reaction to something that upsets us. When very bad news is broken to people, a typical immediate response is for them to gasp, 'Oh, no!'

Instead of becoming angry at your child's seeming indifference, or irritated by his or her apparent lack of realism, then reacting to his or her casual dismissal of your concerns with sarcasm or bitterness, use level one listening to explore his or her true feelings on the subject. What worries, uncertainties, self-doubts or fears underlie the apparently uncaring attitude?

3 Put-down listening Here the listener only seeks an excuse to make some crushing and sarcastic remark – part of a power play intended to demonstrate the speaker's inferiority. Once again, children are often the victims. The focus of hearing is reduced for the same reasons as in dismissive listening, because the purpose is not to take in and reflect on all that is being said, but to pick on specific words or on a certain phrase, which can become the launching pad for a crushing retort.

I remember hearing an earnest, but not very successful sixteen-year-old asking his form master for career advice. After describing his fairly unimpressive progress, he concluded, 'What should I do for the best, sir?' The teacher, who had seemed bored by the boy's account, glanced up from the papers he had been studying, commenting loudly and to the general amusement of the class: 'The idea of your being able to do anything for the best is beyond my imagination.'

Put-down listening frequently indicates a clash of mind styles, as the intellectual thinker dismisses the intuitive approach of the involved thinker, or the action-orientated implementing thinker decries the cautious, analytical approach of the intellectual thinker.

4   *Judgemental listening*   People who listen like this want a chance to pass sentence on the speaker. Linda, whose parents both had to go out to work, had missed a day's lessons so as to look after her sick brother. The following morning she attempted to explain her absence to the form teacher. Before she could do so, the woman said disdainfully, 'You don't need to tell me lies. I know why you missed my classes. It's because you are either too idle or too stupid to keep up with the rest.'

Adults, especially teachers who are primarily left-brain-dominant intellectual thinkers, are often extremely judgemental in their dealings with the other mind styles.

5   *Distracted listening*   This results from trying to listen and do something else at the same time. Rather than stopping work, the person listens with half an ear, making occasional encouraging noises to maintain the pretence of paying attention. 'How interesting, dear,' says the mother absently, as she tries to complete some urgently needed office work. 'I see, that's good,' murmurs the father intent on watching television.

If you believe that what is being said is more important than what you are doing at that moment, stop immediately and listen at level one. If you either cannot or do not want to stop at that moment, never be afraid to explain your preoccupation and fix a later time when you will be able to listen attentively. Although parents hesitate to do this for fear of upsetting or discouraging the child, distracted listening is actually a far greater insult and one which may result in many more confusions, misunderstandings and hurt feelings.

6   *Awe-struck listening*   This occurs when the child feels so intimidated by an adult's power and authority that he or she listens without taking much in, allowing the words to flow unheeded past their ears while a distant, glazed

expression comes over his or her face. If parents or teachers adopt a godlike, aloof and unapproachable stance this is frequently the type of listening that results.

Even when their own school days are no more than a dim and distant memory, parents, too, can find themselves using awe-struck listening when going back to school to talk to their child's teachers. The atmosphere of their surroundings and the attitude of some teachers may strip away the years and turn them into helpless pupils again. As a result, even well-merited outrage over some educational failure may remain unspoken, or be diluted into a mild, almost apologetic, protest.

7 *Anxious listening* This has the same effect as awe-struck listening, in that little or nothing of what is being said is taken in. Often anxious listening is combined with awe-struck listening – the child is made nervous by such an important person condescending to speak to him at all. But it can also occur when the child is only in awe of the adult in terms of his or her ability to cause him pain and humiliation. As soon as the adult starts to speak, the child becomes fearful and seeks to cope with these feelings, usually by psychologically switching off.

8 *Apathetic listening* This results from a 'couldn't care less' attitude; the child does not hear because he just does not want to bother. Such negative listening is usually all too obvious from his expression (ranging from boredom to contempt), his posture and his gaze. He studiously looks away while listening. Often this is simply another response to anxiety: rather than using avoidance to cope with the upsetting feelings, the child uses denial – 'What does it matter what *she* thinks!' – or an attempt at emotional insulation – 'I'm not going to let anybody get through to me; that way you don't get hurt!'

9 Impulsive listening Here the listener, usually a child, is so eager to get started on some exciting activity that he or she simply cannot be bothered to listen to instructions, explanations or warnings. This is particularly likely to affect action-orientated children (implementing or inventive thinkers), when they are eager to embark on a new project. But impulsiveness can also act as a defence against anxiety, with the child eager to get a distressing task completed as quickly as possible. In this case, impulsive listening is just another facet of the anxiety response.

Impulsive listening gives some children a reputation for disobedience. But it is not that they are not prepared to obey – merely that your instructions have never got through to them. I shall describe the most effective way of talking to impulsive listeners in a moment.

As you can see, there are many ways of listening inefficiently, and everybody is guilty of practising most of them at least some of the time.

Level 2 – neutral listening

Here attention is paid to what is said, but there is no attempt to search for inner meanings. There are occasions when such neutral listening is justifiable. Conversations of which the only purpose is to exchange simple, factual information usually work effectively at this level. But even this apparently straightforward task is not always performed as well as it might be, which is why people can forget another person's name only five minutes after being introduced!

Occasionally, to avoid mistakes and to check your understanding of what has been said, repeat the main points of another's comments once he or she has finished speaking. This establishes mutual agreement on the key issues, provides a safeguard against mishearing, and impresses them more deeply in your memory.

Children should learn neutral listening as early as possible, and you can make their task easier by using the special ways of talking to them that I shall be describing in a moment.

Level 1 – positive listening
This involves listening actively and paying attention to the thoughts and feelings left unsaid, as well as to the words spoken. Positive listening is the aural equivalent of reading between the lines and searching for hidden meanings. This is not a difficult skill to master, and by doing so you will understand far more clearly how others feel.

If you want to discover, for instance, why your child has done unexpectedly badly in class, or become miserable about going to school, use *diagnostic listening*. If you want to help your child to understand and express his deep emotions, use *empathic listening*. When listening to children in order to help them communicate more effectively, use *attentive listening*.

Diagnostic Listening

This involves adopting the approach that an experienced doctor uses when making her diagnoses.

Start the discussion by asking a friendly but neutral question, such as 'You seem a bit down today – do you want to talk about it?' While speaking, keep your expression friendly and avoid any hint of criticism. Then, having made the first move, say as little as possible. Even if hurt or upset by your child's replies, try to keep your feelings to yourself for the time being, so as not to inhibit further disclosures. When told by her patient that he smokes heavily, a good GP does not crossly inform him that he has only himself to blame for being ill. Were she to do so, he would be very likely to keep quiet about any other bad habits – facts which might prove essential for an accurate diagnosis – that might influence her diagnosis and treatment. Instead, she makes a mental note of his disclosure and uses that information when prescribing an appropriate treatment.

You should do the same when listening diagnostically to your child. Be very careful to avoid the trap of negative, judgemental listening, an error that is all too easy to make. This *does not* mean that you should conceal your feelings about what has been said or done. But the time to reveal them is *after* you have achieved a clear understanding of the facts and reached a decision about what to do for the best. Also, be attentive to your child's tone of voice and the way in which words are stressed. Does he or she sound slightly miserable, even when recounting good news – 'I'm being moved up ahead of the rest of my class' – or inappropriately cheerful when talking about a disappointment – 'I wasn't made form captain after all'?

Conflicts between what is being said and how that information is expressed often indicate that painful emotions are simmering below the surface. Your child either cannot find the right words to express those feelings openly, or is too embarrassed to admit the truth. Tone is one way of providing a clue about his or her real reactions to events, without actually putting them into words; word stress is another. When a child shrugs off a personal upset with some comment like 'Honestly, it's *nothing*', you can take a bet that it really is *something* and that he does not know how to talk about it.

When using diagnostic listening, never let silences worry you. Most people hate them so much that they rush to fill the void, even though words are often unnecessary and usually unhelpful. Many children, and quite a few adults, have great difficulty in putting their more deeply held thoughts and feelings into words. Your attentive silence, combined with eye contact, a warm expression and obvious sympathy, provide the time and reassurance necessary to accomplish this difficult task.

Attend with your eyes as well as your ears, noting the child's expression and the direction of his or her gaze, together with gestures and postures. Tension in face or body is a clue to hidden stresses which may not be apparent from the words. A brief frown, or wry smile, before somebody or something is mentioned, suggests that they have an importance not always apparent from what is said. Three especially revealing types of body language are:

Blocking The child folds her arms and/or crosses her legs, leans away from you and refuses to give eye contact. These are non-verbal ways of shutting out the other person, and usually indicate discomfort, embarrassment, anger or some other negative emotion.

Fidgets The child displays small, anxiety-revealing movements with the hands or feet. Shuffling shoes on the ground, rubbing one leg against the other, playing agitatedly with a pencil, elastic band or a similar small object – such activities should all be noted. Movements that involve self-manipulations of some kind, such as pulling at the hair or pinching distractedly at the face, can indicate self-anger that cannot find proper expression.

Illustrators Here, movements with one or both hands are used to emphasize points. Sometimes speakers use illustrators like a conductor's baton to beat out the rhythm of their words. This normally indicates that they are comfortable with what they are saying. Notice, especially, the moment when illustrators cease and either fidgets or blocking signals take over. This generally indicates the transition between an easy flow of ideas and the expression of more emotionally charged, and perhaps less honest, remarks.

Pay attention to humour, particularly self-mocking witticisms. Feelings and fears too painful or embarrassing to be expressed openly may be concealed in light-hearted banter. Jokes are very often a cover for talking about activities or feelings which make one apprehensive. Listen, too, for denials like 'I'd never do that' or 'Of course I don't mind'. Often the real meaning is the exact opposite: 'I like the thought of doing it but am afraid to admit it' and 'I mind a lot, but don't want to show how you've hurt me.'

Become aware of pauses and repetitions, since these are often indications of anxiety. When people are fearful of their feelings, they express themselves far less fluently.

THE THREE RULES OF DIAGNOSTIC LISTENING

As your child's learning doctor, trying to diagnose mind-skill ailments, you must follow these rules.

Rule 1 Never criticize during diagnostic listening. Criticism often causes children to adopt one of the defensive strategies described in chapter 10. They switch off and think about something more agreeable, adopt a 'couldn't care less' attitude, or attempt to change the subject. When something is said that you know to be wrong or when an obvious error is made, say nothing immediately. Keep your expression neutral and your criticisms to yourself, for the moment.

Rule 2 Welcome mistakes. Only by adopting this approach will deep confusions and misunderstandings be cleared up. Again we can draw a medical analogy between a symptom, such as a fever, and the underlying cause. No experienced doctor would merely treat that symptom without finding out why the patient's temperature had risen in the first place.

Rule 3   Delay comment or correction. If you are helping your child with a problem in arithmetic, for example, do not jump in as soon as a miscalculation occurs. Make a mental note, or better still, a brief written one, that an error occurred that should be corrected later on. But for the moment probe further by saying something like 'I see. Why does that happen?'

Very often a child's difficulties are multi-layered and need to be explored one at a time, each one taking you closer and closer to the root of the failure. Keep your tone neutral and encourage an honest exchange of ideas by putting the child at ease. Use such comments as 'That's interesting', 'I understand', 'You've explained that very clearly', but talk far less than you listen. By remaining silent while encouraging the other person to continue talking, and by nodding and showing interest, you provide an opportunity to explore his or her ideas more deeply.

If your child is unused to being listened to like this, early sessions may be slightly stressful for you both. She or he may be made wary by the unfamiliar situation, and you may not always be certain how to proceed. But by using diagnostic listening routinely, when seeking to find out about problems, these initial difficulties will soon be overcome.

Empathic listening

The purpose here is to help your child to explore, clarify or come to terms with deep emotions. By doing so he or she can achieve insight and a greater understanding of these emotions and moods. While sharing his or her grief or happiness through empathic listening, you are less concerned to understand exactly what has gone wrong (if such is the case), and why, than with diagnostic listening, since your main function is to provide an attentive ear. But once again, say as little as possible.

By keeping your remarks relevant but short, you show that you really have been listening. Check that you have understood correctly, without distracting the speaker from exploring ideas or emotions more deeply and honestly. When you do speak, try rephrasing the comment that has just been made. As well as showing, again, that you really have been paying attention to what was said, this provides the child with feedback about how his remarks sound. Often it is very hard for a speaker to know exactly what impression his words are making. Child: 'It's just horrible the way Jenny treats me now – I always thought she was my friend.' Parent: 'It's upsetting when a friend treats you badly.'

Avoid asking too many direct questions, but if you feel the need to do so, follow the advice on page 133 for *effective talking*. You might also want to remark on the way the person is speaking, so as to draw attention to particular thoughts: 'It sounds as if it was really hard for you to tell me that . . . you seem to have special feelings about it.'

Do not shy away from discussing unhappy events with your child in a realistic way. Some parents insist on trying to play down sad feelings, by dressing up emotionally painful subjects in an artificially cheerful way. Such attempts to provide reassurance, by making the world seem brighter than it is, represent an avoidance response to anxiety on the part of the adult. This Pollyanna outlook prevents children from dealing with underlying fears by denying their existence. Instead of responding with a comment like 'It will be all right, don't worry', say, 'I can see you're sad about what happened. Do you want to tell me about it?' Children whose fears are constantly dealt with by dismissive reassurances suffer conflict and confusion. Painfully aware of their own unhappy feelings, they are being told to smile and look cheerful. And compelled in this way to feel good about feeling bad, they may start blocking their emotions by denying themselves the right to have feelings. In time this can lead to stress-related psychosomatic illness and other psychological difficulties.

Attentive listening

The importance of listening attentively to children of all ages cannot be over-emphasized. Research on the reading ability of children up to the age of eight, for example, has shown that those encouraged to read aloud, by attentive parents, often make better progress than pupils helped by experienced teachers.

Putting ideas into words and then explaining them in the atmosphere of trust, support and encouragement achieved by attentive listening, allows your child to develop such key mind skills as logical thinking, clarity of expression and self-confidence. While listening, use body language to encourage the child to continue, rather than verbal comments, since it is less likely to interrupt his or her train of thought. Adopt the approach used by radio and TV interviewers, who nod, smile and maintain eye contact to show their interest. They know that comments such as 'Go on', 'Tell me more' or 'That's interesting' are unnecessary interruptions of the speaker's flow of thoughts.

So far I have looked at active listening mainly as a skill that adults should perfect. But, of course, it is just as important for children to develop this vital mind skill.

The trouble is that schools provide very little practice in, and offer few rewards for, being able to listen. Inattention is punished, but paying attention rarely draws favourable comment – unlike writing or speaking, which are frequently praised when done well. A child who answers questions correctly after the teacher has provided oral information may be told that she has *learned* it well, but is very unlikely to be complimented for having *listened* efficiently.

To train a child as an active listener, you need to take two main steps:

1 Use level one listening, regularly. Remember that young children are highly imaginative. If they observe you using, and valuing, positive listening they are much more likely to adopt the same approach.

With older children, discuss the ideas and suggestions raised in this chapter, and share your feelings on the subject. Invite examples of the different kinds of negative listening, gleaned from their experiences at school or in the home. Suggest a game in which you each have to notice and identify different forms of negative listening in other members of the family. This helps the child to understand the various kinds of ineffective listening, while at the same time training effective listening. But make certain you keep the mood light-hearted, never allowing it to degenerate into a point-scoring squabble between children. Should this occur, gently point out that both are now using negative listening!

2 Start rewarding attentive listening, instead of taking it for granted.

Consider the ways in which brain dominance and mind styles may influence the ways in which conversations are listened to. As I explained above, level two listening may come more naturally than level three listening for strongly left-brain-dominant listeners, while those in whom the right side of the brain exerts greater influence could find level three listening slightly easier. However, they may be so concerned with the emotional aspect that factual information is overlooked. By attending primarily to either content or colouring, the sense of a message can be distorted. Ideally, therefore, children should become skilled in attending to both the surface meaning and the deeper implications of the words being spoken.

Now let us turn our attention to the second key element in successful verbal communications:

EFFECTIVE TALKING

Because people devote a great deal of time to talking does not always mean that they are especially good at it! My research has shown that verbal instruction occupies about 80 per cent of class time. Yet, alarmingly, much of that instruction proved either ineffective or even damaging to the growth of mind skills. Many of the comments made were a direct result of adults indulging in one of the types of negative level one listening described above. But even when they tried hard to talk constructively to children, mistakes still occurred.

For one thing, I found that most grown-ups spoke too slowly, at around a hundred words per minute or less. Since the brain can process verbal information at rates of up to five hundred words per minute, this painfully slow delivery reduces attention and leads to boredom. The brain, fed up with being forced to work at a snail's pace, drifts off, tunes out, daydreams, shoots away at mental tangents and generally misses the point.

Away from home, your child will probably have to learn how to cope with this problem by filling the time constructively through the use of visual imagery and association. These are mind skills that greatly enhance the retention and recall of information, and I shall be describing both in chapter 9. At home, speed your rate of delivery, if you feel you sometimes talk too slowly. Most children prefer listening at around 250 or so words per minute – while blind children, whose active listening is more highly tuned, prefer a delivery of some three hundred words per minute.

What is said, of course, is just as important as how it is said, and here research suggests that the content of the conversations adults have with children is often very unhelpful. In a study carried out at Bristol University by Dr Gordon Wells, a group of children was followed from fifteen months to the age of ten. On occasions these youngsters were 'bugged' by being fitted with miniature radio transmitters which allowed recordings to be made of their conversations at home and at school. At the same time language development was evaluated by the use of standard assessments. The results showed that the level of language ability in children depended on the quality of adult talking. Family background, parental education and economic status were not significant factors. Dr Wells explains:

What helps children to learn is simply to be a courteous conversationalist. With young children you may have to keep checking that you've understood what they are trying to tell you. But that's very different from correcting a child – although it may look similar. It's treating the child as someone whose thoughts matter, as an equal conversational partner.

Although by the age of five, all the children were able to understand what their teachers said to them, difficulties still arose due to the content and style of those conversations. While recordings made in the home showed mothers responding sensitively to their children's interests, providing relevant information, expanding the children's contributions and generally creating a constructive atmosphere, transcripts of conversations between children and teachers revealed a very different exchange. In the classroom, it was far less likely that a child's views would be acknowledged, or their contributions taken seriously or given positive recognition. Instead, the teachers usually adopted an over-rigid style of presentation which took little account of feedback from the children themselves. 'All teachers who have heard recordings of themselves in the classroom have been horrified,' comments Gordon Wells.

A major cause of concern here was the way in which questions were asked. Teachers spend up to 75 per cent of class time asking questions intended, amongst other things, to evaluate learning, correct misconduct, give directions and test knowledge. Questions are used least often to stimulate the growth of mind skills. Studies have shown that most questions asked demand only a very low level of thought – usually little more than a simple exercise in memory. In fact, good questions are an extremely effective way of motivating, stimulating and – as we have already seen – diagnosing the causes of learning difficulties. By asking the right sort of questions at home you can enhance the development of a wide range of mind skills.

Questions may be asked informally, to share knowledge that your child has just acquired, or more formally when, at his request, you test his understanding of a recently studied topic. When asking your child questions, make certain that they:

1 Are *clear*, leaving no doubt about their purpose
2 Are *sensibly stated*

3 *Relate* to your child's experiences
4 Are *relevant* to educational goals
5 Sustain *interest*
6 Provide an opportunity for *reflection and critical thinking*.

Questions to avoid
Some questions, because they are badly phrased or thought out, confuse rather than stimulate the child. Among the most frequently encountered are:

Vague questions, which provide no criteria for a satisfactory answer – for example, 'What do you think about pollution?' One study showed that 40 per cent of the questions asked in class are of this type.

Spoon-feeding questions, where the answer is so obvious that there is little point in asking them – for example, 'Is England larger or smaller than America?' The frequent use of such questions leads to lazy thinking and a decline in the desire to learn.

Confusing questions, which include too many elements for the child to be able to consider at one time – for example, 'When, where and why did the Civil War start?'

Narrow questions, which have only one right answer and test the child's powers of recall rather than her ability to think efficiently. The presentation of narrow questions frequently cues the child about what sort of reply is expected, and where the information is likely to be located in her memory. For example, in the question, 'When did William the Conqueror land in England?', the 'When' alerts the child that a historical date is being requested, while the name and place indicate the subject headings under which to search in the memory store.

For bright thinking, ask broad questions

Broad questions are those which have many equally valid answers, but no single correct one. Instead of testing general knowledge and recall, they stimulate creative thinking. For instance, the question, 'What would you expect the Normans to have brought with them to England?', offers a less obvious clue to the type of answer expected. Instead of involving a reply of just a few words, it requires a far fuller and more elaborate response. Because it contains no clear directions as to exactly where such information might be stored in the memory, the broad question, rather than being merely an exercise in remembering, obliges a child to search for information in various locations, to draw together themes and associate different ideas, thereby stimulating imagination and creativity.

Because children are much less familiar with broad than with narrow questions, your initial attempts to stimulate their thinking in this way may produce no more than an awkward silence, followed by a plaintive 'We haven't learned about that yet.' When the question is broadened still further to 'How might English history have been different if King Harold had won the Battle of Hastings?', the confusion, and resistance to answering, may be even greater. 'He lost,' a twelve-year-old boy told me angrily, 'so how can anybody know?'

The way the three questions above were posed – 'When did . . . ?', 'What would . . . ?' and 'How might . . . ?' – demonstrate how a change of phrasing and emphasis transforms the intellectual task from making demands on recollection to requiring increasingly complex and important mind skills.

Table 15 *The questions you might ask*

Form of question	Type of question	Mind skill needed
'When did . . . ?'	Narrow	Recall
'What did . . . ?'	Broad	Analytical thinking
'How might . . . ?'	Very broad	Reflective thinking

Broad questions are unpredictable and allow a range of acceptable responses. They require the child to infer, offer opinions, express feelings and pass judgements. They demand longer, more thoughtful and more carefully structured responses. You can use them as a means of encouraging your child to explore subjects more deeply, to experiment and gain fresh insights, to develop attitudes, beliefs and ideals. When used properly, broad questions compel the child to judge, justify, evaluate or defend a position.

Broad questions often use phrases such as: 'How do you feel about . . . ?' 'What do you think about . . . ?' 'Do you agree that . . . ?' 'What is your opinion about . . . ?' 'What do you think are . . . ?' Do not be surprised or disappointed if, at first, your child resists answering these questions. Schools offer so much more practice in answering narrow questions, that many children feel uneasy and threatened by questions not directly linked to a clearly indicated area of knowledge. As a result they become anxious, and seek to escape from the situation through avoidance. They may also express outrage that you are somehow being unfair and not playing by the accepted rules, as this exchange between an English teacher and her class of fifteen-year-olds illustrates:

Teacher: 'What do you think Dylan Thomas meant when he wrote "rage, rage against the dying of the light"?'

Students: No response.
Teacher: (After a long silence) 'Well, how did you *feel* when you read that line?'
One student: (Crossly) 'Why don't you just give us the answer?'

The fact that children are often dismayed by such questions does not mean that you should avoid asking them, or assume that they are incapable of coming up with interesting, informed and creative answers. All it takes is practice and persistence, in a friendly and supportive learning environment.

Always allow children plenty of opportunity to reflect on the question and come up with their answer. Often adults become so anxious themselves by the silence which follows the posing of a question, that they provide the solution far too rapidly. One study of response times in American classrooms showed that, on average, a teacher waited only *three seconds* between asking a question and either providing the answer or moving to another child. This is especially damaging to intellectual thinkers who, as you will recall, need time for reflection as well as having a strong need to be regarded as intelligent. Their inability to answer in the time allowed leads many children to conclude that, unless they are able to respond instantly, they must be slow and stupid.

Be patient and make it clear to the child that you are not in any hurry for him to answer. Show no irritation, either verbally or through your posture and expression.

Since, as I noted above, many people find silences oppressive, and the anxious child may come up with any answer just to bring the ordeal to an end, you should encourage your child to think aloud by saying everything that comes into his or her mind while seeking a solution. Thinking aloud is an extremely powerful mind skill, which benefits both adults and children. I have already mentioned that the process of transforming ideas into words imposes a structure on those ideas and means that they are expressed clearly. By using diagnostic listening as your child talks herself through a problem-solving or decision-making task, you can also identify weaknesses in her thinking process, irrational conclusions, illogical assumptions, gaps in her knowledge and so on.

But if children are to be encouraged to continue speaking while thinking, it is absolutely essential that you never make them afraid to voice their thoughts aloud. Criticism should be kept to an absolute minimum, and do avoid being pedantic. What matters is not whether children dot every 'i' and cross every 't', but that their ideas are interesting, lively and original.

Give your child time to get used to what may well be a novel way of asking questions for you both. Once he or she accepts that it is not going to be a punishing experience, and that you have a genuine interest in sharing his or her knowledge and experience, such sessions should become a great deal easier. Use games to help him develop an interest in, and an ability to answer, broad questions. These must not become general knowledge tests – which, as you will now realize, comprise highly cued narrow questions testing only recall – but rather explorations of imagination which all can play because they do not depend on any particular knowledge. For example, you might decide to find answers to what would happen (would have happened) if . . . dogs and cats learned how to talk; . . . all the grass in the world was killed off by a new disease; . . . television had never been invented; . . . aircraft had been around at the time of the Roman invasion of Britain.

Avoid asking too many questions at one time. Rapid-fire questioning prevents the child from thinking clearly and developing clear expression.

*　　*　　*

To summarize: effective listening and talking are probably the two most important ways of enhancing mind skills that you can employ. In fact, were you to close the book at this point and do nothing more to help your child than adopt the procedures contained in this chapter, I can guarantee that motivation would be increased, self-image strengthened, anxieties reduced and intellectual perform-ance significantly improved as a result of your new approach.

Become more aware of the different sorts of negative listening that can occur. Consider how your own brain dominance and primary mind style are likely to influence the way you and your child talk and listen to one another. Listen at level one when your child is telling you some-thing important, and avoid the negative habits of hearing I have described.

Gain practice in asking broad questions, but do not become impatient if at first your child finds these much harder to answer than the narrow ones with which he or she is almost certain to be far more familiar. Encourage him to ask broad questions himself, since you, too, are likely to need practice in creating the far more compli-cated answers that these demand. But never allow ques-tion and answer sessions to become stressful occasions, during which the child feels on trial. As we have seen, the two most common responses to anxiety – avoidance and denial of reality – create powerful barriers to successful learning. Be playful in your approach; even children whose primary mind style is that of the intellectual thinker learn more easily when a subject, while treated seriously, is presented in an enjoyable way.

8

Seeing Is Achieving

Before your child can have bright ideas or creative insights, before any effective thinking is, in fact, possible, the brain has to be provided with the raw materials of thought. These consist of information taken in through the five senses. The secret of success is to know what is worth paying attention to and what should be ignored. To do this, your child should step into the first of the three roles I described in chapter 2, and become an adventurer. Leonardo da Vinci wrote:

I roamed the countryside searching for answers to things I did not understand. Why thunder lasts longer than that which causes it, and why immediately on its creation the lightning becomes visible to the eye while thunder requires time to travel. How the various circles of water form around the spot which has been struck by a stone and why a bird sustains itself in the air. These questions and other strange phenomena engaged my thought throughout my life.

Before your child can think, therefore, he or she must learn to perceive; to engage in a constant quest for fresh ideas and original insights by travelling away from the well beaten track of conventional wisdom, by seeking his or her own explanations and understandings, instead of unquestioningly accepting the answers of others. While engaged in this adventure, developing personal theories and juggling new concepts around in their minds, children are not bored or afraid, but enthusiastic and fascinated. Think about something you really enjoy doing – perhaps your job, a sport or a hobby. You will certainly have noticed that, while you are absorbed in this activity, time speeds past; you are not worried by distracting thoughts because your mind is sharp and clearly focused. It is the same with your child.

When children fail in school and tell you that they are bored, that a subject is irrelevant or stupid, that they cannot concentrate or that they become tired after just a short period of study, or when they put off doing work assignments, they are saying one thing in many different ways – 'I'm not involved.'

Unfortunately, a great many children find a very great deal of what goes on in class extremely uninvolving. Sometimes the teachers are to blame for presenting information in a brain-numbing rather than mind-enhancing manner. Sometimes it is society's fault for expecting schools to teach subjects which have very little relevance to the kind of world the children live in, to the sort of aspirations they have, and to the goals they seek. Sometimes it is the child's fault for not giving either teachers or lessons a chance. Many subjects do take time to get into, at first requiring you to work hard without much excitement or reward, to slog away and put in a lot of effort, while taking it on trust that some day it will be all worthwhile. Learning to play a musical instrument, to be a skilled footballer, athlete, actor or singer, to speak another language, to write complicated computer programs, are just a few of the many skills which depend on a tremendous investment of time and energy before you start seeing any real results.

There will be occasions when parents and teachers have to insist that children buckle down to tasks that bore them, because they know that these subjects are essential stepping-stones to future success. Whenever possible, however, you should try to help your child feel personally involved in what he or she is doing. Presenting information in a way that matches brain preference and mind styles, by following the approaches in chapter 6, will help. You can also improve performance and increase motivation by encouraging the skills your child needs in his search for information.

As we saw in chapter 4, the first stage in thinking is perception, the input of the information that is to be processed. The final stage of this activity is performance, when the individual acts on the results of his brain work.

We will start by enhancing the major mind skills concerned with perception. There are seven of these, and all can be stimulated by means of games. Select those which appeal to you; because this book is intended to assist the parents of children falling within a wide age range, some may seem either too juvenile or too advanced for your own child. Set aside any which appear over-complicated for the moment, and employ them when your child is older. Games which you fear he or she would reject as being insufficiently challenging, can mostly be modified with a little thought and imagination.

To think efficiently we must start by perceiving clearly. We must use our five senses in such a way that knowledge supplied to the brain is:

1 Comprehensive
2 Accurate
3 Reliable.

Children, and adults, frequently fail because they attempt to solve problems or make decisions on the basis of incorrect or inadequate information. We all view the world through the filter of our preconceptions, rather than confronting reality directly, as many believe to be the case.

A simple experiment to demonstrate how expectations

colour perceptions can be performed using the three drawings in figure 10. Show one child drawing (a), while covering drawing (b). Show another child drawing (b), but not (a). Now let both look at (c) and ask them to find a hidden figure.

Children who see (a) first nearly always say it is a pirate, while those who were shown (b) usually tell you that it is a rabbit. By preparing their perceptions to identify either the pirate or the rabbit, you have created what psychologists call a *perceptual set*.

These mind sets arise because our brains make sense of the world by comparing incoming information with an already existing mental pattern. You notice this when finding your way around a strange town, gradually building up an internal model of how different streets are joined together, where various landmarks can be found, and so on. In time you rely so heavily on this internal map that you hardly notice your surroundings any longer, except when something unexpected happens – a building has been painted a different colour or a familiar landmark demolished, a shop has changed hands, and so on.

Fig. 10   The interplay of perception and expectation

Mind sets are essential in order that our brains may make sense of an enormously complex environment. If we tried to pay equal attention to everything in our surroundings, the brain would become overloaded, incapable of performing efficiently. To prevent this catastrophe, areas of the brain function like newspaper sub-editors, reducing the millions of items of information which arrive every second to just a few deserving of our consideration. The result, however, is that we often perceive not what really is happening, but what we would either like, or anticipate is going, to happen.

When a particular mind set becomes rigid and impervious to change, it leads to stereotyped thinking. A highly prejudiced person, for example, focuses very narrowly on any information that seems to support his bigotry, while refusing to perceive anything that might challenge those perceptions. In other words, he sees what he expects to see.

This blocking of incoming information by negative habits of thought is well illustrated by the failure of astronomers to discover the planet Uranus, despite thousands of years of intensive sky-watching. The planets as far as Saturn had been known since earliest recorded history, creating a mind barrier which made people believe that there could be no further planets in the universe. It was a rigid perceptual block which prevented them, not from looking, but from seeing, from giving credence to the evidence in front of their eyes. No further planets could exist, therefore none did exist! On several occasions before its eventual discovery by William Herschel in March 1781, astronomers had noticed a star in the position of Uranus; in fact, one had seen it on four successive occasions without perceiving the motion, against the background of stars, indicating that it was a planet. Even after Herschel had observed that the body possessed a visible disc – further clear evidence of its being a planet – he initially believed it to be a comet, and reported as much to his colleagues.

One area where mind sets play a major, and often very unhelpful, role concerns the way we perceive our abilities and evaluate success or failure. A child who has become convinced that he or she is hopeless at schoolwork will focus on failures, while the child who has confidence in her ability in class will pay more attention to achievements. To break a negative mind set, present contradictory information as often as you can. This means giving the failing child as many chances as possible to succeed in situations where failure was anticipated.

Unfortunately, this is not what normally happens. Knowing that Tommy or Jane is poor at sums and has little self-confidence, the teacher gives him or her very easy ones. This can be done with the best of intentions, to avoid distressing the child or to introduce a little success into his or her life. But the outcome is usually very different, with motivation and self-esteem declining still further. And it is not hard to see why!

If you give a child locked into a failure mind set a task that is too easy, success will have little meaning. Not being the least bit stupid, the child knows that success was handed to him on a plate and therefore has no merit. Far from encouraging motivation, this patronizing approach actually diminishes it. Imagine how an employee would feel if the boss handed various tough assignments to his co-workers, but then passed an extremely easy one to him. Instead of being grateful for not having to face the same degree of challenge, he is likely to feel insulted at the boss's low opinion of his abilities. If he is already lacking in confidence, then this strategy can only undermine him still further. It is the same with the failure-orientated child. On the other hand, to give such a child a hopelessly difficult task is equally unhelpful.

It is by providing tasks that are sufficiently hard to present a genuine challenge, while offering a realistic chance of achievement, that you gradually improve the clarity of a failing child's self-perceptions. Now, instead of focusing on mistakes and set-backs while largely ignoring successes, the child starts taking more notice of the things that he or she is doing right.

But distortions due to the preconceptions, prejudices, attitudes and opinions that make up mind sets are not the only reason why the information given to the brain to process is insufficiently comprehensive, inaccurate or unreliable. These faults often arise because too little attention is paid to sensory inputs – to the sights, sounds, tastes, smells and tactile sensations by which our senses keep us in contact with the outside world. Thinking about the four mind styles, you can see how this failure of perception might occur. The involved thinker may be so close to her feelings that she misses the facts, the intellectual thinker so intent on gathering the facts that he pays no heed to his feelings. The implementing thinker can be so busy considering the practical aspects of a problem that its more theoretical implications escape his notice, the inventive thinker so eager to get going that impulsiveness prevents her from taking in more than a small proportion of the available information.

An important mind skill for your child to perfect, therefore, is the careful, accurate observation of his or her surroundings, so that information from the senses is perceived with great clarity. In this way the strengths of each of the mind styles are combined, and their inherent weaknesses removed.

MIND SKILL 1 – CLARITY OF PERCEPTION

You can help your child to perceive more clearly and accurately by playing entertaining games during which attention is focused on different aspects of the surroundings. Since these involve more right- than left-brain thinking, you may find that children whose scores suggested that preference initially show greater aptitude. However, given some encouragement, even those with strong left-brain dominance will enjoy playing these games. And by doing so they will enhance their ability to think with both sides of the brain.

The paying-attention game

Select one of the five senses – for instance, sight – and explain that for the next few minutes you are both going to concentrate on using it as fully as possible. During this time the child is to pay as little attention as possible to all sensations of hearing, smell, taste and touch. How long you play for depends on the child's age and level of interest – never go on too long, because short games frequently repeated are better than occasional longer sessions.

Looking For this version of the paying-attention game, choose some reasonably complicated object, either natural or man-made, and ask the child to look at it as carefully as he possibly can. When playing with several children, try to have a sufficient number of similar objects to give one to each – for instance, picture postcards, photographs, pine cones, fallen leaves, rocks, fossils, flowers, rotting timber, fungi, carvings, pieces of crystal or sea shells.

The objects chosen should have plenty of detail and be small enough to hold and turn over in the hands so that they can be closely inspected from all angles. Each child studies the object as carefully as possible for a few minutes without saying anything. They then take turns at describing what they have seen. This is not a test of memory – they can keep on studying the object as they speak. Encourage the children to make increasingly precise and detailed observations, so that every feature is subjected to an intense scrutiny.

At first, their comments will probably focus on the more obvious aspects of the object, but after a while they will start seeing things that were originally overlooked – a tiny patch of algae on the underside of the piece of crumbling timber, the regular rib patterns of a fallen leaf, or subtle colour shifts in a lump of crystal as the light falls from different directions. Objects can then be swapped around among the children to see if they can spot things that others missed.

Expeditions can be mounted to suitable locations – the beach, woods, meadows, parks and so on – in search of objects to be used in this game. But make sure that the children look for a while (right-brain skill) before they speak (left-brain skill), so as to stimulate and exercise both hemispheres.

Listening   In this version of the game, the children are told to ignore everything but sounds. Where this can be done safely, they will find it helpful to listen with eyes closed, so as to focus all their attention on the sense of hearing. The idea is to detect as many different sounds as possible, close and far away, faint and loud. Again, these are not to be mentioned for a few minutes, while all those playing concentrate on listening. Then the sounds are described and discussed as before.

Tasting, touching, smelling   Some further preparation will be needed when playing this version. For taste exploration you will need different kinds of foods: salty, sweet, sour, dry, moist and so on. For touch exploration, use objects that provide interesting tactile sensations: for example, sandpaper, a mirror, modelling clay, dough, warm and cold water in bowls, different kinds of fruit and vegetables. For smell, choose not only obvious things such as perfumes, but also such items as dried grass, flowers and cooking ingredients. Have pleasant as well as less pleasant odours. Very often objects collected for 'seeing' practice can be used for other games as well.

When exploring taste, touch and smell it may help, as with hearing, if the children are blindfolded. But the purpose of the game is *not* to guess what is being tasted, touched, or smelled. Nor is it to pass an opinion about whether that sensation is pleasant or unpleasant. What is required is keen observation and accurate description rather than verbal labelling.

Left-brain-dominant children may have trouble with this at first, as they are so used to thinking by naming. Such a child will tell you: 'That's perfume.' You: 'But what does it smell like?' Child: 'Like perfume!' You: 'I'd like some more details of the way it smells. Does it remind you of anything?'

The same game can be played without using specific objects. While walking down a familiar street or through a country meadow, for instance, you can encourage the child to see, hear, smell or feel as intently as possible. When playing the paying-attention game you will be surprised at how different a well-known neighbourhood or landscape suddenly appears. Listen to traffic sounds, birdsong, the chatter of passers-by, a distant aircraft. Concentrate on smells: traffic fumes, wild flowers, cooking odours wafting through the open window of a restaurant, fresh bread in the bakers, and so on. Finally, focus on the sensations of touch: sunshine on the face, a breeze ruffling the hair, the way shoes pinch, the roughness of gloves on the hands, or clothes rubbing against the body.

* * *

This game helps children to become more perceptive about their surroundings, to observe more carefully and accurately, not only with the eyes but with all their senses. By allowing time for looking, listening, smelling, tasting and touching, before a word is spoken, the right side of the brain is able to respond to the incoming information in a more general way, before the left brain labels those perceptions by putting them into words.

The game trains another, no less important, mind skill – that of building up mind scenes which include sounds, tastes, touch sensations and smells in addition to visual images. In the next chapter I will explain how you can use this to give your child a powerful memory, to aid logical thinking, improve problem-solving, overcome anxieties and heighten motivation.

MIND SKILL 2 – METHODICAL EXPLORATION

Information must be explored in an organized manner in order that the brain can understand what is being perceived and so be able to identify gaps in knowledge or understanding at an early stage. Without method, the brain may be overwhelmed by fragmented perceptions, many of which, removed from their original context, make little or no sense. This is the state of mind we are in while dreaming, when a wild parade of disconnected ideas drifts around the mind. Children frequently feel the same way in their waking states, with a confusion of disjointed scraps of information, sights, sounds, smells and tastes spinning around in their minds, producing increasing uncertainty and bewilderment. A fundamental rule of successful learning is never to try to commit any information to memory until and unless you fully understand it. There is no point in cramming your brain with data which makes no sense, in the hope that somehow the mind will be able to work out what it is all about. The consequences will be mistakes, misunderstandings and frustrations.

In order to make sense out of large amounts of information, children must learn to classify knowledge under different headings, so that facts and figures may be accessed quickly and easily when required. Provide practice in this mind skill with games which require items to be classified in various ways, as well as explaining how this can help to make studying easier.

In My Zoo   Here is a game which provides this practice. It starts with one of the players saying something along these lines: 'In my zoo I want only four-legged animals.' The players then either have to name or write down the kinds of animals which could live in the zoo, such as lions, tigers, polar bears, zebras and so on.

The next player introduces a second requirement for being in the zoo, such as: 'In my zoo I want only four-legged animals which eat meat.' Any non-meat-eating animals – zebras, for instance – are expelled from the zoo, and it is now the turn of another player who says, for instance: 'In my zoo I want only four-legged, meat-eating animals with long tails.' Once again, more of the animals have to drop out. The purpose of the game is to end up with just one breed of animal in the zoo, and the player who achieves this is the winner.

Variations include 'On my farm', where you use farm animals, and 'In my store', which looks at groceries and other products. For children who prefer doing things to talking about them, for instance implementing and inventive thinkers, the game can be played by moving toy animals about (or they can be made out of modelling clay just for the game).

While travelling by car, plane or train, this game can be played as a modified form of I-Spy: one player opens up a classification, such as 'everything painted red', and you watch out for as many red things as possible. Then a second requirement is introduced, such as 'red things which can't move around', so eliminating vehicles from consideration. And so on until no more objects can be found for a set of descriptions.

Creating a schoolwork archive

School subjects also benefit greatly from being organized and classified. When children are able to draw together information from a great many sources, the subject becomes more interesting, and they can view it from a broader perspective. It is especially helpful with left-brain-dominant thinkers who, as we have already seen, tend to study the trees but miss the forests. All that is needed is a large drawer or box, with cardboard partitions dividing it into major subject areas. They may relate to different school subjects, such as history, biology or chemistry, or to important subdivisions within a single topic, such as imports/exports, industry, language, geology and so on, within geography.

Folders provide further subdivisions, and in these are collected classroom notes, cards listing references to pages in books, diagrams, charts, tables, illustrations copied from books or cut out of old magazines, articles, clippings from newspapers, postcards and photographs. Children with an interest in photography can be encouraged to take their own pictures to illustrate suitable subjects – for instance, when visiting sites of historical interest, museums, zoos, botanical gardens and archaeological digs. Tape recordings of radio programmes might also be included. This library of mainly printed material may be cross-referenced to a collection of physical objects associated with the subject – for example, books of pressed flowers, rocks, fossils, animal skeletons and models of all kinds. Implementing and inventive thinkers, especially, find this an enjoyable and motivating way of learning and remembering. When the time comes to write an essay or prepare for a test, the relevant files can be extracted and studied.

Classifying information in this way is not only a time-saver when searching for facts – it also helps the child to organize the material in his mind, so making its recall far faster and more accurate.

Younger children, especially implementing and inventive thinkers, may find this idea more appealing if, rather than storing pieces of information in boxes, they make a display of them in their rooms. You can help by showing them how to make a learning ladder, which is made of a sheet of stiff cardboard about 2 feet × 3 feet, with the five rungs and tapering struts made from coloured tape held in place by drawing-pins. Allow your child to select which topics should be included in the ladder. Starting by organizing the information relating to a leisure activity helps make a game of constructing and using the ladder rather than letting it become a school-related chore.

Now, various facts are written out on cards and fixed between the rungs of the ladder. Between the top two rungs are placed a few cards which provide general facts about the chosen topic. Between the next two rungs the child fastens cards on which are written more detailed and specific information. Proceed down the ladder in this way, with the wider spaces of lower rungs containing increasing detail.

In addition to cards with facts written on them, your child should be encouraged to create or search out illustrations and other related material – for example, small samples of different rocks for a learning ladder concerned with geology, or feathers and leaves for a natural history ladder. These can be stuck on cards which are then fixed outside the rungs of the ladder, using tape to link the samples to the relevant fact cards. But all the cards and items should be removable, so that the same ladder framework may be used for a large number of topics.

Constructing a ladder takes time, with your child adding information cards and other material gradually over a period of weeks. Additional facts and illustrations can be tracked down, and cards replaced, as new knowledge becomes available. Organizing information in this way makes it far easier for the child to understand and learn the facts and figures it contains, because the process of collecting, classifying, writing down and pinning up the information helps to arrange and establish it in his mind. To get the best results from the ladder:

1 Let your child decide where the cards are placed.

2 Encourage an active search for fresh information.

3 Keep the learning ladder displayed in a prominent place, such as bedroom or den, so that it can be glanced at from time to time. This casual review of the material will help fix the information into the memory more firmly.

4 Each ladder should cover a single topic only. Trying to include too many items of information is confusing and counter-productive. If the idea appeals to your child, there is no reason why a number of ladders on a variety of subjects should not be made and displayed at the same time.

On completion, leave a ladder in place for several weeks before replacing its contents with a fresh subject. All the information cards, together with any illustrations, maps, drawings, charts, notes, samples of material and so on, can be filed away in large envelopes and stored in a file box for future reference. When the time comes to revise a subject, perhaps for a test or examination, the ladder can be reconstructed without difficulty to provide an invaluable revision aid.

MIND SKILL 3 – DESCRIBING

Until your child is able to describe something clearly it is impossible for him or her to think about it clearly. When teachers or parents complain that a child is a 'woolly' thinker, it often means that she or he cannot form a strong mental picture of any given topic.

Develop this skill through discussions in which you actively encourage the child to describe different events, activities and objects, using both careful observation and creative imagination to produce powerful images. Vary the requests for descriptions, sometimes asking for a factual account of what was seen or heard, while on other occasions encouraging flights of fantasy. Two enjoyable and stimulating games which enhance a child's descriptive powers are 'Identikit' and 'Finish my story'.

Identikit Your child selects someone who is well known to the other players, perhaps a local shopkeeper, a relative, a friend or a personality from a popular TV show, and describes him or her as vividly as possible. The others have to try to guess who it is. Variations include choosing animals, objects, buildings or places to describe.

Finish my story For this game you decide on a number of elements that are to be included in the tale. These might be a haunted castle, windswept moor, steamy jungle, ocean liner and so on. You note them down on cards.

At the start of the story the hero or heroine arrives at the place mentioned on a card, selected at random from the pile by one of the players. That scene, together with what happens to the characters, must then be described as vividly as possible. When the story-teller gets stuck or wants to pass the turn on, he or she simply says, 'Finish my story', and the next player selects a card, transports the characters to a new location and, as before, makes the descriptions as imaginative and detailed as he can.

A variation on 'Finish my story' is to construct three trigger-word cards, as shown in table 16. One card contains thirty-six adjectives, the second thirty-six nouns and the third thirty-six verbs. You and your child select words from the cards at random, by throwing a dice six times. The first throw gives a number from the top row, the second a number from the left-hand column. Together these will identify one of the trigger words. For instance, on the nouns card in table 16, a throw of a 6 and a 2 means the chosen word is 'devil'. If a 5 and a 3 had been thrown, the word selected would have been 'dragon'. The first two throws are used to pick an adjective, the second pair a noun, and the third a verb. You can use the words shown on the cards below, but it is far better to create your own in collaboration with your child.

When three words have been chosen, you or your child must invent a story which describes the scene conveyed by the three words. Encourage fantasy by asking your child questions about the story he or she is creating.

Table 16   Trigger cards

1   Adjectives

	1	2	3	4	5	6
1	red	silly	floppy	thin	giant	damp
2	cold	blue	huge	ugly	pink	nude
3	hot	hungry	cruel	tiny	green	warty
4	dim	slimy	happy	tough	kind	black
5	clever	sad	jolly	soft	short	crimson
6	tall	fat	yellow	brave	white	spotty

2 Nouns

	1	2	3	4	5	6
1	pig	horse	worm	eskimo	witch	robot
2	ghost	fish	lion	car	dog	devil
3	mouse	duck	boat	bike	dragon	lizard
4	doctor	newt	whale	fairy	snake	fox
5	robber	spy	hunter	diver	tiger	Martian
6	rocket	ant	teacher	monster	bear	submarine

3 Verbs

	1	2	3	4	5	6
1	jump	hide	leap	run	crawl	eat
2	spin	climb	fly	fall	swim	sneeze
3	faint	kill	help	hurt	fight	save
4	destroy	burn	dive	sail	build	dig
5	cry	laugh	chew	sit	fear	drag
6	raise	drop	swallow	paint	dread	love

Suppose your child threw two 6s, then a 2 and a 5, followed by a 3 and a 2, this would give 'spotty', 'spy' and 'fly'. His or her task would now be to invent an imaginative story about, for example, a spotty spy who had to fly away on a mission.

Help your child to break out of mind sets by getting him to describe various details of the scene and to invest them with as much fantasy as possible. What sort of a spy was he – tall or short? How was he dressed, and how could people tell he was a spy? How did he fly – with wings fitted to his back, or in an aircraft? And if the latter, what kind of an aircraft – a modern jetliner or an ancient biplane? Get your child to draw the spotty spy in flight, or model him in plasticine, but only after he has been described in words.

MIND SKILL 4 – FLEXIBILITY

Children must learn to perceive things from more than just one viewpoint, or they run the risk of getting trapped by an inflexible perceptual set.

The frame game An enjoyable game for stimulating flexible perceptions can be made from a sheet of card with a 1-inch square hole cut out of it.

Your child uses the frame to view small areas of different objects in the home and outside. The idea is to search for interesting views which people normally miss, and restricting the range of vision by using the frame makes this task easier. A child might find, for instance, intriguing patterns on the flaking paint of an old bench, fascinating colours in an oil-streaked puddle, or strange fissures on the bark of an ancient tree. Help your child to see things from different viewpoints. Older children may enjoy taking photographs or making a drawing of the new shapes and designs spotted through their frame.

View switch Mind sets can be loosened, and stereotyped habits of perception broken down, by inventing stories in which your child must switch viewpoints. For example:

There's a car rushing past. What would it be like if you were the car's front wheel? How would the road look, and the people? How would the road feel, and what happens if you run over different kinds of surface – cobbles, smooth highways, country lanes, gravel drives and so on?

There's a fly on the wall. What does the room look like from up there? What does a loaf of bread look like as the fly drops towards it?

There's a bird overhead. How do we look to him? What does the house look like? How far can he see?

There's a fish in the pond. What view does it have of us, standing on the edge staring down? How does the depth of the pond appear? What do the tangle of weed, a bug swimming across the surface, or another fish, look like?

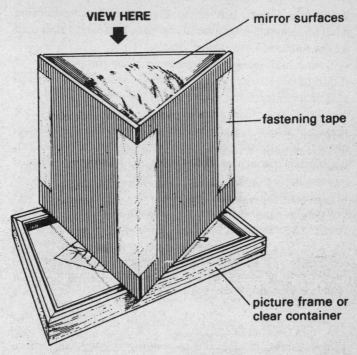

VIEW HERE

mirror surfaces

fastening tape

picture frame or
clear container

Fig. 11 The mirror toy

Mirror toy This is an easily made and amusing toy which appeals to many younger children, and helps them to see everyday objects in new ways. Construct a teleidoscope, which works like a kaleidoscope, by fixing three small mirrors together, as shown in figure 11. Use sticky tape to hold them in place.

Place this triple mirror on a frame of clear plastic, or glass. A transparent box lid or a picture frame are suitable (although you must, of course, be careful if using glass when playing with young children), so that the light shines through from underneath. Examine leaves, rocks, house-

hold items, flowers and so on. Ask your child to describe
what the objects look like in the different views reflected
by the mirrors.

MIND SKILL 5 – READING AND PERCEIVING

Approximately 75 per cent of formal learning takes place
through reading, which means that success in life and, to
a large extent, enjoyment and understanding as well
depend on the ability to read efficiently. It is true today
and it will be true tomorrow, no matter what the advances
in computer-assisted learning may be.

Efficient reading is not just a matter of speed. Woody
Allen jokes that after taking a rapid-reading course he
finished Tolstoy's *War and Peace* in three minutes. 'It's
about Russia,' he says. The important thing is to be able
to read at a speed which allows the desired level of
comprehension.

Teaching reading fluency
Early practice is essential to reading fluency. The more
you read to your child and have your child read to you,
the more skilled she or he will become. Some experts
believe that even children as old as eleven still derive
benefit from reading aloud and being read to. As with the
teaching of all mind skills, it is essential that reading be
done in a happy atmosphere.

Do:
   Keep sessions short, no longer than fifteen minutes for
   a young child and up to twenty for older ones, depending on their attention span.
   Keep sessions regular – if not daily, then every other
   day.

Keep your patience. Children would sooner not make mistakes, so irritation and criticism will not help.

Keep sessions relaxed. Unwind, both yourself and your child, using the relaxation procedure described on page 179, before each session.

Don't:

Turn what should be a game into a chore.

When slips occur – and children of all ages are bound to make occasional mistakes while reading – be tactful, since continuous correction slows down the pace and makes the sessions more anxiety-arousing and far less enjoyable.

Persistent mistakes indicate that the reading material is pitched at too high a level, so look for a slightly easier book. It is much better for the child to recognize and correct his own errors rather than to rely on you all the time. Sometimes a child comes across a word which she understands but cannot pronounce, and gets around the problem by substitution. If her chosen word has the same meaning, let it go.

When the child comes to a complete halt, you can (1) take over and read out the word that has caused the block, or (2) suggest returning to it later, or (3) provide clues to help solve the problem. For example, suggest that she breaks the word down into its component parts, which she might even write out on a scratch pad with hyphens indicating the splits – for instance, 'inspiration' could be written as 'in-spir-ation'. Any illustrations accompanying the text should be studied, to see if they offer an explanation for any word which the child can read but does not understand.

Understanding can also be aided by asking broad questions, such as 'Why do you think he did that?', 'Who do you think made that happen?' and 'What do you suppose will happen next?' Diagnostic listening can also be used to explore the root cause of a misunderstanding. Sometimes, for example, the child gets confused because he mistakes the meaning of a word and cannot work out how it fits into the story. Such a mistake is likely to affect his ability to read future texts correctly, unless it is identified and corrected now.

Which approach you adopt will be determined mainly by your child's preferred mind style. As we saw in chapter 6, some would sooner be nudged in the right direction, whilst others feel frustrated unless allowed to arrive at an answer unaided.

Ask older children to write down any words they do not understand and then look them up in a dictionary. Every child should have her own dictionary, clearly printed and with paper thick enough for it to be used with ease. Indeed, the use of dictionaries and similar reference sources should be taught and encouraged as early as possible, so that the child becomes familiar with the procedures. Looking up words can be the basis of a game, played between children or between a child and an adult, in which players take turns to choose words at random from the dictionary while the other tries to guess the meaning.

Although some of these words will certainly stick in the mind, it is not important that they remember them, since the purpose of the game is first to learn how to track down words and secondly to allow the children to discover certain rules about word structure which make it easier to guess the definition of new or unfamiliar words. They may realize, for example, that the prefix 'ex-' indicates 'out of' or 'exclusive of', and that strange words can sometimes be understood by breaking them into their component parts.

Playing word games of all kinds, from crosswords to

anagram puzzles, is an excellent way of improving fluency in and understanding of language. But as you probably realize, it is also a game more likely to appeal to left- than to right-brain thinkers.

For right-brain-dominant children, words can often be made easier to remember if, instead of trying to recall them as strings of symbols with a particular meaning, they are seen as pictures. The spelling of difficult words, too, is often made easier for right-brain thinkers if they attach an image to each letter of the alphabet – for example, *a* = apple, *b* = ball, and so on. But instead of just reading the letter and word, *a* becomes an apple in the mind, *b* evokes the image of a ball, *c* a mental picture of a cat, and so on. Then spelling a complicated word becomes a matter of stringing images together, to form a bizarre kind of film. To remember that 'balloon' has two *l*'s and two *o*'s for example, the child might be asked to imagine a brightly coloured *ball* balanced on top of a rosy-red *apple* which has two *legs* protruding from it, and that each leg is painted bright *orange* and standing in a bird's *nest*.

Although this may sound rather bizarre, especially to the strongly left-brained, it has considerable appeal for many children, and further uses of imagery as a way of remembering complex information will be considered in the next chapter.

Motivation is the key to reading efficiency, as it is in every other sort of activity, so provide your child with incentives to read by choosing the books and magazines that interest him, rather than those you feel he ought to read. If a book seems boring and hard to understand, its literary merits will never be sufficient to arouse interest. The probable result is that not only will the child not read that book, but he will come to regard all reading as boring and best avoided.

As noted earlier, it is important, while learning, for

children to read aloud, so that their proficiency can be evaluated and errors corrected. Once fluency and confidence have been achieved, it is time for them to master more advanced forms of reading, since only by achieving a high degree of sophistication in this skill can they hope to meet the heavy demands of later studies.

Teaching advanced reading skills

Start by encouraging your child to think exactly why she is reading a particular text. She must get into the habit of asking herself the simple question, 'What is my *purpose* in reading this book?' The answer may be 'to find enough facts to answer test questions', 'to know the text sufficiently to write an essay on it', or 'so that I understand exactly what was in the author's mind'.

Reading *purpose* determines reading *style*. There are three styles, and your child should become proficient in them all:

Skimming – glancing briefly down the text to pick out single-word answers to questions already in your mind.
Scanning – here you still read rapidly, although not quite as fast as when skimming the page. This is the method to use if you want to obtain slightly fuller information from the material.
Studying – the slowest method of all, and only necessary if you want to understand the text in great depth.

The golden rules of efficient reading

Never skim when your reading purpose requires you to scan.
Never skim or scan when your reading purpose demands study.
Never waste time studying when skimming or scanning serve your reading purpose as effectively.

Where to start

Look through the material, and note any subtitles or cross-headings, illustrations, charts or tables. This need take no more than a minute or two. Then put the material down and ask yourself just what the author can tell you. This is similar to flying over an unfamiliar country before exploring it on foot. You get a general impression of the difficulty of the terrain, and notice the location of various features.

Skimming　Move through the text swiftly, while seeking general ideas or specific ideas. Skimming is intended to provide short answers to questions which ask *who? what? when? where?* Hold the question in your mind while skimming, and the right answer often jumps out of the page at you. Teach your child to skim by allowing her eyes to run across the sentences until a key fact has been located. Then it can be noted, or written down. This process continues until all questions appropriate to skimming have been answered.

Some people find it easier to pace themselves during early practice, by moving a card swiftly down the page, uncovering one line at a time. They then follow the card down without making any conscious attempt to take in the words, yet holding in their minds the questions to which they are seeking answers. It is remarkable how, when that answer appears, the brain registers the fact and the card halts its rapid downward progress for a moment, while you take aboard the desired information.

The *purpose* of reading can often be served by this method. Train your child in this mind skill by getting him or her to go through a text that must be read for school, identifying a dozen or so key facts, dates, places, people and so on, and then making up questions based on them. For instance, skim questions derived from a science text might include: 'Who first sent telegraph signals across the Atlantic?', 'When was this done?', 'Where were transmitter and receiver located?' and 'What message was sent?' Then give her practice in uncovering these facts from the text as quickly as possible.

Scanning This involves reading quickly but carefully while searching for answers to rather more complicated *how?* and *why?* questions, where the information required can be found in not more than two or three sentences. This demands more time and effort, however, since the material must usually be ordered correctly before the answers can be located. It helps to have key words in your mind while scanning. For example, a child scanning a geography text to find out about the main industrial processes in a country, might have the key words *industry* and *manufacturing* in mind.

You can help your child to master this skill by preparing a text as for skim practice, but this time asking him or her to seek answers to more involved questions. Using the same type of text as that described above, two scan questions could be: 'Why did the telegraph prove such a useful invention?' and 'How was it used?'

Studying This is the most thorough, but also the slowest, style of reading. Its purpose is to discover longer, more detailed answers to *how?* and *why?* questions. It involves absorbing facts, making judgements, analysing content, reflecting on ideas and concepts, being critical and constantly questioning. It requires the child to read between the lines and to pause frequently so as to make certain that he or she understands what is in the author's mind. Such reading is necessary when the child is asked to go beyond the information given in the text and provide an interpretation of it.

In an English class, for example, students might have

to consider why a writer uses a particular phrase, or introduces a certain character at a critical point in the narrative, or how some incident early in the story influences the heroine's later actions. Finding the information for answers like these requires the text to be studied, rather than skimmed or scanned.

Key points for advanced reading
Determine the *purpose* for which the material is being read. Teach your child to ask: 'What do I want to get from this text?' before opening the book. The *purpose* determines the reading style to adopt, and in order to satisfy it the child should keep the following points in mind:

1 It is not always necessary, nor even efficient, to start at the beginning. Your reading purpose usually guides you as to the most useful starting-point.
2 The pace of reading should be varied according to the reason for reading the text and the complexity of the material.
3 Keeping brief notes helps. Start by jotting down the idea most relevant to the purpose. List key facts, figures and ideas in order of their importance. Use brief notes about people, places and events to jog the mcmory. Show your child how to produce pattern doodles, using the procedures described in the next chapter.

MIND SKILL 6 – LEARNING

Perception and learning are closely linked. We only become aware that something has been perceived by remembering the perception. For this reason, I consider remembering and recalling information in this chapter rather than in the next, where we explore the processing of information once it has been perceived.

Research shows that when children fail to remember things that they have tried hard to learn, the fault lies not in the mechanisms of memory so much as in the way those mechanisms have been put to work. Imagine the chaos that would ensue if a careless librarian scattered new books randomly among the other titles in a billion-volume library. While none of these books could be said to have been lost, locating a particular title would obviously depend on luck rather than logic. The same thing happens when storing information in the memory: once it has been properly filed away, there is virtually no end to what can be memorized and recalled, even under exam pressure.

Your child can prove this for himself by reading through the following list just *once*, and then attempting to write down all twelve words, in the correct sequence, from memory: elephant, umbrella, bicycle, hamster, ice-cream, bus stop, dolphin, lighthouse, frog, harmonium, jelly, deckchair. If you or your child are able to recall only a few of them, do not worry. That failure certainly does not mean that your memory is faulty – only that it is not, at present, being used correctly.

By following the procedure I describe, your child will find it possible not only to remember all the words in the correct sequence after just one read through, but also to recall the list in reverse order, or start and finish at any point chosen.

The list should be read through a second time, but now, rather than attempting to commit the words to memory, tell him to create a vivid mental image of each one, and then link this to the next in as bizarre a way as possible – to create a mind movie. He might, for example, imagine a giant blue elephant holding aloft a gaily striped umbrella on one huge leg, while balancing precariously on a bicycle. Next, he might see in his mind's eye the elephant crashing headlong into a giant hamster, who is eating ice-cream from a large tub while waiting at a bus stop. But instead of a bus, along comes a dolphin with a lighthouse on its back. The keeper in charge is a large, brilliant-green frog, who sits before a harmonium made out of jelly in a comfortable deckchair, which has been placed on the back of the big blue elephant.

To remember that list, your child simply recalls those images. Then, as the crazy movie unwinds in his mind, he will find that every object is remembered quickly, clearly and correctly. All he needs do to remember the list backwards is to run the film in reverse order, starting with deckchair and on through to elephant. Similarly, the list can be picked up at any point by recalling one image and then picturing the images either side of it.

Because the last object, *deckchair*, was associated with the first, *elephant*, the list has been transformed into a loop, which means that your child is able to start anywhere and proceed either forwards or backwards with ease. Get him or her to try it. Most children are thrilled to discover what good memories they actually have, and so become much more self-confident about their ability to remember things at school.

Images are easier to recall than words, because each of those familiar nouns is already stored away in your child's memory. But because no direct links exist between them, remembering one does not bring any of the remainder to mind. By creating bizarre images, you first introduce some new and unforgettable visual memories. You then join these together, producing a unique addition to the vast and complex mechanism of memory that we can call the brain's *knowledge network*.

The knowledge network in action

The network contains all the facts that you have ever learned, with related items of information being more closely associated than unrelated ones – which is why it takes a person only a fraction of a second to tell you that a canary is yellow, but longer, in most cases, to confirm that it is an animal.

You experience this knowledge network in action whenever you struggle, without success, to remember a friend's name, a favourite quotation, or somebody's 'phone number. It is on the tip of your tongue, but remains stubbornly in the background of the brain. Frequently it is only after abandoning the attempt and turning your attention to another task that the elusive fact emerges. What happens is that, once your brain has instructed the memory to trace some item of information, a search starts in the knowledge network and continues until either the task is abandoned or the required fact surfaces. As the brain is under less pressure when you are asleep, it quite often happens that something apparently lost for ever the previous evening comes into your mind on waking.

You may also have noticed that, just before coming up with the correct information, you recall things that are similar to, but not identical with, the facts that you are seeking. The name wanted is Brown, and the first one that you think of is Black, or Braun. This happens because that section of the network in which Brown has been stored also contains closely related facts.

Knowledge networks comprise not only words, but images, sounds, smells and tastes as well as sensations of touch and movement. By triggering one type of memory you often evoke a vast number of others. Birdsong, for example, may bring to mind a happy childhood in the country; an antiseptic smell may recall the misery of a stay in hospital.

When committing new facts to memory, your child should always try to store them in as many different memory locations as possible, especially in the visual network, which adults tend to neglect because the older we get the more left-brain, word-dominated, our thinking becomes. So while studying, your child should:

1   Repeat the information aloud – sound-memory storage.
2   Write it down – visual- and muscle-memory storage. The brain remembers which muscle movements are required to produce the words.
3   Create bizarre images – visual-memory storage.
4   And, whenever practicable, employ taste, touch and smell memories as well. This is why I suggest that a child's knowledge archive should include photographs, sound recordings, drawings, diagrams and actual examples of the things being studied, as well as models.

Creating external knowledge networks

Complex learning tasks become far easier to tackle when advantage is taken of the brain's internal network of memories. This can be done by showing your child how to create an external network, containing all the information to be recalled on a particular topic, that can then be slotted into mental storage as a single entity. By doing so, what was previously a 'shopping list' of facts and figures becomes a unified whole – just as the list of disconnected nouns was far easier to remember accurately after each had been linked to its neighbour. Here is how to do it.

1   Your child should take a sheet of paper about 30 cm by 25 cm and draw on it at random fifteen oblongs, approximately 6 cm by 4 cm. The easiest way of doing this is to cut the shape from a sheet of stiff card, and then use it as a template for the oblongs. If your child prefers to use the TV memory box, described on p. 177, as a further aid to learning, then the screen of this device should be used to produce the oblongs.

2   A topic is selected and your child extracts the facts, which must be learned using the skim, scan or study methods.

3   These facts are then written inside the oblongs (one fact per oblong). The limited space means that information must be kept to a minimum, and so your child should use abbreviations, initials and so on. Once one sheet has been filled up, a second is completed and then a third, until the topic has been covered and a sufficient depth of knowledge achieved. For many subjects it is necessary to create a large number of networks. This task should be approached logically and with thought, so that each of the networks is as self-contained as possible – that is, each covers a sub-topic within the subject being studied. If your child were studying human biology, for example, one or two networks might be sufficient to provide all the information needed about, say, the functioning of the heart or kidneys. Similarly, were the subject the geography of North America, one or two networks might be enough to cover the sub-topic of agriculture in the mid-West.

4   The final step is to link the facts together in any way that appears logical, by drawing lines between the oblongs until all have been connected. Check this by ensuring that each oblong has just two lines joined to it, as in Figure 12.

A list of facts has now been transformed into a network, just as the list of nouns was turned into a network by linking the last to the first before memorizing it. As we have seen, the advantage of a network is that one can start at any point and move in either direction when recalling the facts it contains.

5   There are two ways of transferring the external

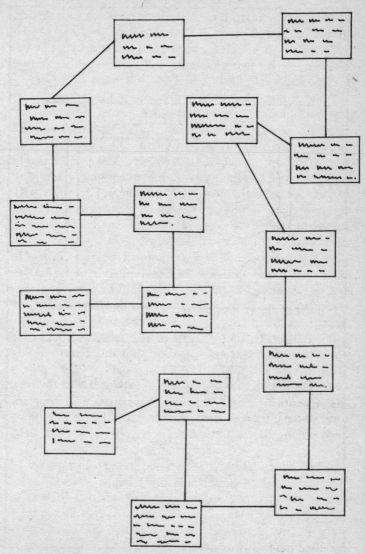

Fig. 12   A completed external knowledge network

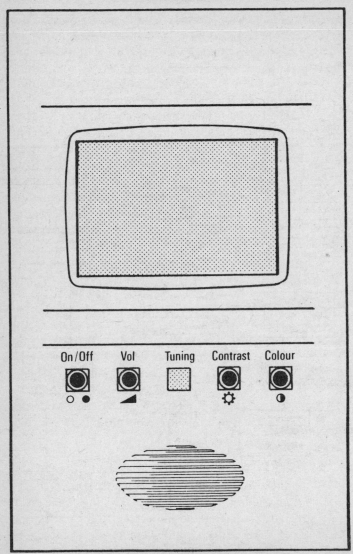

Fig. 13   The TV memory box board

knowledge network into the long-term memory. Your child can simply read through the facts in each oblong, moving to the next by following the lines, until all have been memorized. After reading all the boxes two or three times, he should use a piece of card to cover all but one of the oblongs (it does not matter where he starts). The child now reads the facts in this oblong and tries to recall the information contained in either of the adjoining boxes. This is then checked, by moving the card, and the process repeated. He can move in either direction around the network, but having started to travel in one direction he must continue along this route until all the information has been either recalled or reread. After a few trips around the knowledge network, he should have little difficulty in accurately remembering all the facts it contains. When using images, bear in mind that the more unusual they are, the easier the recall process. I shall be discussing such visualizations more fully in the next chapter.

A more effective and interesting way of tackling the same task is to use the TV memory box. This not only adds an element of entertainment, which younger children, especially, seem to enjoy, but also aids recall through the process known as *anticipation learning*. Here the memory can be jogged by providing the brain with clues to any facts which refuse to come to mind.

Constructing the TV memory box

Start by photocopying the illustrations of the TV board and shutter (figures 13 and 14), and pasting them on to stiff card. Alternatively, you can copy or trace the designs on to card. With a sharp knife cut slots A, B and C (see figure 15). Remove the shaded area of the screen on the TV board, and cut out the small locating hole D below the screen. Cut out the shutter mechanism, and remove the shaded area E. Finally, slide the shutter mechanism through slot A of the TV board, then through slots B and C. You should now find that when the shutter mechanism is drawn upwards, in the direction of the arrow, the screen area is gradually uncovered.

Using the TV memory box

When constructing the oblongs for the knowledge network, use the screen area of the TV memory box to provide the template, as suggested above. Once the network has been filled with facts to be learned, and these have been read through two or three times, the device is placed over it, so that the information in one oblong can be viewed on the TV 'screen'. (As before, the child may start at any point on the network.) This is now read, and an attempt is made to recall the facts in either of the adjoining boxes. Next, the shutter is slid into place, blocking out the network. Using the small locating hole, the child finds the line connecting the original oblong to either of its neighbours, and slides the TV memory box along until the screen has been positioned above the next item of information to be recalled.

If the child gets stuck, he can move the shutter up a little to reveal a small portion of the facts beneath it. Often these few words are sufficient to jog his memory and allow all the information to be remembered correctly. If recall still eludes him, the shutter can be moved up a little further, so uncovering a few more of the words. This continues until either the facts have been remembered, or the shutter has been fully removed, the whole oblong revealed and the elusive facts read out. The shutter is then slid back into place, and the locating hole is used to move the TV memory box over the next oblong. The procedure is repeated until the whole of the network has been studied. After just a few trips around the oblongs, all those facts will have been stored away in your child's memory. By allowing him to anticipate what has to be recalled, and by jogging reluctant recall with a few facts, the TV memory box offers a simple but powerful aid to recollection. Because each item of information is linked to its neighbour, remembering any one fact makes it far easier to bring the next to mind, exactly as in the list of nouns above.

Later in the book I will describe ways of using knowledge networks in order to answer exam questions more easily and successfully.

Relaxation and learning
Your child may find these learning sessions easier and more successful if they are preceded by the brief relaxation exercise described next. Research suggests that a brief period of relaxation, lasting only five minutes or so, can improve retention and recall by up to 50 per cent. But it is not a procedure every child enjoys, so if yours becomes bored or impatient abandon the procedure, at least for the moment. Compulsory relaxation is an impossibility!

Learning to relax

This is a skill which can be mastered in a couple of weeks of regular practice. About four sessions per week are usually sufficient, although it is impossible to be exact because some people – both adults and children – relax far more easily than others.

Avoid clashes with favourite TV programmes or times when the child would expect to be playing. If she is very active, carry out the training after she has been playing

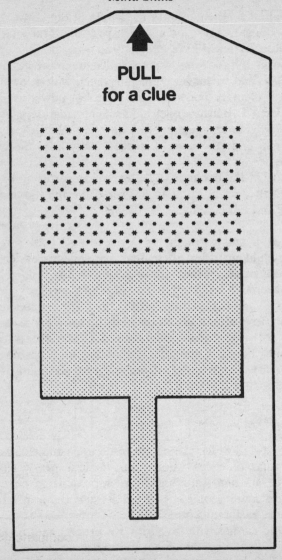

Fig. 14 The shutter mechanism of the TV memory box

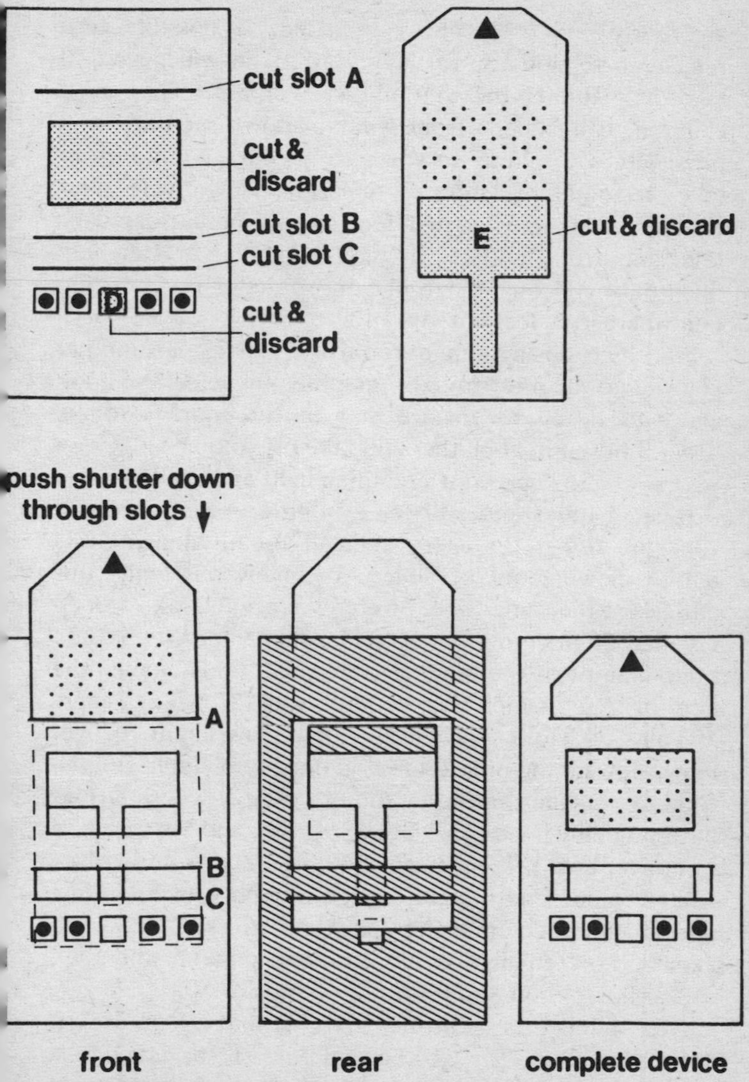

cut slot A

cut & discard

cut slot B
cut slot C

cut & discard

E cut & discard

push shutter down through slots ↓

A

B
C

front

rear

complete device

Fig. 15   How to make the TV memory box

vigorously and feels physically tired. If possible turn relaxation sessions into a family affair, in which you all take part. Remember that adults, even more than most children, can benefit from winding down mentally and physically. By joining in you also encourage children to take the training sessions more seriously. Motivate older children, who may at first feel slightly embarrassed or reluctant to participate, by explaining that it can help them during exams, when playing sports or in any situation where they feel nervous.

Start by choosing a quiet room and making certain that you will not be interrupted. Take the 'phone off the hook and hang a 'Do not disturb' sign on the door! Sit or lie down. Loosen tight clothes and take off your shoes. Close your eyes and keep your breathing light and shallow.

Remain quiet and still for a minute or so. Focus on your breathing: on every exhaled breath imagine the tension flowing out of your body. Now tense all your muscles at the same time. Stretch your body, take a deep breath, flatten your stomach and clench your fists. At the same time press the back of your head firmly against the floor or chair, hunch your shoulders and frown as deeply as you can. Hold this tension for a slow count to five. Now allow all the muscles to flop out completely. Tell the child to imagine that he or she is a puppet whose strings have suddenly been cut. Notice yourself, and ask the child to notice, how it feels when the body relaxes and is free from tension. Continue to concentrate on your breathing and imagine becoming less and less stressed with each exhalation. Remain like this for one minute, and then repeat the tension and relaxation sequence.

Rest quietly for a further sixty seconds, focusing on your breathing. For another minute or so, imagine a pleasant setting in which you feel secure and comfortable – perhaps a sun-warmed beach or a quiet country meadow. Picture these images, as vividly as possible, in your mind's eye. Lie still, focusing on this mental image while keeping your breathing slow and regular, for another sixty seconds – longer if you prefer, although many children tend to get a bit fidgety if asked to lie still too long – before getting *slowly* to your feet (you may feel a little giddy if you stand up too quickly) and returning to your normal activities.

At first you may need to help children create vivid mental images, by describing various features of the chosen scene. If it is a beach, for example, you can draw their attention to the sounds of the sea, the smell of tropical flowers, the feel of the sand under their bodies. In the next chapter we shall be using relaxation and mental imagery to enhance learning, studying and the recall of information, so it is a skill well worth mastering.

Perceptions in class – lessons and lectures

Efficient recall here depends on rehearsing in the correct way what has been heard. Teach your child the following procedure.

As the lesson or lecture proceeds, keep brief written notes. He should never try to copy down verbatim everything that the teacher or lecturer says. In addition, he should keep a record of the number of important points to recall. Some ten minutes after the lesson ends, he should find a quiet place, relax and go through the key points, silently, to himself. Tell him not to become concerned if he appears to have forgotten several of them. The next recall lesson should take place about one hour later. This means that morning lessons can be recalled at lunch, and afternoon classes when school ends. He should have further recall sessions immediately before going to sleep. At each session your child should find it easier and easier to remember more key points accurately. This clear

Mind Skills

memory can then be maintained by a couple of rehearsals per week. While attempting to remember what was said, the child should remain relaxed and not force his brain to come up with the information. He should take some fact that he remembers, think about anything that that reminds him of, and then follow the train of associations produced. Often this brings the elusive fact clearly to mind.

By helping your child to develop these six vital mind skills, you enable him or her to become a confident, energetic and successful adventurer, exploring both the outside world and the landscape of the imagination in search of fresh conquests of understanding. The comprehensive, accurate and reliable perception of information ensures that your child's brain will have worthy material on which to work. What this work involves, and how the second – processing – stage of thinking can be significantly enhanced, we will be exploring in the next chapter.

9

The Art of Successful Thinking

In this chapter we shall consider the second stage of thinking, during which your child's brain processes the information taken in through the five senses. Here, as I suggested in chapter 2, the mind skills needed for successful thinking are very similar to those of the artist. And this applies whether the task involves scientific reasoning or a flight of imaginative creation – because art is not, essentially, about things but about ideas. The end result, whether a painting or a play, a sculpture or a symphony, is the physical expression of ideas that have been manipulated and transformed by the human mind.

Successful thinking is the highest form of intellectual artistry. It is a talent that we are all born with and can learn to exploit if we choose to do so. By helping children to realize their true potential as artists of ideas, you will be endowing them with probably the most precious – certainly one of the rarest – gifts that anyone can possess: a truly creative mind. 'The artist is not a different kind of person,' says the sculptor Eric Gill, 'but every person is a different kind of artist.'

Describing successful thinking as an art does not mean, however, that it should be regarded as a haphazard process – far from it. Behind the apparent spontaneity of most great ideas one generally finds careful preparation. There is a lot of truth in the old saying that genius is 90 per cent perspiration and only 10 per cent inspiration.

Without planning, the processing of information becomes random and confused. Yet this is the way many children learn to think. Given an intellectually challenging task, they set off in search of a solution with no real idea of where they are going or how to get there. Having arrived at a conclusion or found an answer, they are frequently unclear, if it turns out to be right, why it is right, or if wrong, where they went wrong. Faced with a challenging task, such children often become unhelpfully anxious. Their minds fill with negative ideas, such as 'I don't know where to begin', or 'I can't cope with this sort of problem', which inhibit constructive thinking.

By learning the strategy of *mind-planning*, these confusions and anxieties are avoided, your child feels more in control of his thought processes, and answers are found by brain work rather than guesswork. Mind-planning can be applied to any kind of mental activity, whether practical or theoretical, related to school subjects or to personal problems. Because the strategy is equally helpful to adults, I suggest you try using it for yourself, at home and at work. Apart from allowing you to tackle a wide range of activities more easily and successfully, there is no better way of interesting children or of convincing them that something is worthwhile than to see it being used by adults.

Mind-planning involves three stages, each posing a question for your child to ask and answer:

Stage 1 – Fact-finding   Ask: What do I know?
Stage 2 – Goal-setting   Ask: Where do I want to go?
Stage 3 – Action-taking   Ask: What do I have to do?

To illustrate the procedure in action, we will apply it to the fairly trivial mental task of converting a temperature in degrees centigrade to Fahrenheit. As you may remember, the conversion involves multiplying the temperature in degrees centigrade by 9, dividing the result by 5 and then adding 32 (Fahrenheit=(centigrade $\times \frac{9}{5}$) + 32).

Suppose your child is given the problem: The temperature outside is 20 degrees centigrade. What is the Fahrenheit equivalent?

At stage 1 of mind-planning – *fact-finding* – your child asks: What do I know?

In this case:

The temperature in centigrade = 20 degrees.

The formula for making that conversion = $(C \times \frac{9}{5}) + 32$.

Stage 2 – *goal-setting* – raises the question:

Where do I want to go?

Here the answer is straightforward:

From degrees centigrade to Fahrenheit.

Stage 3 – *action-taking* – asks the question:

What do I have to do?

This draws your child's attention to the manipulations and transformations that must be performed on those *facts* in order to arrive at the desired *goal*. Here, all that he has to do is to apply the formula correctly. That is to say:

$$F = (20 \times \frac{9}{5}) + 32$$
$$F = 36 + 32$$
$$F = 68$$

When applied to so straightforward a problem, mind-planning may seem like an over-complicated way of thinking. Yet even with such simple tasks, many children make careless mistakes, especially when their mind styles lead them to respond impulsively to mental challenges.

Here, confusions could arise at stage one, where a hasty reading of the problem might cause the child to convert the wrong temperature, or at stage three, where he might apply the formula incorrectly – for instance, adding the 32 *before* multiplying and dividing.

So even with a basic mental task, mind-planning is

useful. Where the level of thinking demanded is far higher, the strategy helps to ensure that information is processed fast and effectively. So let us consider each of these three stages in more detail, to see exactly what is involved.

STAGE 1 – FACT-FINDING
ASK: WHAT DO I KNOW?

This question can also be phrased as: 'What don't I know, at this moment, but must find out to arrive at the correct answer?'

Most complex problems require these extra steps to be taken, as you gradually move from what is known to what may be deduced or reasonably concluded from the facts provided.

Encourage your child, when dealing with anything other than a trivial problem, to write down on a sheet of paper all the facts that have been provided, can be remembered, or may be assumed from the problem. Having done so, the first point to consider is the reliability of the information.

How reliable is the information
Working from inaccurate or otherwise unreliable information is a trap into which even experienced thinkers fall. In the early 1950s, for example, a group of medical scientists carried out pioneer research into the link between exercise and heart disease. It was, in fact, the landmark study which was to spawn jogging, marathon-running, aerobics and popular concern over keeping fit. Yet, as other scientists were soon to point out, this carefully conducted study contained a flaw which made the evidence unreliable.

Read through what was done, discuss it with older children, and see if you can discover why this was so.

Bus drivers vs bus conductors
To find out whether exercise affected heart disease, Dr Jeremy Morris and his colleagues analysed the health records of 31,000 men aged between thirty-four and sixty-four, working as either bus drivers or bus conductors for London Transport. They found that sedentary drivers were much more likely to have heart disease than active conductors, who were on the move all day collecting fares.

But even though the differences were highly significant, the conclusion – that exercise prevents heart disease – was questionable. Why?

The source of the error lay in the fact that bus drivers and bus conductors might well have differed from the start in their degree of fitness. It was possible that stouter, less active and, perhaps, less healthy men sought employment as drivers, while more active, energetic and potentially healthier men decided to become conductors. As the American humorist Henry Wheeler Shaw remarked more than a century ago: 'The trouble with people is not that they don't know but that they know so much that ain't so.'

Encourage your child, from an early age, to question what she is told and to examine information closely before trusting it, to probe beneath the surface and to develop a healthy scepticism, especially where figures are concerned. Lively discussions about the evidence being used to support projects or proposals under public debate in the newspapers and on TV are a good way of developing this skill. You do not need to be an expert on the particular subject in order to explore the strengths or weaknesses of the arguments for and against. All it takes is a critical mind trained to notice possible flaws or dubious assumptions.

Teaching this skill can be made into a game, with one child arguing in support of the plan and another trying to find weaknesses in the evidence used to justify the proponent's viewpoint. A useful technique is to score the available information on a scale of 0–5, where zero indicates great uncertainty and 5 shows that there can be no doubt of its accuracy. These items of information can then be written out again under one of three headings, depending on how they were rated: certain (4–5); fairly certain (2–3); uncertain (0–1).

Facts receiving low scores should be carefully rechecked. With the available information clearly evaluated, and either checked or rejected (if of dubious reliability), your child should explore it in greater detail by asking three questions:

1 Have I considered all the possible meanings and implications of each item of information?
2 Am I making any unjustified assumptions about any items of information?
3 Could I look at any of those items differently?

Teach your child to review all the facts, by posing these questions before moving to stage two of mind-planning.

Making unjustified assumptions about the information is a very common source of error, as figure 16 illustrates. Your problem here is to reproduce the design from just *one* sheet of card, without using any kind of adhesive.

You will find it instructive to try your hand at this problem before reading further. It will also help you to understand mind-planning more readily if you tackle the task using the three-stage process. Stage two, the *goal*, is clear. Stage three, the *actions* to be taken, form the heart of the task. Here is the hint: be very careful about the facts you have, or assume, about the nature of the problem.

You will find the answer at the end of this chapter. The chief barrier to finding a solution is the assumption that you are dealing with the same surface of the card on either side of the flap. Only after this idea has been rejected does it become possible to create the required result.

Creative thinking (which we will be considering in more detail later in this chapter) involves viewing the facts from a variety of perspectives, in order to discover different ways of linking things together, of modifying, adapting, adding to or subtracting from what is available.

The final problem draws attention to the possibility of there being additional facts to be deduced from the information available. Figure 17 gives an example of a 'concealed' fact.

An ant is making its way along a length of elastic 100 cm long, at a rate of 1 cm per second. After one second the elastic stretches to 200 cm, after two seconds to 300 cm, after three seconds to 400 cm, and so on. How long, if ever, before the ant reaches the end of the elastic?

Visualizing what happens to both elastic and ant should make it easier to spot the essential hidden fact. Again, I will provide the answer at the end of the chapter. If your child tries this problem and gets stuck, suggest that he or she makes a model of the problem, using an elastic band with a blob of plasticine or something similar representing the ant.

The problems just described are the sort that children normally only encounter late in their school careers. Yet the vital mind skills involved can, and should, be mastered by children at as early an age as possible.

Even when the facts themselves are accurate and reliable, it is perfectly possible to draw quite the wrong

Mind Skills

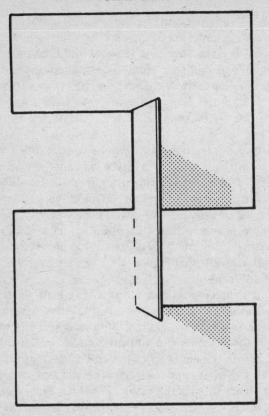

Fig. 16   The card problem

conclusions from them. So in addition to checking any information provided, before starting to process it your child should also learn to test the propositions being advanced.

How sound are the arguments?
There are many forms of dishonest argument which people use, knowingly or unintentionally, in order to

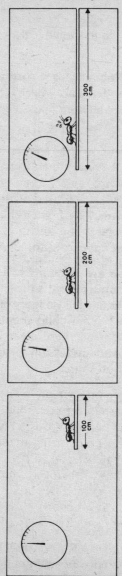

Fig. 17 The problem of the ant on a piece of elastic

support a weak case. Here are six of the most often employed which your child should learn to spot and reject from an early age.

1 All or nothing 'Politicians are corrupt.' 'Union leaders are wreckers.' 'Students are idle.' Train your child to notice statements in which *all* has been implied, when honesty demands the use of *some*.

2 Worm words 'Peter is firm; John is obstinate; Martin is pig-headed.' Words convey emotions as well as information, and 'worm words' and 'worm phrases' to describe people or events are always used with the purpose of nibbling away at reason. Teach your child to substitute a neutral word with the same meaning, and then see whether the argument appears as forceful and convincing.

3 Diversions These are attempts to lure people away from the main point under discussion – for example, 'It's all very well to talk about the dangers of flying, but what about road accidents?' Your child should be encouraged to notice and comment on these diversionary tactics, of which TV debates and discussion programmes on the radio are usually a good source.

4 Distractions Here one person focuses on some minor factual error, in an attempt to discredit the other's arguments, even though the mistake is trivial and makes no real difference to the point being made – for example, 'You said the crime rate was up 15 per cent. In fact it has risen by only 12 per cent. Obviously you don't know what you're talking about!' Your child should learn to evaluate the strengths of such distractions by asking whether the criticism, even if true, actually makes any difference.

5 Laughing them down Rather than answer the point, the dishonest arguer tries to make a joke, intending to make either his opponent or his opponent's argument appear trivial, or so ridiculous that it does not deserve to be taken seriously. A mother who complained that her young child had to travel twenty miles each day after being moved from a local school, was told by her local authority: 'Perhaps you would prefer it if the teachers held their classes in your front room?'

6 *Irrelevancies* Here a problem as serious as the one being discussed, but having no relevance to it, is introduced in order to attack the speaker for not doing anything about it – for example, 'It's all very well to talk about drug abuse, but what about famine in Africa?'

A mind-straightening game

The tricks used in dishonest arguments – and those listed above are just a few out of many (Dr J. P. Thouless, author of *Straight and Crooked Thinking*, has identified nearly forty) – are best described as CRAP, an acronym for Considered – Regarded As Puerile. Every child should be provided with a first-class CRAP-detector. You can ensure this by having regular CRAP-detecting sessions to see who can spot the greatest amount in newspapers, magazines, TV and radio programmes, as well as at school and even during family discussions.

The person who claims to have detected a dishonest argument registers the fact by holding up one hand, with three fingers folded down, while the thumb and little finger wiggle vigorously and the child emits a sharp beep . . . beep . . . beep to indicate that the CRAP-detector has detected a puerile argument. Having identified a CRAP item, the child must then explain why it qualifies, and – if possible – propose an alternative more accurate or more honest way of making the same point.

Keep a record of the number of CRAP pieces spotted each week, perhaps pinning some of the more horrible examples on the family notice-board. One point can be awarded for each CRAP item a person detects, but a point is deducted if that person is found to be using dishonest arguments himself.

Evidence-testing and argument-evaluating are two of the most important basic mind skills any child can learn. Together they comprise the neglected art of critical thinking.

Teaching critical thinking

'Mastery of the art of thought is only the beginning of the task of understanding reality,' notes Dr Thouless. 'Without the correct facts it can only lead us into error.' Critical appraisal of available information is rarely taught in school, where students are usually expected to accept what they are told as true, and rarely encouraged to question received wisdom too deeply. Dr Thouless continues:

Education has, in the past, often fostered the tendency to acceptance of predigested thinking. John and Richard III were 'bad' kings – not merely bad 'on the whole', but in all respects – oppressive, cruel, and tyrannical in their public lives and with no redeeming features in their home lives. Edward III and Henry V, on the other hand, were examples of 'good' kings.

To counter this threat, teach your child to think for himself by subjecting ideas, opinions and proposals to critical analysis, no matter how authoritative the source. This may not make him a popular student – many teachers dislike having their statements queried. But only in this way can the brain be educated in the art of thinking, rather than schooled into passive conformity.

* * *

I have devoted quite a lot of space to the first stage of thinking, because many mistakes in evaluating the information on which the mind will work is critical. So important are the procedures described above that your child may find it helpful to copy the summary in table 17 on to a piece of card small enough to slip into the pocket, to prompt him about the questions to ask when faced with a task demanding serious thought.

Table 17   A mind-planning prompt card

Stage 1 – Facts
Ask: What do I know?
   What must I find out?
Ask: How accurate and reliable are my facts?
   How sound are the arguments?
Ask: Have all meanings and implications been looked at?
   Am I making any unjustified assumptions?
   Could I look at the facts differently?
   Are there hidden facts to be discovered?

STAGE 2 – GOAL-SETTING
ASK: WHERE DO I WANT TO GO?

This question can only be answered once the nature of the problem is clearly understood. Able children may fail not because they do not know *how* to think, but because they correctly work out the right answer to a different problem!

Such errors are easily made when working under pressure. As I suggested in chapter 2, one of the challenges of a computer-dominated working environment is that, increasingly, information will have to be mentally processed under just such conditions. The only safeguard is a methodical examination of the task, to ensure that no such misinterpretation occurs. The questions your child should ask at this stage are: 'Do I fully understand what is being asked?' 'Could other, equally valid, answers exist?'

In the question, 'What is half of 2 + 2?', equally correct answers could be either 3 *or* 2. If you did not give both possible solutions, it could be because you failed to identify that two valid outcomes, or goals, existed.

STAGE 3 – ACTION-TAKING
ASK: WHAT DO I HAVE TO DO?

This is the stage of thinking where the information is processed to achieve the desired result. Your child should ask: 'What can I do with what I know?' 'Have I looked at all possible ways of using what I know?' 'Do I need to have further facts before continuing?'

Since the most appropriate action to take must depend on the goal sought, strategies for improving the mind skills involved in stages two and three can best be explored together.

Just as a skilled artist will have many techniques for transforming raw materials into a finished work, so should your child learn a variety of mind skills for manipulating ideas and concepts. What actions are going to prove most appropriate, and which kind of goals will be involved, however, depends on the type of problem being tackled.

Some problems can have only one correct solution, and these are called *convergent* problems. Others, known as *divergent* problems, have a number of equally correct or useful solutions. Let us explore each in turn, to see how mind-planning will help your child to identify the correct goal(s) and decide on the most appropriate actions to take.

Problems with one right answer
The centigrade to Fahrenheit conversion task described on page 186 is an example of a convergent problem. The

right answer is 68 degrees Fahrenheit, and no other is acceptable. Many of the problems children face at school are of this type, although they are not necessarily so trivial.

Convergent problems demand methodical analysis and logical reasoning to solve them. Usually the goal is clearly stated as part of the problem, and the questions tend to be narrow ones starting with *When, Where, Why* or *Who* – for example, 'When did the Pilgrim Fathers land in America?' 'Where did Wellington defeat Napoleon?' 'Why does ice float?' 'Who made the first solo crossing of the Atlantic?'

Convergent problems are usually tests of knowledge rather than of thinking, and demand accurate recall of information. The mind skills for enhanced learning, which I shall be describing a little later, will help your child to do well on this type of task.

Problems with several possible right answers
On 13 April 1970 the crew of Apollo 13, on their way to the moon, called NASA ground control at Houston, Texas, and announced: 'Hey, we've got a problem here!' The problem was that their spacecraft had just exploded! Here, in magnificent understatement, is a clear example of a divergent problem. The task facing the mission controllers was to find a way of bringing those astronauts down safely. Many possible options were available to them, and they had to identify and implement the one with the greatest chance of success.

But divergent problems come in all shapes and sizes. For instance, your child is being bullied at school, but does not want you to say anything to the teacher because he might be picked on even more. What should you do for the best? Give your child judo lessons? Tell him to stay out of trouble? Complain to the parents of the boys concerned? Encourage a friendship with a stronger boy who might offer protection? I am sure you can see flaws in all these suggestions, and can come up with other ways of helping the boy.

Solving this kind of problem is often more of a right-brain than a left-brain skill, and not one which your child may be given much opportunity to practise in class. Nevertheless it is important that he or she gain experience of divergent problems, since they are far and away the most common ones encountered in real life.

A useful procedure for developing the mind skills needed for tackling divergent problems, and one which can easily be practised at home, is *brainstorming*. This involves sitting down in a friendly atmosphere and dreaming up as many answers as you can to a wide range of problems.

How to brainstorm

Every session is divided into an *idea production* and an *idea-editing* stage. During idea production, three rules must be strictly followed:

Rule 1 Any sort of comment is forbidden, whether encouraging or critical. You just keep a note of the ideas as they are produced, without saying or doing anything that might stem the creative flow.

Rule 2 The more humorous, uninhibited and free-wheeling the ideas that are generated, the better. Never let your child become fearful of expressing a thought, however crazy or unworkable it may appear. Cultivate an emotional climate in which he or she is happy to say anything and everything that comes to mind.

Rule 3 Produce as many ideas as possible. It is always easier to edit down than to build up. Linus Pauling, the Nobel prize-winning scientist, has commented: 'The best way to get a good idea is to get lots of ideas.'

As you probably realize, this means switching *off* the left, analytical hemisphere and switching *on* the right side of the brain. As a result, you may find that left-dominant children, especially when their favoured mind style is that of the intellectual thinker, at first find brainstorming hard to get into. Their strongly logical way of thinking will tempt them to interpose objections: 'That couldn't work . . .', 'How absurd . . .', 'You must be crazy to think that's possible . . .'

Apply the rules of *idea production* firmly. Tell him or her that all these objections must wait for the second part of the brainstorming sessions, when you switch from right- to left-brain thinking and move into the *idea-editing* stage. Now you return to the ideas and proposals generated during the production session, and review each of them carefully. Any that are obviously impracticable should be rejected, but before doing so see whether they might not be made workable in some way by combining them with other ideas, inventions or innovations. Here are some of the questions that might be asked during the editing stage:

Could it be used in some other way if modified?
Would it help to make it bigger, thicker or stronger?
Could it be improved by becoming smaller, thinner or weaker?
Could some parts be rearranged to make it more practicable?

As an example of how brainstorming can produce answers to divergent problems that might not yield a satisfactory solution if tackled in any other way, consider the challenge recently confronting a group of engineers when they were set the task of designing a lorry jack. The specifica-

tions called for a jack sufficiently compact to fit into a box
only four inches wide, but capable of cranking out to
three feet while supporting the weight of a four-ton
vehicle. During the idea production stage of brainstorming, one team member joked that they were being asked
to perform the Indian rope trick. (In this illusion, a coil
of rope becomes rigid enough to support the weight of a
child.)

During the editing session the whole team explored this
seemingly impractical idea to see whether it could provide
the basis for a working lorry jack. The solution which
emerged was to have two chains, similar to cycle chains
but flexible in only one direction. When cranked up, these
chains unrolled from the box and were forced together to
create a solid rod.

Brainstorming can be used to solve family problems,
with everybody working as a team. One mother, worried
about how to entertain her two children during a long
car journey, brainstormed with them to produce games
and entertainments. The seven-year-old came up with
more than thirty suggestions, the ten-year-old with over
fifty. Some of them were so good that she had them
typed out and circulated to friends and relatives with
young children, for use when they faced the same
problem. Brainstorming can also be the basis for two
enjoyable games.

Find a use for   Take an ordinary object, such as a cotton
reel, a house brick, a matchstick, a zip, a paper-clip or a
safety-pin. The aim is to dream up as many extraordinary
uses for the object as possible, the more imaginative the
better. See how many different uses can be found in sixty
seconds.

Life games   These require more preparation, although
once set up they can be used on many occasions. Here

you take a real problem, such as running a factory or leading a country, and give each player a specific role – managing director, union leader, politician, financier and so on. To make the game more interesting and to stimulate a greater sense of involvement, the child might be asked to design a factory or 'create' their very own country by making drawings or models. The various players can also be drawn or modelled and moved around the game area. This greatly appeals to implementing and inventive thinkers.

You start the game by posing a problem, which can often be lifted straight out of the headlines: a strike, a leak of dangerous chemicals, a civil uprising, the loss of crops in a monsoon, and so on. Each player then either works out a possible solution, or responds to the answer proposed by another player. If acting out the parts appeals to your child, then the game can become even more exciting.

Apart from developing mind skills directly concerned with problem-solving, life games train children in the presentation and communication of their ideas, in arguing and justifying, in planning ahead and persuading, as well as making them more aware of the consequences of their actions and of the fact that a problem can appear very different when viewed by somebody else. Intellectual thinkers can also learn valuable social skills, by working in groups on a particular problem, sharing ideas and collaborating in the creation of strategies.

Brainstorming helps to enhance several of the mind skills essential for creative thinking:

1 Fluency – the production of relevant ideas
2 Flexibility – the ability to see what is familiar in an entirely new way
3 Originality – the essence of all great art

4 Elaboration – the blending of many different concepts, themes and associations in producing the final idea.

Frequent brainstorming sessions enhance right-brain skills in the left-brain-dominant during the idea production stage, and left-brain skills in children with a more dominant right hemisphere during the idea-editing stage. In this way your child's ability to exploit the whole of his brain is increased. You can also enhance right-brain skills by showing your child how to use visualization (thinking with images) when tackling a wide range of problems.

Thinking with images

One day in 1865, after spending many months in a fruitless attempt to unravel the mystery of the chemical structure of benzene, the German chemist Kekulé was relaxing by a fire and staring casually into the flames licking upwards from a blazing log. Suddenly, as he studied the leaping tongues of fire, Kekulé was reminded of snakes chasing one another's tails. In a flash of insight he realized that benzene, like the snake flames, must have a ring structure.

We have already looked briefly at the ways in which images can be used to improve the recall of a list of words, and to produce a relaxed mental state. Now I will explain how to employ visualization in an even more powerful way.

Most young children have very powerful visual abilities, which they experience spontaneously while daydreaming or fantasizing. The creation best known to most parents, and a cause for concern to many, is the fantasy friend who shares the games of a solitary child. Often this invisible companion is vividly described and has a clearly defined personality. If your own child has such a friend, do not worry. It is a perfectly normal and natural part of growing up. Far from discouraging these fantasies, you should share them with your child as a means of stimulating imagination and visualization.

Imagery training

Keep early sessions short – no more than five minutes or so. As with the relaxation training described in chapter 8, choose times when your child does not want to play with friends or watch the television. Start by selecting some suitable objects for visualization. Those used when playing the 'Paying attention game' (page 149) are often ideal.

You may find it helpful, during early sessions, to begin with a few moments of physical relaxation. This is not essential, since visualization is itself an extremely relaxing activity. However, some adults and children find that they can banish distracting thoughts and focus their minds more easily if they first reduce bodily tension. Practise the following technique for yourself, before trying to explain it to your child.

Sit still for a few moments, eyes closed, and focus on your breathing. On each exhaled breath imagine the stress and tensions leaving your body and the muscles gradually unwinding and becoming more and more relaxed.

Study one of the chosen objects, carefully, for about twenty seconds. During this time try not to use words to describe what you are seeing, but simply allow the impression to form in your mind. Now shut your eyes and attempt to re-create the object as a clear mental image. Once again, it is important not to name any of the parts or identify the object in words, since this stimulates the left hemisphere while the intention is to enhance the powers of the right. Accept the images as they come to mind; never try to evaluate or resist them. Any attempt to analyse what is happening alters your state of consciousness.

With only a little practice, you will find it fairly easy to create and sustain a mental impression of the object just studied. After a while the image should become so clear and steady that you can move it around in your brain and, as if viewing a hologram, make observations from different angles.

If you or your child are a left-brain-dominant intellectual thinker, be prepared for this skill to prove slightly harder to master than for right-hemisphere thinkers with other mind styles. In a family where there are several different ways of thinking, it is quite normal for some people to become proficient at visualization earlier than others. If you or your child find it tricky at first, do not give up. Remember that by stimulating the right side of the brain, left-brain thinkers are releasing previously neglected mental power and creative energy.

The next step is to imagine something without the initial stimulus of actually observing it; or, if using a physical object as the source of the imagery, to imagine it changing in some way. You might, for example, create an image of a plant, seeing it in your mind's eye first as a shoot, then growing, putting out more leaves, blooming, and finally withering away.

While holding this image, focus on specific details, such as colour, shape and texture. Return to images visualized earlier and notice any changes that may have occurred. In one American study, a group of eleven-year-olds was asked to picture their favourite flower on three occasions. Each visualization lasted about half a minute, with a ten-second gap between them. Every time they returned to their flower, the students saw a different picture. On the first occasion, one visualized her flower on the ground, surrounded by other, equally beautiful, blooms. The second image was of her flower wrapped in multicoloured paper. In the last, she saw it being worn by her father as a buttonhole.

When helping your child to learn visualization, I suggest that you begin, as described above, by using actual objects as the image stimulus. The procedure can be introduced as an addition to the 'Paying attention game' in chapter 8.

Next, encourage him to focus on images of scenes or objects recalled from memory. Start with visual imagery, but later introduce sounds, tastes, touch and smell. Once again, you will find the training in careful observation, provided by the 'Paying attention game', helpful.

Now introduce scenes which involve a sustained chain of images with action and movement. These animated 'mind movies' could include a shopping trip, a visit to the seaside, a flight on an aircraft, or a ride on a roller-coaster. Ask your child to discuss his visualizations with you, to describe what can be seen and heard, tasted, touched and smelled.

When he or she has grown used to working with these vivid images, the procedure can easily be adapted to enhance performance in virtually any activity. To improve speed and accuracy on the sports field, for example, a child should rehearse different types of stroke or play, using imagery, before an actual game. One method is to work backwards from the desired outcome, such as a basketball landing in the net, through the different actions that would be necessary to achieve that result.

In learning and studying, visualization greatly enhances the retention and recall of information. Here your child can use images in much the same way as when committing that list of words to memory in chapter 8. In order to remember the exports of a particular country, for example, he or she could take an imaginary trip around the docks, and picture huge cargo vessels being loaded with goods. On the sides of the vessels, in bright-red lettering (this colour sticks especially well in the mind), are their destinations, while on the sides of the various objects being exported – machine parts, bales of wheat, crates of sugar and so on – have been written the value or quantity. In order to recover those facts, your child need only take a mental walk around the same imagined harbour. While creating the images, he or she should ensure that they are as bizarre as possible. As I explained in the last chapter, the more unusual a series of mind pictures, the easier they are to recall.

To reduce examination nerves, your child can use visualization to run through all the events leading up to the exam. His mind movie might start on the morning of the big day, then include travelling to school, waiting outside the room and finally taking his seat behind the desk and watching the question papers being handed out. Any anxiety aroused by this imagery may be dealt with by switching to the soothing images of beach or country-side created at the end of the relaxation training sessions. Ask the child to talk about his or her feelings, and notice any negative thoughts or ideas. Do not comment on these at the time, instead, use either the diagnostic or the empathic listening approach described in chapter 7. Make a mental note of any unhelpful thoughts he or she may mention. Then, on a later occasion, help the child to think in a more positive way by together talking through his or her fears.

To enhance self-image or improve motivation, images can be created in which the child pictures himself succeeding, despite setbacks, in some challenging activity. Visualization in a relaxed and emotionally secure state of mind is an extremely powerful procedure, with the ability to enhance a wide range of skills. Merely by becoming proficient in these ways of using the brain, your child also perfects the all-important mind skill of concentration. 'Concentration,' says sports psychologist Timothy Galloway, 'is the supreme art, because no art can be achieved without it, while with it anything can be achieved.'

ENHANCING YOUR CHILD'S CREATIVITY

In chapter 2 I suggested that the attitudes which characterize great artists must always include imagination and intuition – the 'ability to see beyond the boundaries of what "is" to discern what might be'.

This may have given the impression that creativity is a haphazard process, that it occurs spontaneously and in ways which are beyond our ability to control. This is certainly the view of many parents, who consider that unless a child is born with the spark of creative genius it must be for ever denied him or her. Such an assumption is damagingly wrong, since every child has the potential to be highly creative if given the opportunity to practise and perfect these skills. American music teacher Don Campbell notes:

To be creative is to develop manners of association which are new. There is an endless flow of curiosity. It lies outside the practical, disciplined and step-by-step manner of expression. Creativity is not dependent on education or qualifications, but on the manner of approach and how things are considered. Creativity takes advantage of the unknown, the unexpected and the peculiar. Being right is not as important as being aware.

Sadly, in our culture getting it right is far more important than awareness, so the creative talents of the young child get strait-jacketed by conformist thinking. Yet successful thinking is almost always creative thinking, and in the decades to come, as computers take over most routine, non-creative mental activities, the creative mind will come to be increasingly prized and rewarded in every aspect of human endeavour.

Since, by definition, the creative mind is concerned with the original, the unorthodox and the unfamiliar, creativity is an extremely difficult – some psychologists would say impossible – mind skill to measure. Dr P. A. Guildford of the University of Southern California has identified sixty-one separate intellectual talents, and suggests that there may be as many more again yet to be discovered. Yet IQ tests measure, at most, about eight of them. As a result, even creative children who are highly intelligent, as they usually are, may score poorly on such tests and be judged less able by adults than their convergent-reasoning, intellectual-thinking, left-brain-dominant companions.

Curiosity, the driving force of creation and innovation, should be curbed as little as possible, and then only to keep your child safe and you sane! Stimulate the curious child by not giving over-simple answers to his constant questions, and try not to become irritated by this endless desire to discover. Children who receive encouragement to be creative are constantly inventing and improvising, especially when implementing and inventive mind styles make this their preferred way of thinking. They may take a little of something that they saw an adult do, add a pinch of an idea from a TV programme, adapt what they watched another child create and mix them all together to produce something entirely original.

The best way of enhancing creative mind skills is to give your child the tools and then let him or her get on with it. Unless you have an extremely good reason for intervening, such as the physical safety of the child, the less you get involved in his creative exploration the better. Your role is to observe and guide, to fill in the gaps of missing information, to separate harmful facts from playful imaginative fantasy, to provide the raw materials of creative endeavour. Allow your child as much freedom as possible when creative game-playing.

Remember that it is not the end product that matters but the process of creation, so you must not always expect a picture for the den wall or feel angry if an intricate construction is dashed to the ground amidst peals of excited laughter.

Provide plenty of materials for creative expression. Simplicity with variety is the key to success: paper plates, straws, empty plastic bottles (to fill with dried peas or gravel to make music with, or to make fantastic shapes), cardboard boxes, cast-off clothing, old magazines, worn-out sheets and pillow-cases, left-over decorative tiles, carpet samples, ribbon, string, empty cotton reels – the list is endless.

While it is necessary, at first, to show the child how to use materials, try to leave him to his own imaginative devices as much as possible. Too much supervision represses creativity, as the child learns that you are more concerned about her making a mess than interested in what she has created. Avoid the temptation to pick up the brush yourself and change his interpretation of reality by 'correcting' that 'funny-shaped nose you've given to Grandma'. Remember that reality is relative. Picasso was once showing a portrait he had painted to the sitter's husband. Seeing his bewilderment, he asked if anything was wrong. 'Well,' replied the man uncertainly, 'it's just not like her.' Picasso inquired what she looked like. The husband proudly extracted a small picture from his wallet. 'This is a perfect likeness,' he said. After studying the snap for a moment, the artist remarked quietly, 'Tiny, isn't she!'

Really look at what is being produced, rather than using distracted viewing and distracted listening, paying lip-service to requests for your reactions with 'Oh yes, very nice, dear – what is it?', as you hurry past the table. Pick up the picture, model, or poem. Study it carefully and ask about how it was done. With genuine interest, watch a play that your children have staged for you. Ask about the characters and where the idea came from. What will happen next? How can the plot develop from here? In other words, provide positive, constructive feedback of the type described in chapter 7.

If your child is eager to keep a particular creation for the time being, overcome your desire to have everything in order before tea time and do not worry too much about a little mess.

This is not to argue against all restrictions, but rather that fairness and firmness provide a framework for living and learning. It can be difficult to accept democracy in the home, and sometimes tiresome to have to discuss why certain restrictions are necessary to ensure acceptable living conditions for all concerned. Yet learning to cooperate, to accept majority views, even while disagreeing with them, and taking responsibility for one's own actions, are all essential mind skills.

It is also important to remember that creativity requires not only space and freedom to flourish, but also a large measure of self-confidence – that is, the ingredient that stimulates the desire to try and try again – on the part of the potential young creator.

Sensitivity is an important aspect of creativity. Does your child spend a lot of time experiencing the beautiful things that he sees? Does he try to express colour or texture by explaining how it touches his mind? When listening to music, does she see pictures and want to share them with you? And if she does, are you willing to devote time to level one active listening, or will the child be fobbed off with, at best, neutral and, at worst, one of the forms of the negative level three listening described earlier?

Parents sometimes worry because a highly creative child is very sensitive to sadness in their friends and relatives of all ages. Welcome that sensitivity, and allow him or her to share these feelings with you honestly and openly. This is often harder for boys, especially when either parent has stereotyped notions about masculinity. If sensitive boys run the risk of being branded feminine, the strongly independent streak found in most creative children often results in girls being criticized for being over-masculine.

Creative children have other characteristics calculated to incur the wrath of adults who feel threatened by their independence, which they often interpret as impudence; such adults are easily annoyed at their stubbornness, which they regard as impertinence, and angered by their non-conformist attitudes.

Enhance your child's sense of security by including him or her in adult decisions and plans. If you are going to redecorate the living-room, the changes you will make will involve feelings about colours, textures and spaces. What is it about that carpet that irritates you so? How long do you have to put up with serviceable, practical furniture, when you would love to have bamboo tables and a peacock chair?

Try sharing these feelings with your children. Sit down as a team and exchange ideas. Explain your views and seek theirs. You will probably be pleasantly surprised at the alternatives they propose and the furious activity that will be stimulated. Show interest in and enthusiasm for their ideas, thus encouraging future cooperation and input. And follow the same approach for planning all family activities: buying clothes, preparing food, leisure pursuits, holidays abroad, laying out the garden – or planting the window-box. It is not the size or scale of the operation that matters, but the opportunity of having their creative ideas taken seriously.

Remember that thinking and dreaming, logical reasoning and creative imagining, are your child's natural birthright. Adults can enhance these by providing the right world of learning, or they can destroy them almost entirely through their attitudes and actions.

Solutions to problems

1   Card problem   The card should be cut and folded as shown in figure 18.

2   Ant problem   Although it may seem as if the ant will have to keep walking for ever, in fact it will be carried forward as the rubber is stretched.

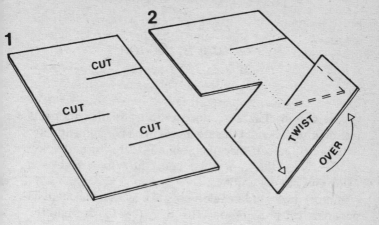

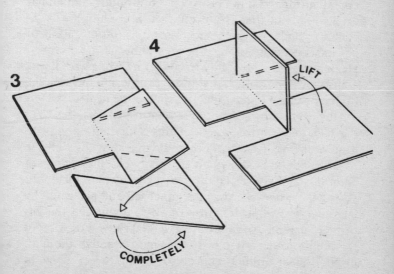

Fig. 18   The solution to the card problem

10

Thinking in Action

As we saw in chapter 2, success in translating thoughts into actions demands the attributes of a champion athlete: determination, self-discipline, and a desire for perfection which causes the individual constantly to stretch and extend his mental abilities.

Your child should develop both the intellectual stamina necessary for pressing onwards despite setbacks, and the sprinter's capacity for short, fierce bursts of speed in order to breast the tape ahead of the opposition. There must be a will to win, confidence, and assurance in one's own potential for attainment when confronting unfamiliar challenges. But that is not all! For your child needs, in addition, skills of communication, so as to present his or her ideas persuasively and convey enthusiasm to others. He or she needs the ability to cooperate while working as a member of a team, but without ever losing the courage to think and act independently, should the need arise.

This may seem a dauntingly long list of qualities. Yet the vast majority of young children have the ability to acquire them all, and to a high degree. For, like all the other mind skills described in this book, these are not natural talents conferred through an accident of birth, but skills which, because they are practised and perfected by learning, lie within the grasp of every infant and the gift of every parent. And they are essential skills. For without the ability to act effectively, the most creative thought, inspired idea, brilliant concept, startling theory or great vision will have no meaning. Either the individual assumes responsibility for its successful and vigorous implementation, or it never sees the light of day. And this, sadly, is the fate of most ideas. 'The reason is that generating the idea is the easy part,' comments industrial consultant Roger Von Oech. 'Making it reality is another story. The world of imagination is filled with endless possibilities and boundless resources. The world of action is different. It has finite resources and still less of that single most important commodity – time.'

In my experience, children, and adults, can be divided into two main categories. There are those who, when confronted by any new or unfamiliar challenge, will tell you, 'I can't do that!' And there are others who explain, 'I don't know how to do that!' For the first kind of child the world is filled with impossibilities; for the second, with possibilities. As soon as a child learns to say, 'I can't do that', it is as if steel barriers were raised across the brain, shutting out all possibility of understanding. But saying, 'I don't know', is only to admit that, at the moment, the mind skills needed for accomplishing a daunting task are not in one's possession. The possibility – indeed the probability – remains that, given sufficient motivation those mind skills could be mastered. And this is certainly a correct assumption. For, while there *are* clearly theoretical limits to the human brain's capacity for learning, adapting and achieving, such limitations are of no practical significance, since nobody has ever encountered them.

So never allow your child to undermine his mind by the things he says – and strenuously avoid doing so yourself. How often, for example, have you used, or heard your child use, such comments as 'I've got a terrible memory', 'I've no head for numbers', 'I'm hopeless at languages', 'I can't do that', 'You are stupid', 'You are clumsy', 'You are useless'?

I call these, and many similar remarks with which children are bombarded at school and in the home – often

day after day, month after month and year after year –
GIGO statements. GIGO is computer jargon for 'Garbage in – garbage out'.* The most sophisticated computer
in the world is only as good as the programs, the set of
instructions fed into its electronic brain, on which it
operates. Feed garbage in, and garbage is all you can
hope to get out.

Children's brains are programmed by garbage comments as well. Repeated often enough and over a sufficiently long period, they will be internalized: that is to
say, the child will come to accept them as a fair and
accurate reflection of her true abilities. And when that
happens, she starts to fail, expects to fail, becomes expert
at failing.

Teachers often tell me that they have in their classes
children who are not only good for nothing, but good at
nothing. They assure me that these kids are hopeless and
beyond help, and that there is no subject, no single mental
activity, at which they can succeed. Those teachers are
mistaken. Persistent failures are very good at doing at
least one thing – at failing. They are masters and mis-
tresses of incompetence, with the ability to snatch defeat
from the jaws of victory.

But they are not like that because that is the way their
brains were doomed to perform from birth. They have
learned to fail – as surely and as successfully as the
achieving child has acquired the mind skills that lead to
attainment. But even in the absence of such self-fulfilling
prophecies of intellectual impairment, some children turn
to failure as a means of reducing their anxieties about
succeeding. This sounds paradoxical, yet achievement can
prove more of a threat to some children than their lack of

* For an explanation of how to analyse GIGO comments, see my
book, *You Can Teach Your Child Intelligence*.

success. Achievement raises other people's expectations of you, sets you apart from your peers and gives you a reputation in the eyes of parents and teachers that can prove extremely stressful. If you fail more frequently than you succeed, people stop expecting so much of you and thus the anxiety level is reduced.

Because anxiety, and the defence mechanisms used to protect against its distressing mental and physical symptoms, exert such a powerful influence over performance, the starting-point in this examination of ways of helping your child to translate ideas into action must start with an exploration of its causes and its likely effects.

HOW ANXIETY CAN DIMINISH MIND SKILLS

Probably the most common reason why children fail is that they lose their nerve and feel afraid. They become fearful of thinking for themselves, of trusting their own judgement, of making mistakes when solving problems, or of being tempted to question the attitudes and assumptions of others. These fears can easily reach a level where they not only make effective thinking impossible, but they generate a sometimes overwhelmingly powerful desire to escape from the situation. Unfortunately, over-anxious children may find it impossible to discuss their feelings, even with sympathetic and caring parents, out of embarrassment, an inability to frame their fears in words, or from concern that they will be laughed at or not understood. And they are often right to worry about such a response, for many fears which engulf the child seem insignificant to grown-ups.

Anxiety has been described as fear spread thin. But however thinly spread, its capacity for causing damage to all kinds of mind skills is considerable. The bodily symptoms, such as rapidly beating heart, churning stomach, dry mouth, and fast, uneven breathing, are so distressing that it becomes virtually impossible to think clearly or act decisively. At the same time the mind fills with negative thoughts about failing to cope and being humiliated. Even well remembered facts and figures seem lost beyond recall, while the ability to solve problems and make decisions declines sharply.

Many children experience these high levels of anxiety at the start of a new term, when changing schools or moving to a different form, on the day of a test, and, especially, while taking exams. The result is that previously capable students fail to achieve expected goals.

But even when the level of anxiety is so slight that you may not realize that your child is other than confident and content, it may be sufficient to impair performance and act as a barrier to attainment. The progressive rise in mental and physical symptoms typically follows the pattern shown in figure 19.

Once this spiral goes beyond a certain point, the symptoms are extremely difficult to control. And merely telling yourself, or being told by others, to calm down and keep cool is no help either. That part of the nervous system responsible for arousal, the so-called 'fight or flight' response, is an ancient mechanism which evolved at a time when the dangers that threatened mankind were all too real. As they hunted in the jungle or lived in constant threat of attack by hostile neighbours, early humans needed to fight or flee in order to survive. Today, although the threats which confront us are very different, the anxiety response remains unchanged.

HOW ANXIETY CAN ENHANCE MIND SKILLS

It may seem strange that, having explained how harmful anxiety can be to performance, I should now suggest that

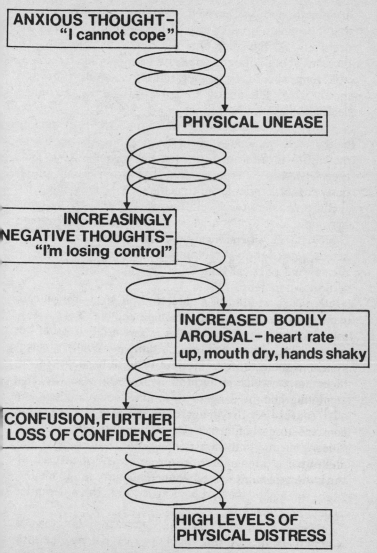

Fig. 19   The spiral of anxiety

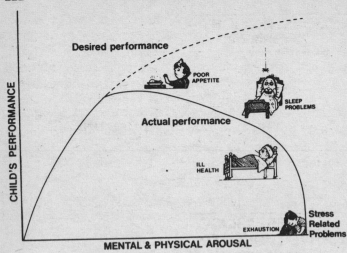

Fig. 20   The relation of arousal to performance

exactly the same kind of mental and physical arousal can also enhance a child's ability to think and act. Yet for any task, a certain level of arousal is essential in order to remain alert, interested and attentive. Whether such arousal is going to prove helpful or harmful depends on the extent to which it occurs and on what your child is attempting to do.

As you can see from figure 20, up to a certain point increased arousal enhances performance, but beyond that critical limit there is an abrupt decline. The greater the intellectual challenge, the lower the level of arousal at which the best work can be done. The more mundane the chore, the higher the levels of arousal at which it can be carried out efficiently.

Imagine a child who has been told to copy out a list of exports over the past ten years. The list is long, the task dull and the child's concentration likely to wander. In order to copy the list accurately, a high level of arousal will be needed. Now imagine he is trying to recall these exports in order to write an exam essay. The level of arousal at which the copying was done successfully will almost certainly prove far too high for efficient recall.

The secret, therefore, is to know how to regulate anxiety so as to allow it to rise by the right amount to ensure a good performance, without any risk of it running out of control. The levels of arousal experienced depend on three main factors:

1 The child's unique response to that particular task. As parents and teachers know only too well, children vary considerably in the way they react to an identical situation.

2 How much prior experience he or she has of similar tasks. Practice with examination questions or items in an IQ test, for example, increases the scores significantly through a reduction in anxiety, brought about, in large part, by familiarity with that activity.

3 The way the child views the likely outcome. The more certain either success or failure appears, the lower, as a general rule, the anxiety aroused:

Success certain –   low anxiety – high motivation
Success impossible – low anxiety – low motivation
Outcome uncertain – high anxiety – average motivation

Consider the state of mind of a child who has worked hard, revised carefully and enters the examination hall confident of doing well. Under these circumstances the chances are that she will not be unduly anxious, and will feel highly motivated to take the exam. Another student who, having done little work and no revision, knows he is certain to flunk the exam treats it with indifference.

Finally, we have a student who has worked hard but lacks confidence in her ability to succeed in the subject. She believes that, with luck, there is a chance of getting through. But if she is unlucky with the choice of questions, failure will be equally likely. As a result, she feels extremely anxious and only moderately motivated to take the exam.

The majority of children are in this position. They can rarely predict the outcome of an examination with any certainty. Indeed, one of the most tragic aspects of modern education is how little insight so many pupils show into their own abilities. In order to help your child to control his or her levels of arousal and to use them to enhance mental skills, you need to understand:

1 Why the anxiety is being triggered
2 How to bring unhelpfully high levels of arousal under control.

There are three major causes of anxiety in children, and we will consider each in turn to see how they affect your child's attitude to intellectually demanding tasks.

1 Anxiety caused by challenges
In adults this type of anxiety is generated by a wide range of activities and situations. Confronting problems at work, being put under pressure at home, marital difficulties – all contribute to an increased arousal level.

In some people fears are aroused by specific situations or circumstances; in others they exist as free-floating anxiety, a background of distress which affects everything they attempt. Such feelings make it very hard to cope with frustrations and difficulties, while many challenges will be avoided entirely. As we have seen, anxiety impairs concentration, reduces motivation and undermines self-confidence. Excessive anxiety, which has been reported in children as young as four, can lead to symptoms of over-tiredness, emotional upsets, psychosomatic illness and reduced immunity to infectious diseases.

For many children, the challenge of school is a major source of anxiety. There, either unintentionally or as a matter of deliberate policy, adults often increase stress levels as a means of exerting authority and exercising control over pupils. The American author and teacher John Holt comments:

We adults destroy most of the intellectual and creative capacity of children by the things we do to them or make them do. We destroy this capacity above all by making them afraid, afraid of not doing what other people want, of not pleasing, of making mistakes, of failing, of being wrong.

Thus we make them afraid to gamble, afraid to experiment, afraid to try the difficult and the unknown . . . we use these fears as handles to manipulate them and get them to do what we want . . . we find ideal the kind of good children who are just enough afraid of us to do everything we want, without making us feel that fear of us is what is making them do it.

The damaging consequences of this type of anxiety are often both wide and deep. Children who fall behind in class may never be able to catch up again – such is the pace and pressure of an examination-driven educational system. Serious gaps in their basic knowledge make it impossible for them to cope with or comprehend more advanced studies, so deepening their ignorance and increasing their fears. They may come to see themselves, and be seen, as unintelligent. Self-fulfilling prophecies are created at home and in the classroom, leading to an ever more rapid downward spiral of motivation, expertise, self-confidence and success.

Even a short period of excessive anxiety, especially during the early months at school, may be sufficient to brand the child a failure for the rest of his educational career – and sometimes for ever. Nick Millman, now an engineering student, clearly remembers the fear generated by one of his teachers some ten years earlier. 'I was never a bright pupil but I did try hard,' he explains. 'I was learning how to tally up – you know, mark down five ones and put a line through it. I was quite young, maybe seven or eight, but this to me was a difficult art which did not make sense.'

His teacher was a daunting woman in her fifties, whose face appeared to be set in a permanent scowl. 'She always looked at you over the top of her thick-rimmed glasses, rather than through them,' Nick recalls. 'You notice these things when you're young.' Reluctant to ask her for help, but afraid of falling even further behind in the class, he timidly approached her desk and said he did not understand. She demonstrated the method again, and then asked him to do one. He tried and failed:

It was only my panicking that was confusing me. Mrs Brown went mad. She threw my book onto the table and told me I was stupid not to understand that. The rest of the class stared at me. That hurt me even more than the teacher did . . . By the end of being in her class she led me, and my parents, into thinking that I was lacking in intelligence and a defeatist.

How you can help

Involved thinkers, because of their greater sensitivity to physical sensations and their well-developed intuitive abilities, are especially likely to suffer from this form of anxiety. If you have reason to believe that school anxiety is harming your child, use diagnostic and empathic listening (chapter 7) to identify the root causes of his or her distress. Having established the main reason, or reasons, for the unhappiness, it may then be possible to bring about the necessary changes: for example, by drawing the principal's attention to the activities of a bullying master, by arranging extra coaching to help the child catch up with the rest of the class, and so on.

By improving his or her thinking skills, using the procedures described in the previous two chapters, you should also be able to help build greater self-confidence and ability in class. In addition, you could use visual imagery and relaxation training as means of dealing with more general anxieties.

2   Anxiety caused by social demands

I shall describe two of the most commonly encountered types of social anxiety and the behaviour which results. Your knowledge of the child should make it fairly easy to decide whether either of them could be causing difficulties.

Refusers   These children hang back and only join in social activities, games, playing, group projects and so on, with the greatest reluctance – usually only when compelled to by adults to do so.

Incompetents   These children make an attempt to join in games and play but are so clumsy and/or lacking in skills that others are unwilling to accept them into the group and often do so only with protest and under adult pressure.

It is not hard to see how this anxiety response inhibits the growth of mind skills. To learn from life, children have to work and play with others. While the loner may excel intellectually – as I pointed out earlier, children whose primary mind style is that of the intellectual thinker are often at greatest risk here – he may fail to acquire no less essential social skills.

Bertrand Russell recalls in his autobiography how, during the greater part of childhood, 'the most vivid part of my existence was solitary. I seldom mentioned my more serious thoughts to others, and when I did I regretted it . . . throughout my childhood I had an increasing sense of loneliness, and of despair of ever meeting anyone with whom I could talk.' While Russell's loneliness was not due to social anxiety but to the unusual circumstances of his upbringing, his words perfectly describe the feelings of many children whose fear of others leads to an equally powerful sense of isolation.

Sometimes children are reluctant to join in because they have a low self-image, considering themselves inferior to their companions and therefore unworthy of their attention. They may also be afraid of being bullied. When an adult tries to help, by virtually ordering a group of children to play with a friendless child – 'Do let Billy join in, he looks so lonely' – the others are unlikely to admit him willingly, and very likely to edge him out again as soon as possible.

Although kindly meant, such an intervention is harmful both to the solitary child, who feels his sense of inferiority even more acutely, and to the group, whose often complicated network of relationships is disrupted. They may also feel that being obliged to play with the unpopular child is a form of punishment, which makes it far less likely that either will want to have anything to do with the other in future.

Finally, the anxious child never learns the skills of introducing herself into a group and of winning popularity through cooperation and inventing interesting activities. Frequently, children become playground wallflowers largely because they lack the ability to make friends. Like virtually everything else in life, this is a mind skill that has to be acquired through experience and perfected by practice, in order to be used successfully. The anxious child, who uses avoidance to cope with social fears, denies herself the chance to master these skills. As a result, a vicious circle is set up, whereby incompetence leads to isolation, which in turn restricts social competence.

Children who attempt to join a group but fail because of lack of playing competence may find the experience so unpleasant that they give up trying. As with making friends, the notion that children have to be taught how to play may seem curious. But the fact is that even the apparently least structured and most uninhibited playing actually demands a number of skills, together with an understanding of its unwritten rules.

For example, during what is known as 'rough and tumble play', young children will engage in mock fights. These are highly ritualized encounters in which the essentially peaceful nature of the combat is signalled by a whole range of subtle body-language messages, including a relaxed, open mouth.* But when children have never learned how to send out or interpret such signals, things can quickly get out of hand, with the child becoming either needlessly frightened, bursting into tears and fleeing from the scene, or unintentionally aggressive and using an inappropriate and possibly painful degree of force.

This can give rise in adults to a suspicion of bullying, especially when the child concerned is male and taller or stronger than his companions. Bullying is, indeed, one of the strategies sometimes used by the socially incompetent child who has failed to make an impression by other means. And although it is seldom recognized, children who resort to aggression to gain the attention of others are often made extremely nervous by social encounters.

---

* See my book *The Secret Language of Your Child*.

In their case, however, they have learned to channel the high levels of physical arousal generated by such activities into the expression of anger and frustration rather than anxiety and fear.

The popular child is usually the one who can think up exciting activities and take the lead in them, or else play an effective supporting role in another's game. By never staying long enough in a group to acquire these skills, an incompetent child is obliged to remain on the sidelines.

How you can help

An effective way of assisting the socially anxious child is to set up a play session involving him and other children, which requires cooperation and communication and is both entertaining and rewarding. (Notice that this is not the same as attempting to force the unwanted child into an already established game.) Select an activity requiring the active participation of all, but avoid anything involving competition, between either individuals or teams. Tasks such as setting up a camp, pitching a tent, building a tree-house or a bridge across a stream, are all suitable outdoor pursuits. Indoor activities could include constructional toys, racing cars and model train sets; cooking, painting a group mural and putting on a play or making a video film. Select an activity for which the solitary child shows some aptitude, since this will increase her or his confidence and self-image.

Coach the children in taking turns, sharing toys or materials, in making suggestions and in reaching decisions as a group. Encourage them to talk, to swap ideas and exchange information, to praise one another when someone does something especially well.

Start with a small group – the solitary child plus two or three others of about the same age. Try to include socially skilled children of both sexes in the group, but prevent the more dominant ones from taking command. If you know other parents in your neighbourhood who are worried about their children's seeming inability to make friends, you might like to form a group with them. Avoid turning a play session into a period of formal instruction – indeed, there should be no awareness of its true purpose – and fade from the scene as soon as possible.

It is essential that the child joins in, rather than looking on admiringly as you do everything for him. The object is not to demonstrate your own competence, thereby emphasizing the child's lack of it, but to provide learning experiences under the most encouraging and reassuring conditions possible.

With older children, sporting expertise is frequently a passport to self-confidence and social success. Not everyone enjoys team games, and there is no reason to force such a choice on an unwilling child, however much pleasure you personally derive from these pursuits. There is a wide range of sports where there is no need to engage in competition, such as sailing, swimming, running, riding BMX bikes and so on, where the child can enjoy the company of others and make friends with similar interests.

Parents who are left-brain-dominant intellectual thinkers may dismiss physical pursuits, or any activities which do not seem to lead directly to classroom attainment, as a waste of time. I cannot emphasize too strongly how mistaken this view is. The mind skills acquired through play include self-confidence, a strong self-image, the ability to persuade and communicate with one's fellows and to collaborate to achieve shared goals, an independent outlook and a willingness to confront unfamiliar challenges.

3   Anxiety caused by expectations

This can have many causes: for example, an uncertainty about satisfying the ambitions of parents or the hopes of teachers; a desire to win friendships, to be admired, respected and loved, or to gain the cooperation and trust of others. People made especially anxious by the prospect of meeting the expectations of others often have a rather negative self-image so far as some particular activity is concerned, although confident and competent in other areas. For instance, a child with little interest in school-work, whose parents value academic success highly, could become extremely anxious about satisfying their hopes for him in class. At the same time his skill on the football field might be such that he would feel no anxiety over meeting the expectations of coach and other team members.

Adults can be made anxious about living up to the expectations of a demanding employer, an ambitious part-ner or competitive parents. If you often become anxious at the prospect of satisfying other people's expectations, it could be that your fears are, at least in part, causing a lack of confidence in your child. Equally it may be that your own high levels of skill and confidence in certain areas are leading you to impose unrealistically high standards on your child. A fear of meeting expectations makes it more likely that those expectations will not be met, for all the reasons given above. In addition, as I shall explain in a moment, a widely employed strategy for coping with anxi-ety is to avoid the situations which cause it.

How you can help

Help by reviewing your attitudes towards:

   1   *Goals*   Are your aspirations unrealistically high? Parents often want their children to satisfy their own

unrealized ambitions in life, or to become mirror images of their success story.

2 *Pressure* Are you stressing your child, quite unintentionally, by placing too much emphasis on certain tasks? A recent study of British primary schools showed that many of the younger children were highly stressed by having to follow the same task-oriented curriculum as their older companions. Conflicts between the major mind styles of parents and children are frequently the cause of this type of pressure.

More and more ambitious parents, eager that their children should begin formal education as soon as possible, are starting them on full-time learning as early as the age of four. The proportion of children in this group rose from under 20 per cent in 1979 to almost 70 per cent by 1983, the majority in nursery classes attached to primary schools. These children's fears were expressed through inventing violent and vivid tales about children who were eaten by monsters or thrown into prison for making mistakes in class. Older children, too, are under increasing pressure from parents worried about their chances of finding work unless they achieve the best possible academic credentials.

While such concerns are understandable – indeed, it is unlikely that you would be reading this book at all were it not for a strong desire that your child should succeed – applying too much pressure can prove as self-defeating as showing too little interest in his or her intellectual attainments. The trick – and it is one which requires a great deal of perception, sensitivity and skill – is to achieve a balance between pressing too hard and not pressing hard enough just when a little extra effort is needed. I hope that the ideas contained in this book will have given you new insights into how this subtle task might be accomplished.

I have spent some time looking at the effects of anxiety on performance, because I consider it to be the single most important influence on the growth of mind skills. But, as is clear from the list of abilities given at the start of this chapter, your child needs to practise and perfect other skills as well, which I will now consider.

GETTING THE MESSAGE ACROSS

A muddled presentation always reveals confused thinking. Some children believe that merely expressing their thoughts as they occur to them will, in some miraculous way, impose order on mental chaos. Students often have a touching faith that even when they have not a clue what their answer to some question means, adults will understand it.

Effective communication involves many mind skills, including self-confidence and the ability to control one's anxiety, but above all it demands clarity of expression. And that in turn means organized thinking.

Communicating by writing

In chapter 9, I explained how to structure information in such a way that it slots comfortably into the brain's copious knowledge network and can be easily recalled when required. The best way of organizing written information, such as an essay or examination answer, is to reverse this process by producing what is called an *ideogram*. This simple, but powerful aid to recall can be learned by even young children and will prove an invaluable practical procedure both in school and later at work.

Imagine a child answering an examination question. A

few nights earlier she revised that topic using a number of knowledge networks and the TV memory box. As you will recall, the network is created by writing brief facts inside oblongs which are then joined by lines in such a way that the items are linked together in a logical sequence.

Having read the exam question carefully, and having used the three-stage mind-planning procedure described in the last chapter, she takes a sheet of scrap paper and notes down every item of information that she can recall on that topic. Because of the way the external network stored that knowledge in her memory, recalling just a single fact helps her to remember all the rest. She writes down each brief fact until the networks relating to that topic have been recreated on the scrap paper. Now she searches these notes for a suitable idea with which to begin her answer. This she numbers '1', and then circles it. Next she looks for a second item which follows logically from the first, numbers this '2', circles it and links it to circle 1 with an arrow. She continues in this way until all the information she wishes to use in her answer has been ordered and numbered. The resulting ideogram serves two very important functions in answering the question.

First, it provides a blueprint from which a well argued, sensibly structured essay can be produced. As any examiner will confirm, students often lose marks – and perhaps even fail – not because they lack the knowledge, but because of the haphazard, sometimes incoherent, way in which their information is presented. We can compare the difference the ideogram makes with the difference between two houses, one constructed without any plans and at the whim of the builder, and a second sensibly built from a well thought out plan. In the same way, an answer built according to the ideogram blueprint moves smoothly from the initial idea to the concluding paragraph. This strategy is often helpful in a second, less obvious, way as well. Having finished the question, the child should cross out the ideogram, to make it perfectly clear that these are working notes and not the finished answer. Having done so, she may well hand in the deleted ideogram with the answer sheets, since because it has been crossed through, no marks will be deducted for any errors it contains. On the other hand, if an important fact has been noted there but omitted from the actual answer – perhaps for reasons of time – it is possible that some credit may be given. The extra couple of marks gained in this way may be all that is needed to turn a failing grade into a pass.

Communicating by talking

Children often have to present ideas verbally, when taking an oral examination, attending an interview, speaking in a debate and so on. In all these situations, and to an even greater extent later in life, an ability to talk clearly and persuasively is a valuable skill. A youngster who interviews well often gets a chance denied to the equally qualified applicant who does not know how to put his thoughts into words. Indeed, some students have the ability to 'sell' themselves so effectively during interviews that they achieve more than others who have obtained better results in written work.

To acquire the mind skills of confidence, anxiety control and quick thinking under stress, children need to start practising as early as possible in life. Encourage your child to:

1 Join a local drama or operatic group. Most amateur companies are pleased to welcome younger members.
2 Learn voice production, and take part in singing or poetry festivals.

3 Join his or her school's drama and/or debating society.

4 Take acting, singing or dancing lessons.

If none of this is possible, perhaps he can put on plays at home, maybe helped by friends and watched by an audience of relatives. A video camera and recorder will enable him to make his own full-colour sound movies at low cost (once the initial expense of the equipment has been borne). But if the equipment is too expensive for you alone, why not see if other families would be interested in setting up a neighbourhood movie company for the entertainment and instruction of as many children who want to take part?

COPING WITH SETBACKS AND FAILURES

'If a job's worth doing it's worth doing badly!' Perhaps that sounds like lousy advice, and certainly not the sort of lesson you would be happy for your child to learn. Yet when he was an infant, this approach was central to his prodigious learning success.

To achieve anything in life children must first learn to fail correctly. Failure may be distressing, but when put to constructive use, it is a far better teacher than easily earned success can ever be. The trouble is that most children – and adults – spend so much time trying to avoid failure that they never appreciate what powerful allies setbacks and let-downs can prove.

Consider the most complicated learning task the human brain ever accomplishes – understanding and using language. For toddlers it is child's play, for adults a task so challenging that only a minority ever become really fluent in another tongue. One of the chief reasons why languages become increasingly difficult to master is that, as we get older, our fear of failure increases. We become more concerned about looking silly and feeling foolish, should things go wrong. Infants lack any such inhibitions. They happily garble their sentences, muddle up the tenses, and use incorrect words without feeling the least upset or embarrassed.

Indeed, it is only through making and correcting their mistakes that they become word-perfect. Before very long, however, this positive attitude is replaced by a powerful concern over making blunders. Failure is seen not as an inevitable milestone along the road to success, but as something that has to be avoided at all costs. To fail is to invite pain, emotional or physical, to be criticized and reprimanded, to feel foolish or incompetent. As we saw earlier in this chapter, a fear of not meeting the expectations of others can be a major cause of anxiety for children.

A popular method of avoiding failure is what, in the terminology of war games, is called a *minimax* strategy. Faced with a challenge, the child using this strategy chooses that course of action calculated to reduce losses to a minimum, should he fail, while maximizing gains in the event of success. For example, when asked a question in class the minimaxing pupil may decide that the safest course of action is to stay silent, especially when he knows that the teacher considers him bright and capable.

It is easy to understand why silence seems preferable to chancing an answer, once the underlying strategy is appreciated. The subconscious calculation goes like this: 'If I answer, there is a better chance of my being wrong than right. A mistake will make me feel embarrassed, the teacher disappointed and the rest of the class delighted. Should I answer correctly, the teacher won't think me any brighter. By saying nothing the teacher will probably believe I really knew the answer and so I shall still keep in her good books.'

While this strategy reduces the risk of failures, it also makes the child reluctant to venture an opinion, suggest an idea, answer a risky question, or take any other kind of chance. In other words, all those challenges so essential to learning mind skills are avoided when they should be confronted. Children with a high level of anxiety over meeting adult expectations are especially likely to adopt a minimax approach.

Start by helping your child to identify and avoid five major failure traps. These are attitudes of mind which children all too easily slip into, but find it very hard to clamber out of again. The wrong response on the part of parents and teachers may, indeed, make escape almost impossible.

Failure trap 1 – the hair shirt

The child who falls into this trap believes that mistakes can only be purged by punishment, either self-administered or inflicted by others. Instead of reflecting on what went wrong and trying to work out how to avoid similar errors in future, he seeks purification by physical or psychological pain, rather in the way religious fanatics see flagellation as the only road to salvation. You can identify this trap by the fact that the child recounts everything he did wrong in detail, inviting not forgiveness but condemnation for all his 'terrible' faults. A child is wearing her errors like a hair shirt whenever you hear such comments as 'I'm really stupid', 'I'm just hopeless', 'I can't be trusted to do that'.

Help by using diagnostic listening to pinpoint the true reasons for her difficulties, and then suggest practical steps by which they can be corrected. Empathic listening is not always helpful here, because the child *wants* to be reassured that she is right to feel wretched about her lack of success. Go along with this, and you run the risk of entrenching a negative opinion even more deeply.

Failure trap 2 – the guilt goad

Because failure and blame often go together, mistakes can become powerful goads for guilt. This negative emotion distorts your child's perception of his failings, magnifying them out of all proportion.

Just as a teenager may become convinced that his social hopes are dashed for ever by a pimple on the nose, so a child caught in this trap may convince himself that a few failures mean he can never hope to succeed. Children who are made over-anxious by trying to meet adult expectations are especially at risk here. You can identify this trap by remarks like 'I've let you both down so badly', 'It's all my fault things have gone wrong', 'I'm the one you should blame'.

Help by not being over-critical, and by reviewing the expectations that you have in order to see if they are unrealistically high or whether you are being somewhat too perfectionist in your demands. Never let the child feel that your love depends on his success, and that by making mistakes in school he is letting you down. Emphasize that failings only make a person into a failure if they are allowed to do so. Point out how errors are a powerful source of information which will ensure better performance next time. But before offering such advice, allow a cooling-off period. Immediately after the mistake the child may be swept along by such powerful and painful emotions that he will be unable to see the situation objectively. This only becomes a trap if it persists long after the mistake that triggered the distress.

Failure trap 3 – the refuge

Some children use failure as a refuge from challenges and stress. For them incompetence and inability are used as a defence against what they see as life's impossible demands. Stupidity can be a great comfort to the anxious child, because, as I explained earlier, once you have achieved the status of class dunce life becomes easier to cope with. Parents and teachers rarely blame you for lack of success or try especially hard to make you do better. You are allowed to sit, quiet and unnoticed at the back of the class, in splendid isolation, whiling away your time as best you can until class is over for the day. Provided you do not make a noise or become a nuisance, nobody may even notice that you are there. Adults have come to accept that there is nothing more to be done. If, by some strange fluke, you succeed, then everybody is delighted and you get praise that the more achieving child might be denied.

Your child has fallen into this trap whenever you hear him say things like 'I'm hopeless at . . .', 'I'll never understand this', 'Don't expect me to do that'.

Help by never giving up on him. No non-brain-damaged child is born dumb (and many children who are damaged in this way have far keener intelligences than adults usually give them credit for), but any child can think himself stupid. Use your knowledge of the child's primary mind style and brain preference to devise tasks in which he can enjoy meaningful success.

Failure trap 4 – no-go area

This results from a total refusal to accept that he has made a mistake, no matter how blatant the error. Children sometimes use this as a defence against anxiety (denial of reality), or else because their knowledge of the subject is so minimal that they really do not recognize the extent of their failure. Not long ago a group of under-achieving fourteen-year-olds was set a very tough intelligence test, one normally used to assess the ability of university students. Not only did the children complete the test in less than half the time taken by undergraduates, but they were far more confident of being correct. In fact their failure rate was higher than that predicted by chance alone. In other words, they would have got higher scores just by guessing. Yet none of them could recognize that mistakes had been made. The consequence of this trap is that no steps are ever taken to prevent future errors from occurring.

Help by not trying to force the child to confront the reality of his failings, since this will only strengthen the defences and widen the no-go areas. Instead, help him to enjoy genuine success in areas where he does have a real ability. Do not be dogmatic about what counts as success. If you are an intellectual thinker you may feel that intuitive or inventive thinking are less worthwhile. They are not. Once the child is genuinely successful, increased confidence should gradually weaken the defensive strategies and make it more likely that he will ask for help to clear up mistakes.

Failure trap 5 – the projectile

Here the child projects on to others any negative emotions generated by failures and setbacks – anger, resentment, guilt or frustration, for instance. Children have fallen into this trap whenever they regularly blame everyone but themselves for things that go wrong. They may accuse their parents of having sent them to an inferior school, or one that is excessively demanding; of placing them under too much pressure, or not taking sufficient interest in their progress. Equally, teachers may be condemned for going too quickly, or too slowly, for making lessons too hard or too tediously easy. The subjects themselves may be dismissed as irrelevant or rejected as overly challenging.

Help by giving careful, objective, consideration to the amount of truth in such allegations. Even children who project blame on to anybody and everybody, except themselves, may have some justification for their accusations. What sort of reputation does their school have among other parents? Have you been pushing a little too hard, or not devoting enough time to their educational needs? Is a teacher held in poor esteem by other students, and not just your child? Check textbooks and class notes to make sure that the level of expertise, knowledge and ability demanded is at the correct level for your child. Ask other parents if their children are reporting similar difficulties.

These inquiries may lead you to conclude that your child is chiefly using blaming as a way of defending him- or herself, against the anxiety aroused by failures. This is an all too frequent human response which allows us to confront mistakes and setbacks without suffering too much emotional distress. The danger of this failure trap is, of course, that it prevents us from learning by those mistakes, so making it less likely that our performance will ever improve.

Use diagnostic listening to identify the true reasons for your child's failures, then help to overcome them either by working with him, or by seeking assistance from the teacher concerned.

At the same time, encourage your child really to enjoy, and take pride in, any activities (sports, hobbies, etc) in which he enjoys a good measure of success. Never be tempted to contrast attitudes towards these tasks with his approach to unsuccessful challenges; for example by commenting: 'What a pity you don't show as much enthusiasm for . . .', or 'If only you spent the same amount of time and energy on . . .'. This only makes the child resentful and more likely to attribute blame for his failures to everyone but himself. By adopting a positive, realistic and constructive strategy you can encourage your child to escape from this widespread trap. In time he or she will come to recognize that a 'blaming' attitude is both unreasonable and unhelpful.

An action plan for attainment

Your child has just failed and is feeling miserable. What can you do to help? First, use diagnostic listening to discover why the mistakes were made, or empathic listening to help him unburden himself. Just talking over what went wrong to a sympathetic listener often helps to put the failure into perspective. At the same time, do not go along with any of the comments that indicate that he has fallen into a failure trap. Gently but firmly correct that false impression about the nature or extent of the problem.

Help your child to step back from the mistake, not by refusing to accept its importance – something that sounds very trivial to you may seem like the end of the world to him – but by recognizing its significance and showing your readiness to work with him towards a practical solution. Allow him no more than ten minutes in which to indulge in anger, outrage, despair, guilt or whatever other emotions he needs to release in order to reduce the psychic tension created by having failed. Distractions and diversions, a change of scenery, seeing a film, going to a party, can all help prevent him dwelling on the mistake. Negative thoughts only serve to increase anxiety and lower self-esteem. Anger is best channelled into some physical activity, such as going for a long walk, swimming or playing a strenuous game.

After your child has had enough time to distance himself from the failure, and the emotional turmoil has subsided, he will be ready to think about positive steps to learn from that mistake.

Get a sheet of paper and draw a line down the centre. Now ask him to write two headings, one on either side of the line, at the top of the page – 'What went wrong' and 'What went right'. Alone, or with your assistance, he should fill in as many details as possible about what was attempted and what went wrong. While preparing the list, your child must avoid any evaluation of his performance, whether good or bad. For instance, he should not write down, 'It was stupid of me to . . .' or 'I was smart to understand that . . .'

Read through the 'What went wrong' list and help him to expand on what happened, if the details seem too general. For instance, suppose he has written, 'Stood up to read my essay to the class but couldn't get the words out', ask exactly how he felt. Was his mind confused even though he was feeling physically calm, or was his heart and his breathing so rapid and uneven that he could not speak properly even though his mind was clear? The single worst mistake your child can make when thinking back about failures is to learn too general a lesson from them, such as 'I'm never going to be able to cope with reading out an essay before the class', or 'I'm too stupid to understand science'.

From comments in the 'What went right' column identify the strengths of his performance. Whatever we attempt to say or do, there is a good chance that, like the curate's famous egg, it will be very good in parts. Children who have adopted failure as a means of coping with life tend to focus far more strongly on mistakes than on achievements, and even those who regard themselves as totally unsuccessful do get things right on occasions. Help your child to explore those positive aspects, which will always be present, and to build on them.

Your child's failures, when explored calmly and correctly, will show clearly what steps must be taken in order to ensure future success. As Cardinal Newman observed, 'Nothing would be done at all if a man waited until he could do it so well that no one would find fault with it.'

COPING WITH CRITICISM

Children have to put up with a great deal of criticism. Indeed, with some teachers and parents, virtually everything young people do produces either sarcasm or reprimands. They respond to this with various defence strategies for coping with anxiety: avoidance ('If I keep quiet perhaps I won't be noticed'), denial of reality ('What does he know anyway?'), the projection of their own failings on to others ('It's his fault, not mine'), or emotional insulation ('I just don't care'). The problem is, of course, that these attitudes prevent any constructive comments from getting through to them and helping to improve their performance in the future.

But even the harshest criticism can sometimes prove more helpful than hurtful to your child, once she has learned how to turn such remarks to her advantage. She should start by deciding, with your help at first, whether the criticism merits consideration or contempt. Teach her to do this using the *five-finger test*, which works like this.

Write the criticism on a piece of paper, about two inches square, and place it in the palm of the left hand, fingers splayed. Now explain that she has to ask herself five questions:

Question 1 'Does the criticism deserve my respect?' The answer could be *yes* if the critic has as much (or more) knowledge, skill and experience in that particular area as you do.

However, although a teacher may be a specialist in her own subject, that does not mean that she is more of an authority than the next person on anything else. Your child can accept his maths teacher's criticisms of his multiplying of fractions, but need not regard his comments on morality, for instance, as particularly well informed. If there is no good reason for respecting a critic's judgement on that point, fold the little finger down.

Question 2 'Is the criticism reasonable?' Comments based on negative listening seldom meet this qualification. Also to be disregarded are any criticisms where the evidence is unreliable or where dishonest arguments have been used. Your child's CRAP-detector (see page 195) should be trained to sniff out flaws in a critical comment. If, for instance, the criticism was: 'You don't appear to have worked hard enough on this project', it may well be reasonable and helpful since it explains why the work was not up to standard. But the comment, 'You're completely idle and this project proves it', comes into the CRAP category, and the detector should immediately start beeping.

If your child feels the criticism is unreasonable she folds down her second finger.

Question 3 'Does the criticism seem realistic?' Is the child being blamed for something beyond her control, such as a shortage of supplies in the school, bad ground conditions while playing a sport, tiredness because she is getting over the flu?

If your child is convinced, and can convince you, that

the criticism is unreasonable, she can fold down her third finger.

Question 4 'Is the criticism relevant?' When adults resort to destructive criticism with the object of making a child feel small, they make irrelevant comments: for example, linking mistakes in spelling to long hair, dirty finger-nails or unpolished shoes. If your child feels the criticism is irrelevant she can fold down her fourth finger.

Question 5 'Is the criticism rational?' Your child should ask herself whether it was an objective evaluation, or just an angry or frustrated adult letting off steam. A good pointer here is to ask if the criticism was made quietly and privately, or loudly and in public. If the child feels convinced that the criticism was irrational, then down comes the thumb.

The five-finger test is completed, and the clenched fingers can be used to crumple the valueless criticism into a small ball before placing it where such comments belong, not in the brain but in the bin. If she crumples the criticism physically, it is easier for the child to avoid staying psychologically crumpled. Anger and resentment can be disposed of at the same time as the well crushed scrap of paper.

But what about those times when the criticism fails to pass the five-finger test, when your child agrees that there is truth in the remark, even though he still feels it was unfairly expressed? On such occasions help him or her to identify any positive aspects of the remark, in the same way that you encouraged an exploration of the construc-tive aspects of mistakes. Consider the points raised by any fingers which remain outstretched at the end of the test. Explore them with your child and see how they might help him to improve his performance on later occasions.

Suppose, for example, that the criticism was made by someone whose knowledge he respects and that it is reasonable and realistic, despite being irrelevant and expressed during a burst of rage. Three fingers will remain outstretched, and the comment should be explored further to see what helpful ideas may be learned. Even when there is only one finger left unbent at the end of the test, it can still pay to explore that single positive feature of the criticism.

As with failure, allow a cooling-off period before attempting to help your child explore the merits of critical comments. Suggest he perform the five-finger test the day after being hurt, as well as immediately after the event, to see whether the delay has enabled him to look at the remark more objectively. If there *is* any merit in what was said, he should ask himself: 'What must I do so as not to deserve this criticism in the future?'

Write down any ideas. Now consider how, when and where those changes should be made. Here again it is helpful to make brief notes. Once a course of action has been decided upon, your child should run a final check to make certain that he is clear exactly why the proposed changes will be helpful.

11
Mind Skills and Your Child's Personality

So far we have looked at differences between children in terms of brain dominance and mind styles. But, of course, we are all more than the sum total of our intellects. As a result of traits of temperament, children and adults respond to life in a wide variety of ways, and find pleasure in a range of very different activities. Our largely inborn reactions to life comprise the human personality, and are relatively unchanging across time. Since their influence over the development of mind skills is considerable, it will be helpful to understand the effects they have and how children with differing personalities can best be helped.

HOW PERSONALITY ARISES

As every parent knows, each baby is an individual from the first moment of birth. Research has now shown that the traits which produce that individuality are enduring, so that the most important aspects of an adult's personality are present from the earliest weeks of life. These predispositions are, however, moulded by experiences, and will undergo important modifications as a result of the way a child is brought up. Upbringing is, in turn, influenced by inborn traits, and this results in a complex, dynamic interplay which makes it impossible to know for certain how parental attitudes will affect a child's development. 'Domineering, authoritarian handling by parents might make one youngster anxious and submissive and another defiant and antagonistic,' comments Drs Alexander Thomas, Stella Chess and Herbert Birch, whose

pioneering studies have identified the traits of temperament described in this chapter. 'Such unpredictability
seemed to be the direct consequence of omitting an
important factor from the evaluation: the child's own
temperament, that is, his own individual style of responding to the environment.'

Their research, which involved tracing the development
of more than 140 children from birth to their mid-teens,
established two important facts. The first was that, in a
majority of children, any traits that are found at a few
days will persist for years. Secondly, these traits influence
the style of learning and teaching with which children are
most comfortable. When demands are made which conflict with these inborn responses, a high level of stress
arises. To create an effective learning world, therefore,
you should take account not only of your child's mind
style, but also of his or her temperamental style. This
holds equally true at school and in the home. Where your
personality traits match those of the child, conflicts are
unlikely, although there is a risk of unintentionally
encouraging less favourable aspects of his personality.

Where there is a serious mismatch of personality traits
in a family, the same kind of conflicts that occur between
strong left- and right-brain thinkers, or people with opposing mind styles, becomes more likely.

Thomas, Chess and Birch have identified three main
types of child, whose responses are determined by different constellations of traits. After reading through the
descriptions below, you should have little difficulty in
identifying the type which best matches your own child's
response to life.

The easy child
Easy children are bright, cheerful, usually optimistic
youngsters with regular eating and sleeping patterns, who

respond with low to moderate intensity to events. They approach unfamiliar situations boldly and are usually very adaptable. Some 40 per cent of those studied came into this category.

Alex – an easy child   Now aged twelve, Alex merited this description from the very first. He was described as a 'good' baby by his parents. Moderately active, he wriggled quite a lot when being dressed or changed, and was very regular in his bodily functions. Alex fed on a four-hourly schedule from birth, and was seldom scared when placed in unfamiliar surroundings or confronted with novelty.

By the age of three he was a bold explorer, clambering eagerly over the furniture, and confident when playing with friends, although he was equally happy amusing himself. His regular patterns of sleeping and eating were maintained as he grew older, and he quickly adjusted to nursery school.

Today Alex remains a lively, adaptable youngster always eager for new experiences and fresh challenges. Rarely moody, he takes criticism and teasing in his stride, and laughs uninhibitedly when amused.

Helping the easy child

Although their ability to adapt quickly and readily to different demands means that such children respond well to a variety of child-rearing styles, there can be a danger of conflicts arising when the family expectations differ markedly from those found at school or among their peers.

One such child was Robert, whose parents had always stressed the importance of self-reliance and independent thinking. They raised their son to be imaginative and questioning. Having developed these mind skills to a high degree, when he started school Robert soon found himself in clashes with authority. Many teachers considered him impudent for constantly questioning their instructions and insisting on doing things his own way. Because he tried to take charge of games and expected others to follow his lead, his fellow pupils regarded him as too bossy, and he often got into fights. Punishments and unpopularity, not surprisingly, left him confused, stressed and miserable. His work suffered and his position in class made it abundantly clear that he was performing well below his intellectual ability.

Linda had exactly the opposite problem. Raised by fairly authoritarian parents, in a home where she was discouraged from expressing her own opinions, she found herself completely lost when, aged fourteen, she went to a school with a progressive headmistress and a free-and-easy intellectual atmosphere. Here students were encouraged to offer their opinions and to disagree with their teachers if they had valid reasons for doing so. They made decisions for themselves and were generally expected to adopt an independent attitude towards their studies. With no experience of these mind skills, Linda felt quite incapable of rising to the unfamiliar challenges. Her schoolwork suffered, and her parents, who were always highly critical, scolded and punished their daughter for 'being lazy' and 'not trying'.

These two case histories illustrate the possible risks which 'easy' children face in life. If your own child comes into the category:

Do be on the look-out for conflicts as your child moves from one environment to another, such as when going to school for the first time or when changing schools. Review family expectations and standards in the light of demands being made on him or her by school and schoolmates.

While this does not necessarily mean that you should change your expectations or lower your standards, it does suggest that a degree of understanding and tolerance is required. Realize that, in the confusion created by conflicting demands, problems which a more worldly-wise adult might resolve without much difficulty can seem like insoluble dilemmas to a young child.

If difficulties arise, use diagnostic listening to identify their true cause.

Don't respond with outrage or punishment. Remember that the very traits of temperament which made your child so easy to care for could well be responsible for the difficulties that he or she is now confronting.

The slow-to-warm-up child

These are usually less active than easy children, can become grouchy, miserable or pessimistic for no apparent reason, and find difficulty in adapting to changed conditions. They comprised 15 per cent of the children in Thomas, Chess and Birch's study.

Rachel – a slow-to-warm-up child Now aged ten, Rachel was a passive baby, seldom wriggling when being changed, bathed or dressed and sleeping quietly in her cot. She disliked unfamiliar surroundings and fretted until she had become used to them. As she grew older, Rachel became moody, sulking and crying for no apparent reason. She hated playschool and cried every time her mother left, for a whole week. After this she settled down and seemed to enjoy herself, although any variations in routine made her unhappy.

Even today, Rachel hates surprises and is fearful of anything novel. She refuses to eat unfamiliar food, and when the family spend their summer holidays abroad she usually insists on eating the same sort of meals as at home. However, if she can be persuaded to try something new and eat it on a few occasions, she often grows to like it.

She was upset for weeks after moving from her first school, and still cries readily when teased by other children or reprimanded by her teachers.

Helping the slow-to-warm-up child

There is a temptation, with such children, not to oblige them to try things that they appear to dislike. Many parents, after one or two attempts at persuading them to sample a new dish, make more friends, join in games or try their hand at a new sport, give up rather than cause continued distress. Whilst it is certainly wrong to force slow-to-warm-up children to do something against their will – such a tactic can only lead to increased anxiety and decreased motivation – they can usually be encouraged to broaden their experiences provided novelty is presented to them in a non-threatening way.

The secret is to allow such children plenty of time to adapt to new situations and circumstances and while doing so to provide non-coercive support and encouragement. Avoid any sort of emotional blackmail ('Do it for Mummy, darling') or bribery ('I'll give you more pocket money if you do it'), since both tactics have undesirable consequences. The first makes your love appear conditional on their behaving in ways which please you, while for true emotional security these children must realize that these feelings are unconditional. Bribes may produce the desired results, but if used too frequently the children come to do things only to win an external reward, rather than working for inner satisfaction – the only way to achieve true intellectual fulfilment.

Gentle persuasion and unconditional support, together

with a gradual exposure to the new object or activity, are usually effective in bringing about the desired change in attitude or behaviour.

Slow-to-warm-up children can easily become trapped in a mental and physical rut from which it becomes increasingly difficult to free themselves. Bobby, one of the children in the American study, was never given such an opportunity: 'His parents never encouraged him to participate in anything new,' explain Dr Thomas and his colleagues. 'They simply withdrew what he did not like.' When Bobby rejected a new food, they stopped offering it to him. When he refused to play with other children at school, they kept him at home. Before long he found it distressing, or downright impossible, to attempt any unfamiliar activities, whether it involved making new friends or tackling a new subject in class. 'By the age of ten Bobby was living on a diet consisting mainly of hamburgers, apple sauce and medium-boiled eggs,' comment the authors. 'In play he was a "loner".'

Johanna, a child from my own study, had a very similar approach to life. Once she had gained confidence in a new subject, she usually succeeded so long as she was allowed to go at her own pace. In her first school the teachers understood this need, and she prospered. But after moving schools, she was put into a class of high-flyers under a new teacher who was impatient with children who appeared 'slow on the uptake', a failing she construed as a sign of stupidity or idleness – both, in her eyes, the worst kind of classroom crime.

After trying, without success, to cajole Johanna to adopt a faster pace, she simply gave up and ignored the girl, who sat at the back of the class, never causing any trouble to anybody, as she idled her time away. The extent of Johanna's failure only became apparent to her parents when the end-of-year exam results placed their daughter at the bottom of the form in almost every subject. With the help of an understanding teacher, who coached Johanna at her own pace, some of the lost ground was recovered.

If your own child could be described as slow to warm up:

Do be patient. Such children are not unintelligent, but merely handicapped by unhelpful traits. Offer encouragement and make new experiences available to them without any pressure to participate. In other words, open as many doors as possible but never force them to go through. If they refuse even to attempt an unfamiliar task or reject something novel – such as a new food, game or toy – never withdraw it. Instead, make it available on repeated occasions until the strangeness disappears. Teach the kind of behaviour you would like to see – carrying out the task, eating the food, playing with the game or toy – in a relaxed manner.

Don't make sarcastic or unfavourable comparisons between the slow-to-warm-up child and an 'easy' brother or sister. Such comments as 'You are silly not to try that . . . look how much the others are enjoying it', or 'You really are a baby not even to have a go', undermine self-image, reduce motivation, increase anxiety and make it even less likely that the child will make any attempt at that activity in the future.

The difficult child

Difficult children are a trial to parents, teachers and playmates, who have to put up with black moods, depression, anger, tears, and a frequently negative attitude towards life. Also, their behaviour can be very disruptive, and is seldom acceptable to teachers even when it has come to be tolerated at home. Their appetites and sleep patterns are often irregular. Such children formed 10 per cent of those in the American study.

Tony – a difficult child   When he was a baby, Tony nearly drove his parents crazy. He slept very little and spent most of his waking moments bawling his head off. After a doctor suggested that being driven around by car might persuade him to sleep, they would spend half the night motoring through the countryside, returning in the early hours exhausted but with their son as wide awake as ever. Another paediatrician told them with despairing humour: 'Try a bottle of whisky – nothing else seems to put him to sleep!' While lying in his cot, Tony would bang his head so hard that on one occasion he cracked the wooden headboard.

As he grew older this behaviour persisted. His temper tantrums became a family legend, with the slightest setback or frustration sending him into screaming fury or hysterical tears. Tony was always in emotional overdrive. When he cried his sobs filled the house, and when amused he would sometimes laugh so loudly that he developed hiccups.

He was a child of tremendous enthusiasms and equally intense hatreds of people and things. Sometimes, after making a mistake with his homework, he ripped out whole pages. When he blundered while building a toy aircraft, he smashed the almost completed model to smithereens in his anger. Infuriated by teasing, he once attacked his older sister with a kitchen fork after she made a joke at his expense. At school his work was careless and his grades low, and he was often in trouble for bad behaviour.

It is hardly surprising that out of the children in the American study who developed emotional and behavioural problems sufficiently serious to require the help of a psychiatrist, 70 per cent were from this group.

Helping the difficult child

These children are the most difficult to help and the hardest to feel sympathy for. Yet unless you can learn to cope with the difficult child, little positive learning will take place. On occasion the child may become so furious and aggressive that all trace of self-control is lost. What maybe needed is time to calm down and cool off, away from the audience of adults and, perhaps, other children.

All too often, however, adults resort to physical punishment – often, perhaps, more to relieve their own anger than in the hope of preventing such behaviour in future. If your own child comes into this category:

Do try to remain as patient and as objective as possible. The strategies for anxiety reduction taught in chapter 10 should make it easier to remain calm in the face of his or her provocation.

A helpful practical procedure is 'time out'. Here the child is simply removed to another room and allowed to get over his or her emotional outburst. While he or she is calming down, the adult must try to remain calm and as unresponsive as possible, preventing the child from leaving the room but otherwise neither saying nor doing anything. Once the outburst is over, try to understand the true cause of his tantrum. Diagnostic and empathic listening help here. This does not mean that you should approve of his or her conduct, or accept it. But there is a great deal of difference between telling a child, 'I don't like you', and saying, 'I like you but not the way you behave.'

Given time and encouragement, the difficult child can not only learn new tasks but probably become highly proficient at them. Disruptive behaviour, no matter how stupid it may appear, need not be an indication of stupidity. Make demands on such children; they function poorly if left to their own devices. Decide on the standards of behaviour that you require, establish the minimum number of family rules required to attain them, and then ensure that they are imposed consistently.

Because difficult children have a low tolerance of frustration, are all too easily distracted and find it hard to persist for long in any activity, they perform most poorly in an easy-going atmosphere.

Don't be *laissez-faire* in your approach. All the evidence suggests that firmness, when it is based on reason and fairness, provides the most effective strategy. If you find yourself starting to get angry or upset, walk away from the situation until you calm down.

Don't use physical punishment; it will not help, and could easily make matters worse. Avoid dwelling on the child's mistakes, since this can only make him or her feel worse, but focus instead on what should be done another time.

When discussing the child's feelings of frustration, anger, sadness or whichever emotion has led to a particularly negative mood, be careful never to make comparisons with other children. This is a real risk when a brother or sister comes into the 'easy child' category.

THE INFLUENCE OF INDIVIDUAL TRAITS

So far we have looked at the likely effects on thinking, learning and behaviour of the constellation of traits that makes up a child's personality. But within this overall picture there are numerous individual ways of responding to the world – ways whose importance and influence in the development of mind skills are considerable. Here we are going to look at four of them:

1 Energy level
2 Mood
3 Boldness
4 Intensity

1 Energy level

If your child has an above-average level of energy, he will be extremely active – at times, perhaps, over-active, and unable to attend long enough to take his lessons in. Such children are frequently impulsive, blurting out the first idea that comes into their heads rather than pausing for reflection. In class they often act the clown, pester their companions and play around with their books, and they are a generally disruptive influence. Clearly, all these distracting activities make it much harder for them to acquire efficient mind skills. Furthermore, their behaviour may lead to teachers considering them stupid, a judgement they can come to share when frequently repeated. 'If the teacher decides the child does not want to learn and treats him accordingly,' comment Thomas, Chess and Birch, 'the youngster is apt to conclude that he is stupid or unlikeable and react with even worse behaviour.'

How you can help

If you suspect that your child is abnormally active – hyperactive – then start by checking up on his or her diet. Research evidence suggests that hyperactivity may be linked to certain of the additives used for colouring and preserving food; there are more than 3,500 of them, of which most of us consume between seven and sixteen pounds every year.

Children are at a greater risk of developing allergic reactions than adults, since their smaller size means that toxic concentration in their bodies is greater. Furthermore, the foodstuffs with the greatest child-appeal – sweets, cakes and other processed products – are usually those most heavily dosed with additives. Try stopping certain foods to see if any difference in activity levels occurs. In addition, ensure that your child has a balanced diet with as few as possible carbohydrate-rich 'junk' foods.

Do keep teaching sessions short. Find constructive outlets for all that energy. The over-active older child can make an excellent, and very patient, teacher of younger children. Give him or her responsibilities whenever possible. Stay calm and try not to show annoyance. A highly active child often finds it impossible to bottle up all that energy for long.

Don't compel a highly active child to keep still for lengthy periods – it only makes matters worse. Restrict his playtime no more than is necessary: he needs every opportunity for physically exhausting games.

But if your child seems to be lacking in energy, with an activity level that appears far below his peers, you should try to help. Children often suffer a significant decline in energy when under stress – for instance, while studying for exams, when disturbed by family rows or marital problems, while getting over an illness or operation, and at the onset of puberty. Such transitory drops in activity are no cause for concern. But children who are habitually lethargic need help in becoming more energetic and involved.

Low levels of activity are associated with poor motivation, especially in mentally or physically demanding tasks, insufficient persistence and inability to concentrate. At school these children may be penalized for failing to complete assignments, unpunctuality and general indifference to their surroundings.

Helping the low-activity child

A low activity level may mean that your child would rather sit down with a book, a computer or a game of chess than run around with his or her friends. While such intellectually stimulating activities are to be encouraged, since they help to build mind skills, problems can arise when the brain is worked harder than the body. This is compounded when the pursuit is a solitary one, since children need to exercise physically as well as mentally and to acquire the social skills which can only come from playing with children of the same age. If this applies to your child, encourage more active, cooperative games using the ideas suggested in the last chapter for anxious children.

A low activity level becomes more serious when all your child wants to do is to slump in front of the TV. Setting aside the minimally stimulating content of many popular programmes, recent research suggests that there may be an additional, hidden hazard in over-exposure to TV. This hazard has nothing to do with what is being watched, but relates to the way in which the television picture is generated, using a rapidly moving beam of electrons sweeping across the screen.

In one experiment, children were connected to equipment which measured their level of attentiveness. Signals from the monitoring equipment were fed to a control box which switched a video recorder on and off. The only way they could continue to view a favourite cartoon was by staying alert, but despite their desire to see the programme, the longest any child was able to maintain vigilance was thirty seconds.

This decline in alertness occurs irrespective of the actual programme content, and arises from the way a TV image affects the function in the occipital cortex, the region at the back of the brain where visual information is processed. Prolonged viewing of a TV screen causes all viewers, but especially children whose level of activity is already low, to become even more passive and inattentive. To make matters worse, while in this mental and physical condition, viewers of all ages, although not consciously attentive, are especially receptive to incoming information. This means that the brain is far more likely to absorb a programme's message than it would be in an alert state. Most children, lacking the experience, judgement and knowledge of adults, are, of course, even more susceptible when in this condition.

While the degree of censorship exercised must be a matter for individual parents, all should be aware that any prolonged viewing can have adverse effects on intellectual functioning, no matter how uplifting and educational the material viewed.

Do encourage physical activity. The more active a child becomes, the higher her energy level will rise. Lethargy breeds lethargy. Children need to play vigorously in order to ensure the health of both mind and body. As we have seen, they must also acquire the skills necessary for cooperating with others, and these can only be perfected by inventing games, making friends and asserting themselves in the company of their peers.

Don't use words like 'lazy' or 'idle', however much you may feel they are justified. The risk here is that the child will come to explain her lack of energy by telling herself: 'OK, so now I know why I feel this way – I'm lazy.'

If you are energetic yourself, but have a low-activity child, try to share some of her quieter pleasures while gently encouraging her to join in more physically demanding activities. When doing so:

Don't place the child in a situation where she feels incompetent or humiliated. She may not be very good at sports, for example, and hate being shown up by better-coordinated, stronger, tougher, more agile or experienced companions.

Don't apply too much pressure: never *make* the child join in. If the activity looks interesting enough, and sufficiently non-threatening, she will join in.

If, on the other hand, your activity level is on the low side, while your child is usually full of energy, try taking part in some of his activities as a way of encouraging him to value your own quieter, perhaps more reflective pastimes. Here again there are a couple of important rules:

Never force him to play, or take over and dominate his games.

Don't, just because a leisure activity appeals to you, assume that it will also be attractive to your child.

2 Mood
By this is meant the extent to which life is approached in a positive, optimistic manner or in a glum and negative way. Moods do vary considerably, of course, from day to day and from one situation to the next. But even within these variations, it is usually possible to detect a pattern of behaviour which leads one to describe some children as being bright and cheerful, while others strike one as unhappy or depressed.

If your child usually enjoys a bright, cheery approach to life, then he or she will take great pleasure in most of the activities attempted and look forward to the future with confidence – all qualities that help to make the exercise of mind skills challenging and enjoyable.

It may be, however, that your child has a tendency to

become over-upset by disappointments, or depressed by minor failures. Recognize and counter this tendency by providing plenty of encouragement and support when the child feels down. As most people know only too well, negative moods impair concentration and undermine motivation. So be patient with your child if he or she is passing through a difficult emotional period.

Some children, unfortunately, tend to have a rather too negative outlook on life, and experience longer-lasting moods of depression. They may cry without (at least so far as adults can see) any apparent reason for their distress. Help such a child by being positive yourself. If your child is a boy, do not regard a 'weepy' response to frustration as a sign of weakness, and never ridicule him for his tears. The legacy of the stiff upper lip is frequently an unhealthy detachment from one's emotional self, an aspect of the psyche no less important and valuable than the intellect.

If you have a positive outlook while your child is somewhat negative, your more positive moods may help sustain him or her through especially black periods. Be aware of, and avoid, criticizing him for not sharing your optimism and delight. The only consequence of comments such as 'You're a real misery' or 'For God's sake cheer up' is further to undermine self-confidence and deepen the child's depression. Provide distractions, objective comment, sympathetic attention and empathy, but what you should never attempt is to 'jolly' him out of his mood. Although well intended, such an approach patronizes him by implying that his feelings are not worthy of serious attention. Children have to learn how to accept and stay in touch with their emotions, both pleasurable and painful, rather than deal with unhappiness only through denial or avoidance.

The worst situation of all arises when parent and child share a negative outlook. Here the black moods of one are likely to reinforce the misery of the other. There may well be great empathy between them, with each able to appreciate, from immediate personal experience, the feelings of the other. Yet the net result is often to get even more deeply entrenched in their depression.

There are no simple solutions to these complex emotional interactions. As before, talking about your feelings freely, and without fear of having them used against you at a later date, is a vital ingredient in overcoming negative moods. A recent major study concluded that a warm, trusting, empathic relationship was the most important single safeguard against chronic depression.

3 Boldness

This refers to the degree of willingness with which the child approaches novel, strange or unfamiliar situations and activities. A readiness to experiment and explore is, of course, central to successful thinking and learning. Indeed, neither can occur unless people are prepared to go beyond what they know in order to investigate new knowledge and practise fresh skills.

If your child is bold, he or she will approach unfamiliar challenges with enthusiasm, and not be afraid to venture into the unknown or make mistakes. Some children, however, are temperamentally more timid, with avoidance and withdrawal being more likely responses than approach and confrontation. Such children are prone to homesickness, dislike being away from their parents, become fearful in unfamiliar situations and would sooner not try their hand at novel tasks. Parents who are bold themselves are often slightly contemptuous of, or impatient with, children who do not possess this attribute to the same extent. At the same time, somewhat timid adults may frustrate and inhibit the bold child's desire for new experiences.

If you are more prepared to tackle unfamiliar activities and explore unknown challenges than your child is, recognize that his timidity arises, at least in part, from inborn characteristics. Be patient and allow him time to get used to the new situation. Never toss him in at the deep end and expect him to swim, because if you do he is far more likely to go under. Progressively introduce new tasks and activities.

If your child is bolder than you are, try to become more objective about her need to take certain risks and discover just how far one can go safely. This does not, of course, mean allowing her to stumble into physical danger. But very often the hazards of certain activities loom far larger in the minds of adults who favour avoidance, than the risks justify.

4 Intensity

If children experience life intensely, it is no secret. When they lose their tempers, everybody knows it. They shout, slam doors and smash things. Equally, when amused they laugh loudly and uninhibitedly.

Children who express themselves in this way often find it difficult to make or keep friends, who become concerned by the intensity of their moods and lack of self-control. Also, the learning of mind skills is harmed by their powerful feelings. Mistakes may make them so furious that, rather than patiently trying to discover what went wrong and how to put it right, they abandon – or even destroy – the work entirely.

On the other hand, a marked absence of emotional intensity may reveal itself as either a somewhat cold-blooded approach to life or a rather apathetic attitude. The former is unlikely to impede the acquisition of intellectual skills, although it makes it far harder for a person to develop a warm, empathic relationship with people whose feelings are expressed more intensely. Apathy, on the other hand, will bring about all the problems that we looked at earlier when considering the low-energy child.

Adults who experience their feelings intensely can frighten children whose emotional responses are more constrained. Equally, the uninhibited expressions of happiness, anger or grief of the child who has an intense reaction to life may disturb or distress emotionally controlled parents. There is a need to recognize and respect different emotional styles within a family. Attempts to repress intense feelings can result in psychological difficulties, such as cruelty to animals, bullying, and destructive outbursts, which may be viewed as the displacement of powerful emotions into undesirable physical actions.

Key points to remember

Different personality traits should be seen as points along a continuum rather than as pigeon-holes. Not every child, for example, can be considered easy, slow to warm up or difficult. Thomas, Chess and Birch found that only 65 per cent could be categorized in this way, while the remainder had 'a mixture of traits that did not add up to a general characterization'. These constellations of traits, and indeed my comments about the individual traits, should only be taken as a general guide as to how or why your child may respond in a particular way to different situations.

Finally, it should be stressed that, although apparently inborn, these traits are not immutable. Personality is best seen as developing from a constant interplay between the individual and his or her surroundings. Social, cultural and family pressures will encourage certain predispositions whilst reducing, or repressing, others. By understanding the part such pressures and predispositions play in emotional development, you will find it easier to produce the family environment most suitable for your child's intellectual development; to create a learning world, in which mind skills may be practised and perfected most successfully.

Mind Skills and Tomorrow

By the time they leave school, many children find it easier to sink than to think – and most of them do. Swept away by a tidal wave of confusion and complexity, they disappear into the depths of incomprehension and despair.

I believe that, while some children are harmed more seriously and lastingly than others, the mind skills of the majority are, to varying degrees, significantly impaired by their classroom experiences. Only those fortunate few whose brain preference, primary mind style and personality most closely satisfy the demands of formal education, can hope to emerge intellectually and emotionally unscathed by the experience. After more than a decade of full-time education, most have learned only to fail.

But if too few schools are able to help children acquire the mind skills necessary for survival in a technological, computer-based society, how well do they succeed in teaching the most fundamental mind skills all – reading, writing, arithmetic and basic science? Here, too, the picture is sufficiently bleak for leading educationalists on both sides of the Atlantic to warn of a crisis in the classroom.

CRISIS IN THE CLASSROOM

It is estimated that around three million British adults have some difficulties in reading or writing, ranging from poor spelling to an inability even to recognize letters of the alphabet. A 1981 study by the National Children's Bureau showed that more than 3,000 of a sample of

17,000 twenty-three-year-olds admitted to literacy problems. And it is not only school leavers who are expressing concern. 'It shocked me when I first came here,' says Ian French, an ex-schoolteacher now running a youth training workshop in Northern England. 'The general standard is so very, very low. Of the 60 per cent who get extra teaching, most have writing which is very infantile. Among the others the general level of literacy is very poor.'

In his book *Illiterate America*, Jonathon Kozol revealed that twenty-five million US adults were worse at reading than seven-year-olds, while a further thirty-five million read less well than fifteen-year-olds. Figures released by the US Census Bureau in 1986 showed that 9 per cent of English-speaking American adults are illiterate, while among those whose native language is not English the proportion rises to 48 per cent.

As a result, the US now ranks forty-ninth in the world's adult literacy table, in marked contrast with Japan, 98 per cent of whose population are literate – an unrivalled accomplishment – and who, in 1985, bought 3.6 billion books – thirty titles for every man, woman and child. A 1980 report by the US Department of Education and the National Science Foundation stated that most Americans are moving towards 'virtual scientific and technological illiteracy'. The authors warned: 'The generation graduating from high school today is the first generation in American history to graduate less skilled than its parents', while the Carnegie Council of Policy Studies in Higher Education comments that 'because of deficits in our public school system, about one-third of our youth are ill-educated, ill-employed, and ill-equipped to make their way in American society. It is becoming increasingly apparent that even college graduates cannot write acceptable English or even do simple arithmetic.'

Data collected by the National Assessment of Educational Progress showed that the percentage of high school seniors able to demonstrate competence in a wide range of higher-order thinking skills had declined significantly over the past decade. Ten years ago, 21 per cent were able to complete a creative writing task; more recently the proportion had dropped to 15 per cent, while success in solving maths problems declined from 33 to 29 per cent. The authors of the study estimated that, were present trends to continue, 'by 1990 one to two million seniors will not have the essential skills to compete in the information economy.'

Their forebodings were echoed in a report by the National Science Foundation task force convened by President Carter in 1979: 'Scientific and technical literacy is increasingly necessary in our society, but the number of young people who graduate from high school and college with only the most rudimentary notions of science, mathematics and technology portends trouble in the decades ahead.'

Only 6 per cent of US students obtain higher-education degrees in science, compared with 21 per cent in Japan, where since 1970 the number of engineers trained each year has increased threefold. In the US the number of students graduating in law has tripled over the same period, but those qualifying as engineers has actually declined. 'Japan now graduates each year as many engineers as all of Western Europe, and at least as many as the US, and most of these being recent graduates are just beginning to produce,' says management expert Peter Drucker. Meanwhile, Japanese children have shown increasing scientific aptitude over the past fifteen years, according to a 1985 survey carried out by a Stockholm-based educational organization.

Faced by evidence of such widespread failure, it is

hardly surprising that the US National Commission on Education has gloomily commented: 'If an unfriendly power had attempted to impose on America the mediocre educational performance that exists today, we might have viewed it as an act of war.' In Britain, where 80 per cent of children leave school without obtaining the minimum qualifications necessary for entry into either higher education or high technology, there is equal reason for parental concern, especially where numeracy and an understanding of scientific concepts are concerned.

A recent survey by the National Foundation for Educational Research showed that 40 per cent of children aged between nine and eleven were taught science less than once a week. When sex differences are taken into account, the situation is even less satisfactory. More than 75 per cent of girls leave school with only one science examination pass, or none, according to the School Curriculum Development Committee. 'Despite a commitment to equal opportunity in education for both sexes,' comments the committee, 'male and female pupils receive two different and distinct educational packages.' A major stumbling block, researchers have found, is the highly conservative views of teachers, especially in maths, physical sciences and technical subjects, where the majority are men. While many pay lip service to equal opportunities, only a minority practise it.

But this failure in education is not, as some parents believe, the result of the adverse influence of a trendy liberalism which has swept away the basics and replaced them with a more interesting but irrelevant child-centred approach in junior schools. Dr Barker Lunn, principal research officer at the National Foundation for Educational Research, which recently completed a detailed study of teaching in these schools, comments that their findings were in marked contrast to the popular image of junior education since the 1960s, when pressures for child-centred learning first arose. This led the public to believe that 'progressive methods were being practised by large numbers of teachers and were becoming the norm in British primary schools', she says.

The truth was different. After interviewing more than 2,500 teachers in 732 schools, researchers reported that the majority of nine- to eleven-year-olds spend most of their time in class reading, writing and doing sums.

A possible clue to why such a significant number of those children fail to master those skills also emerged from the research findings, which showed that mixed-ability group teaching was rare while cooperative group work in class was rarer still. One sixth of the teachers interviewed had introduced a system which, the authors of the report claimed, was the equivalent to streaming. They did this by arranging the seating according to attainment. Only a quarter of teachers allowed the children to choose where they wanted to sit. This over-rigid teaching system allows slower children to slip ever further behind if they miss, or fail to understand, earlier lessons. Concerned teachers talk of the unassertive, struggling pupil who falls through gaps in the education net, and who goes through school sitting among the failures, switched off and ignored.

It was, in part, to capture the interest of and to offer more individual attention to students like these that, in the early 1980s, computers began to appear in classrooms and the term 'computer literacy' was bandied around common rooms. Many hailed the micro as technology which would bring about a revolution in teaching and learning, making slow pupils bright while enhancing still further the intellectually achieving. Sadly, it seems likely that in the current climate computers are at best an unnecessary distraction and at worst a damaging irrelevance. For although, in the right circumstances, they have a valuable role to play in school, computers are not what computer literacy is really about.

What computer literacy means
Educational journalist Ken Waddilove comments:

It is interesting to note the emotive use of the term computer literacy. The implication is that those who are unaware of the jargon and the technology are illiterate. You could promote the same feeling about needlework or engineering – but these subjects are too mundane to carry with them any mythology. The notion of computer literacy may well turn out to be the most expensive mythical red herring of our era in terms of educational effort.

There are many teachers who, without being Luddites of the silicon-chip society, agree. But they are in the minority.

The computer has wide appeal. Those funding education are excited by the micro because it is so modern and cost-effective. Why pay for more teachers when computers will give individual computer-assisted instruction at a fraction of the cost, and never get sick, want holidays or strike over working conditions?

Teachers often enjoy computers because they are 'high tech' in a world still dominated by chalk dust and blackboards. Besides, since only a few staff members usually understand much about them, working with computers confers status on the specialist teacher. Similarly, having dozens of keyboards and visual display screens confers status on the school.

Parents like them and put pressure on schools to invest in them (often raising the money from the community to do so), because the media are constantly bombarding them with stories about the limitless opportunities for children who understand computing. To deny your child a chance to become literate in this new technology seems to some tantamount to sentencing him or her to a lifetime's unemployment. Students, too, enjoy computer studies, because they are fun and offer a degree of control and interaction which is absent from most other lessons on the timetable.

Small wonder, then, that every developed nation has begun to introduce computers into schools and computing into the timetable. In Britain there is one micro for every 95 secondary pupils and one per 150 primary school children, and 140,000 teachers have been trained in their use. In America there is one computer for every 75 students. France had installed around 100,000 micros in schools by the end of 1985, making her one of the leading proponents of classroom computing. A recent survey in Bavaria suggested that computers are already in use by 90 per cent of grammar schools. In Japan they are being used by kindergarten children as young as four.

The problem is what to use them for. And if the response is 'to help children become computer-literate', what does that phrase really mean and what price is being paid to achieve it?

Officially, micros were introduced into schools to train the 'keyboard generation'. Since most are supervised by teachers in the science or maths departments, there is an emphasis on learning how they work and on how to write programs. Yet, while this is a useful introduction to computing, it misses the main point. The real challenge of the silicon chip society is not understanding what makes the hardware work or even how to produce software. It is knowing what they can do, what can be done with them, and how to deal with their mass-produced end-product – information. It is about appreciating the role computers have in work and leisure activities, realizing their advantages and being able to recognize their limitations.

Imagine what would have happened if, when motor cars started being produced in large quantities, it had been widely believed that only people who could understand the workings of the internal combustion engine would be able to derive any benefit from the coming transport boom, with the result that everybody had been encouraged to train as garage mechanics. Exactly how many jobs will be directly created by computers is hard to estimate, but in the UK it seems unlikely that more than 2 per cent of the more than 900,000 annual school leavers will be able to find jobs for which classroom computer training would be even remotely helpful. Even students who want to study computing in higher education are not expected to have had prior experience; of the forty-six universities in the UK, only two specify a preference for an examination pass in the subject, and even they do not insist on it. A similar picture can be found elsewhere in Europe and in the USA.

Most jobs associated with computing, involving the use of word-processors, data bases and information retrieval systems, demand no prior knowledge of computing, and operators can be trained in the simple procedures required in just a few days. Before long, even this basic level of expertise will no longer be required, as increasingly powerful computers with ever more user-friendly software do most of the work. On the so-called fifth-generation computers, data will almost certainly be input using voice commands, and highly specialized program-creating programs will generate software needed on the basis of a general outline of the tasks to be performed. Self-diagnostic chips will identify the source of hardware breakdowns, perhaps automatically calling up the service company and providing details of the parts that need to be replaced.

There will, of course, be employment opportunities for hardware engineers and software designers, for program analysts and similar specialists, but the major opportunities must arise from the social changes accelerated by computers rather than from computers themselves – just as, today, there is only a limited demand for motor car designers, engineers and mechanics, many of whose jobs are likely to disappear as a result of automation.

And despite all the effort and enthusiasm of computer teachers, and the sacrifices made by other departments, it is not clear that children really do leave school in any sense micro-literate. A recent study by Dr Steven Pulos at the Graduate School of Education, University of California, Berkeley, showed that a surprising number of American pupils aged eight to thirteen were no better informed about computer technology – and this despite weekly computer classes, computer-assisted instruction, training in computer literacy, and some experience with programming and word-processing.

About half had no idea how computers worked, many believing them to be more intelligent than humans, while others saw them simply as information retrieval systems. Only 29 per cent of children said that they wanted to work with computers on leaving school. 'The supposed popular revolution of kids and computers has not happened,' says Pulos. 'If the current, popular view is incorrect, and children do not have a special aptitude or interest in computers, then we have a very damaging misconception on which we are basing many aspects of computer education.'

But these meagre gains in computer literacy are, in many schools, being purchased at a high cost – at the cost of cutting other departments' budgets for purchasing textbooks, laboratory equipment, musical instruments, art materials and so on. As a result, the computer may come to be seen not as the key to unlocking a child's intellectual potential, but as a Moloch on whose altar vitally important opportunities and skills will be sacrificed in vain. Computers can be useful, especially in helping physically and mentally handicapped children to communicate their thoughts and ideas. There are many excellent programs, proving more patient and thorough than all but the most dedicated teachers, to help such children to learn basic skills. But they are not, and never will be, a substitute for human beings teaching other human beings in an atmosphere of stimulation and trust.

SCHOOLS FAIL, BUT DON'T BLAME THE TEACHERS

Seeking human scapegoats when things go wrong is as old as human history, and can take many forms. Research by American social psychologists Carl Hovland and Robert Sears has shown that between 1882 and 1893 the number of negroes lynched in the American South fell with the price of cotton. Public frustrations over educational failure have not yet resulted in the lynching of teachers, but they have led to their frequent professional pillorying. 'To read some of the more important and influential contemporary critics of education,' says Charles E. Silberman in his book *Crisis in the Classroom*, 'one might think that the schools are staffed by sadists and clods who are drawn into teaching by the lure of upward mobility and the opportunity to take out their anger . . . on the students.'

Yet most teachers, like the majority of doctors, lawyers and other professionals, are sensitive, intelligent and skilled, being no more responsible for the present crisis than are lawyers for crime, or doctors for sickness. They work hard, sacrifice much, do their best under conditions that are typically far more intolerable and stressful than those found in almost any other profession, and are as much the victims of the system as the children they teach and the parents who pay their salaries. 'The shabbiness of the teachers' physical environment is exceeded only by the churlishness of their social environment, a fact that educational critics tend to ignore or to acknowledge only in passing,' says Silberman, attributing the blame for this 'peculiar blight' on several related factors, including teachers' low status in the community and stereotyped characterization in films and literature. 'There is the atmosphere of meanness and distrust in which teachers work,' he points out. 'They punch time clocks like factory workers or clerks and are rarely if ever consulted about the things that concern them most.' Their heavy teaching loads leave no time for reflection; they put up with menial duties, scruffy surroundings and an absence of privacy in which to prepare their work.

But above and beyond all these physical problems, real and discouraging though they undoubtedly are, is the basic philosophical confusion about just what the teaching profession is expected to achieve. Although it is more than a century since the Liberal statesman, William Forster, paved the way for mass instruction with his Elementary Education Act, society still has not decided what purpose schools are supposed to serve. Indeed the vision is growing fainter rather than stronger, since, when schools were first established, their goals, however narrow, could at least be clearly stated. Then their role was to teach basic literacy and deference to the masses, and Latin, Greek and leadership to their social superiors. Since then, conflicting ideas about the purpose of school have led to a crisis of confidence and a loss of direction.

For many centuries the dominant idea underlying Western education has been that of *cultural transmission*. The purpose of teaching, according to this view, is to pass on not only knowledge but also cultural norms and social mores. Knowledge exists, out there in the world, and only awaits discovery. Having been discovered, these truths can then be passed on to children via direct instruction. The child's feelings, ideas and personal view of the world are of no consequence. Robert Maynard Hutchins, an American educationalist, said in 1936: 'Education implies teaching. Teaching implies knowledge. Knowledge is truth. The truth is everywhere the same. Hence, education should be everywhere the same.'

Accordingly, knowledge has to be transmitted to children by instruction and by their imitation of adults. Teaching is formal, and children are rewarded for the right responses and punished when they make a mistake or step out of line. As an anonymous headmaster writing in the September 1970 issue of *Where* magazine explained:

The basic duty of schools is to induce literacy and numeracy . . . I believe that the principle of 'divide and rule' is a sign for education as for empires, and that to blur and confuse areas of study by 'general' this and 'integrated' that or 'interdisciplinary' the other only results in blurring the teacher and confusing the pupil. I believe solidly in examinations as the best test for pupils' competence.

Supporting this view, educationalists C. B. Cox and A. E. Dyson in their 1969 Black Paper, The Fight for Education observed: 'Exams make people work hard. Much opposition to them is based on the belief that people work better without reward and incentive, a naïveté which is against all knowledge of human nature.'

These assumptions about the nature and purpose of education, which are still widely accepted both by parents and by many teachers, have resulted in schools whose style of organization Professor Charles Handy of the London Business School compares with that of a prison: work schedules are disrupted at regular intervals, and pupils change their places of work and supervisors constantly; they have no place to call their own, and are frequently forbidden to communicate or cooperate with one another. In most of the schools Handy visited during his researches the children appeared to be 'invisible'. When he asked head teachers how many people there were in their schools, he received answers ranging from six, in a primary school, to seventy, in a comprehensive. The students were rarely included in the numbers given. Professor Handy also reported that teachers, reflecting confusions amongst the general public, appeared uncertain about the precise role of pupils. During their early years at school they tended to be viewed as workers and were given group tasks to perform under supervision. By the time they were on the point of leaving school they had come to be regarded as 'clients' and were allowed to take their pick from what was on offer. But between eleven and sixteen they were far more likely to be seen as 'products'. 'They are like shoes or bits of metal, which are inspected at the end of the production line, sometimes rejected as substandard and then stamped "English", "history", "maths" and so on,' he comments.

Schools might also be compared to chaotic factories where employees swap work stations and change jobs every forty minutes. In most schools the management style adopted comes closest to what American industrial psychologist Douglas McGregor terms the 'theory X approach'. This assumes that most people dislike work, lack ambition, are essentially passive, avoid responsibility, resist change, and are self-centred and unconcerned with the needs of the organization. As a result, the manager's (teacher's) role is to direct, motivate, manipulate, persuade, control, reward and punish the workers (students) in order to force them to respond effectively to the needs of the organization.

Supporters of the cultural transmission perspective believe that knowledge is the same thing as absolute truth and can be built up bit by bit, subject by subject. The philosophical underpinning of this view is that the world exists independently of man and is regulated by natural laws over which we can exert little or no control. John Locke, the seventeenth-century English philosopher, considered the mind of a newborn child to be a *tabula rasa*, a blank surface on which experience writes the lessons of life. Accordingly, the intellect is passive and the world we perceive is the world as it really is rather than a mentally created construct. From these ideas came the behaviourist school of psychology, where what matters is the stimulus and the response, the rewards and punishments which are thought to shape behaviour. Our environment is seen as input, and our behaviour as output.

Burrhus Frederic Skinner, one of the founding fathers of behavioural psychology, defined learning as a change in the probability of response, and believed, like the Jesuits, that given an infant he could turn out any kind of adult one wished – tinker, tailor, beggar or thief. Teachers were the architects and builders of student behaviour, and education was evaluated by changes in behaviour, not in thoughts or feelings. He wrote in *Beyond Freedom and Dignity*:

We can follow the path taken by physics and biology by turning directly to the relation between behaviour and the environment and neglecting . . . states of mind. We do not need to discover what personalities, states of mind, feelings . . . intentions – or other prerequisites of autonomous man – really are in order to get on with a scientific analysis of behaviour.

In a memorable phrase coined by British psychologist Dr Don Bannister, man had been turned into 'a ping-pong ball with a memory'!

A directly opposing view of education is that of the *progressive movement*, founded by the American philosopher and educator John Dewey. Born in 1859, the son of a New England grocer, Dewey graduated from the University of Vermont and taught in high school for three years. In 1894 he opened an experimental school in Chicago, based on a rejection of authoritarian teaching and what he called the 'spectator theory of knowledge' – the idea that knowledge is a gift to be passively received rather than the reward for effort and active participation by students. 'Education is the work of supplying the conditions which will enable the psychical functions as they successively arise to mature and pass into higher functions in the freest and fullest manner,' Dewey wrote.

Children, he believed, learned through the interplay between their natures and their surroundings. The teacher was an adviser, facilitator and guide in this process, but true education came from life itself. Philosophically, Dewey's ideas reflected a pragmatic concept of knowledge, founded in the British tradition of searching for scientific truth via experiments rather than through theoretical speculation. According to this idea, notions of reality are the result of an interplay between an individual and the environment.

At the opposite pole to those who believe in cultural transmission, followers of the progressive movement, and many other psychologists and educationalists, claim that there is no such thing as absolute, fundamental truth but only interpretations of reality. As a result of this belief, they consider the child's view of the world, and the shaping of that view, to be of central importance. According to American psychologist George Kelly:

Whatever nature may be, or howsoever the quest for truth will turn out in the end, the events we face today are subject to as great a variety of constructions as our wits will enable us to construe . . . All our present perceptions are open to question and reconsideration, and . . . even the most obvious occurrences of everyday life might appear utterly transformed if we were inventive enough to construe them differently.

Similar sentiments regarding the child's unique view of the world were expressed two hundred years earlier by the French philosopher Jean Jacques Rousseau in his novel *Emile*: 'Childhood had its own way of seeing, thinking and feeling; nothing is more foolish than to try to substitute our ways.' This view was later echoed by Freud: 'Only someone who can feel his way into the minds of children can be capable of educating them, and we grown-up people cannot understand children because we no longer understand our childhood.'

More recently, a third influential movement has emerged, which suggests that school does so much harm that it must be either radically reformed or, as some propose, abolished entirely. The main advocate of this more extreme position, Ivan Illich, points out that children learn more important and useful things outside the classroom than in it. He concludes that society should be *deschooled*, by abolishing the institutions and reorganizing learning on a local basis, matching those who want to learn with those who would like to teach.

The deschooling movement resulted in Philadelphia's Parkway Program, the Stantonbury Campus in Milton Keynes, and the growth of organizations such as Education Otherwise in the UK, whose purpose is to help families wishing to teach children at home. Only a minority of those arguing against the present educational system support the complete abolition of schools. Most propose a transformation of the attitude of society and of the teaching professions in order to make education relevant and rewarding to both students and teachers.

Charles Silberman believes that the schools of the future must be places where the rights of children are observed, learning methods are varied, and children work on their own, at their own pace and at tasks of their own choosing. The leaving age would be open-ended and students of all ages, including adults, would come and go as they pleased. Anthropologist Margaret Mead wrote in 1958:

We are no longer dealing primarily with the *vertical* transmission of the tried and true by the old, mature, and experienced teachers to the young, immature, and inexperienced pupil. This was the system of education developed in a stable, slowly changing culture. In a world of rapid change . . . what is needed, and what we are already moving toward, is the inclusion of another whole dimension of learning: the *lateral* transmission, to every sentient member of society, of what has just been discovered, invented, created, manufactured or marketed.

TRANSFORMATIONS

In *The Aquarian Conspiracy*, Marilyn Ferguson describes four ways in which people change their minds when faced with new and conflicting information:

1 The easiest, and most limited, she calls 'change by exception'. An old belief system stays intact while allowing for the occasional exception. People may say: 'Schooling is fine, except for . . .'
2 The second way of changing your mind is a little bit at a time. There is never any point where the old ideas are rejected outright, but instead they get modified. People engaged in this form of change may comment:

'The views I held before were pretty much correct, but now I am entirely right.'

3 'Pendulum change' involves abandoning one closed and certain belief system for another which is equally rigid. 'Pendulum change fails to integrate what was right with the old and fails to discriminate the value of the new from its overstatements. Pendulum change rejects its own prior experience, going from one kind of half-knowing to another,' says Marilyn Ferguson. A person may say: 'I was wrong before, but now I'm right.'

4 The final and most dramatic way of changing, which the philosopher of science Thomas Kuhn calls a 'paradigm shift', represents a true transformation in attitudes. (A paradigm is a belief system shared by a majority of people, essentially a widely endorsed collection of perceptual sets.) When this shift occurs, says Ferguson, 'change is no longer threatening. It absorbs, enlarges, enriches. The unknown is friendly, interesting territory. Each insight widens the road, making the next stage of travel, the next opening, easier.'

In little more than one hundred years mass education has moved from teaching basic literacy and piety to instruction over a wide range of arts and sciences; Neil Postman and Charles Weingartner, authors of *Teaching as a Subversive Activity*, comment:

. . . schools were always presumed to be carrying out the mandate of society, or at least giving it their best effort. They taught for obedience or productivity or whatever trait seemed appropriate at the time, producing teachers for teacher shortages, scientists after the Americans began worrying they were falling behind the Soviet Union scientifically after the launching of Sputnik . . . A society shaken by an implosion of knowledge, a revolution in culture and communication, cannot wait for a creaking educational bureaucracy to sanction its search for meaning.

Under the domination of the present paradigm, schools teach *what* and *how* rather than *why*. Content is all-important, and the key to success lies in the acquisition of 'knowledge' and its accurate representation to teachers and examiners. Facts are true, truth is sacred and information lasts a lifetime. As I have sought to show, not only are such assumptions incorrect, but they are also dangerously misleading. Once a paradigm shift has occurred – and this transformation seems likely to occur in the USA before it does in Europe – the emphasis will be on asking good questions, being open to experience and capable of evaluating, analysing and synthesizing knowledge. Learning will no longer be seen as a product for teachers to produce and children to acquire, within an authoritarian framework which demands conformity and punishes dissent. It will be flexible rather than rigid, with an orientation towards people rather than things. Guessing and right-brain thinking will be considered as important as logical left-brain thinking.

The ancient Greeks had the concept of *paidea*, meaning the educational environment, in which Athenian culture as a whole, the community and all its disciplines became a learning resource for the citizens, whose ultimate goal was to reach the divine centre in the self. Today we may be witnessing the rebirth of such a movement towards education not only as a source of wealth, whether personal or national, but as a resource for individual growth and enhancement. Social forecaster Alvin Toffler, for example, considers that in the 'third wave' of civilization people will be expected to become more creative and flexible, producing, in his optimistic view, the 'first truly humane civilization in recorded history'. 'In a rapidly changing information environment, people will need to move in and out of education throughout their lives,' says Professor Tom Stonier of Bradford University. 'Lifestyles will change, with periods of paid employment alternating with periods of education and leisure activities.'

This changing pattern of employment must be reflected in the assumptions and beliefs underlying education. There must be a movement away from training children to become other people's employees, and towards greater self-reliance and personal resourcefulness, to prepare them for what has been termed 'ownwork', that is, work which is controlled and organized by each individual. As David Howell points out in his book *Blind Victory: A Study in Income, Wealth and Power*, not only are an increasing number of people coming into this category, but many more combine employment for somebody else, either full- or part-time, with informal, self-organized, ownwork for themselves. 'As long as teaching implants the idea that full-time employment by some other person or organization is the goal and that government ought to deliver it, and could if it wanted, it is also nourishing the scrapheap mentality,' he warns.

You cannot, of course, guarantee, by helping your child to confront the future with mind skills capable of meeting the challenges it will bring, that he or she will enjoy a successful and fulfilling career. But you can make it a probability rather than a possibility. As a gambler once observed, 'The race may not always be to the swift nor the battle to the strong, but if you're putting money on the outcome, that's the way to bet!'

Furthermore, by preparing your child's mind to confront and cope with complex intellectual issues, you make him capable of participating in crucial social and scientific debates. When faced with anxiety-generating subjects such as the proliferation of nuclear weapons, atomic energy, the introduction of controversial new drugs and treatments, crime, immigration and so on, people typically respond in two main ways. The first is by avoiding giving the topic any serious consideration, by ignoring it entirely, by adopting a reassuring but unrealistic Panglossian attitude, or – perhaps most dangerously of all – by delegating responsibility to others. The second approach is to become more and more certain of less and less, by reducing the complex to the over-simple and by adopting an extreme view: in other words, by replacing intellectual effort with prejudice and bigotry. Both reduce stress and alleviate anxieties. Both are, in the long term, recipes for personal, political and social catastrophe.

Marshall McLuhan once commented that the reason why so many children dislike school is because it gets in the way of their education. In this book I have tried to explain why such feelings arise and how they might be avoided. The intelligence, creativity, enthusiasm and ability of children is not only any nation's greatest asset, it is also its one enduring and endlessly renewable resource. The Japanese realized that decades ago, seeing that in their overcrowded country with its dearth of mineral wealth they had to cultivate and harvest the only crop which grew in abundance – their people's intellect.

Let us hope that it is still not too late to avert Aldous Huxley's prophecy of a 'brave new world', with its alpha and epsilon classes, by achieving a paradigm shift in popular attitudes towards intelligence and education. But time is short. John F. Kennedy used to tell the story of how the French Marshal Lyautey once instructed his gardener to plant a tree. 'But what's the hurry?' the man protested, 'that tree will not reach maturity for more than a century.' 'In that case,' replied the Marshal, 'do not delay another second. Plant it immediately.'

Start helping your child master mind skills with that same sense of urgency. There is not a moment to lose.

Bibliography

Albrecht, K., *Brain Power*, Englewood Cliffs, NJ: Prentice-Hall, Inc., 1980

Arnheim, R., *Visual Thinking*, Berkeley: University of California Press, 1969

Bagley, M. T. and Hess, K. K., *Two Hundred Ways of Using Imagery in the Classroom*, New York: Trillum Press, 1984

Baistow, T., *Fourth-Rate Estate*, London: Comedia, 1985

Beck, J., *How to Raise a Brighter Child*, 2nd edn, London: Souvenir Press, 1986

Brod, C., *Technostress*, Reading, Mass.: Addison-Wesley Publishing Co., 1984

Burley-Allen, M., *Listening: The Forgotten Skill*, New York: John Wiley & Sons Ltd, 1982

Campbell, D. G., *Introduction to the Musical Brain*, Magnamusic Baton, Inc., 1984

Copple, C., Sigel, I. E. and Saunders, R., *Educating the Young Thinker*, Hillsdale, NJ: Lawrence Erlbaum Associates, 1984

Costa, A., *Developing Minds*, Alexandria, Virginia: Association for Supervision and Curriculum Development, 1985

De Bono, E., *Teaching Thinking*, Harmondsworth: Penguin Books, 1982

Deken, J., *The Electronic Cottage*, New York: William Morrow & Co., 1981

Dewey, J., *Lectures in the Philosophy of Education*, New York: Random House, 1968

Eberle, R., *Visual Thinking*, East Aurora, NY: D.O.K., 1982

Edwards, B., *Drawing on the Right Side of the Brain*, London: Souvenir Press, 1979

Ferguson, M., *The Aquarian Conspiracy*, London: Routledge & Kegan Paul, 1982

Feuerstein, R., *Instrumental Enrichment*, Baltimore: University Park Press, 1983

Greene, J. and Lewis, D., *Know Your Own Mind*, New York: Rawson Associates, 1983

Holt, J., *Teach Your Own*, Brightlingsea, Essex: Lighthouse Books, 1981

Howell, D., *Blind Victory: A Study in Income, Wealth and Power*, London: Hamish Hamilton, 1986

Illich, I., *Deschooling Society*, London: Marion Boyars, 1971

Lewis D., *The Secret Language of Your Child*, London: Souvenir Press, 1978

– *How To Be a Gifted Parent*, London: Souvenir Press, 1979

– *You Can Teach Your Child Intelligence*, London: Souvenir Press, 1981

– *Loving and Loathing: The Enigma of Personal Attraction*, London: Constable, 1985

– and Greene, J., *Thinking Better*, New York: Holt, Rinehart & Winston, 1982

Machado, L. A., *The Right To Be Intelligent*, Oxford: Pergamon Press, 1980

Matterson, E. M., *Play with a Purpose for the Under-Fives*, Harmondsworth: Penguin Books, 1977

McCarthy, B., *The 4-Mat System*, Illinois: Excel Inc., 1980

McGee-Cooper, A., *Building Brain Power*, Dallas: Ann McGee-Cooper, 1982

McLuhan, M., *Understanding Media: The Extensions of Man*, London: Routledge & Kegan Paul, 1964

Mead, Margaret, 'Thinking Ahead: Why is Education Obsolete?', *Harvard Business Review* XXXVI (1958)

Merritt, G., *World Out Of Work*, London: Collins, 1982

Mullen, F. and Chaffee, J., *Checkpoint 83*, Denver, Colo.: Urban Ed. 2000 Study Group, 1986

Naisbitt, J., *Megatrends*, London: MacDonald and Co., 1984

Nickerson, R. S., Perkins, D. N. and Smith, E. E., *The Teaching of Thinking*, Hillsdale, NJ: Lawrence Erlba, 1985

Novak, J. D. and Gowin D. R., *Learning How To Learn*, Cambridge: Cambridge University Press, 1985

Oech, R. Von, *A Kick in the Seat of the Pants*, New York: Harper & Row, 1986

Radford, J. and Burton, A., *Thinking: Its Nature and Development*, Chichester: John Wiley & Sons, 1974

Ruggiero, V. R., *The Art of Thinking*, New York: Harper & Row, 1984

Schaefer, C. E. and Millman, H. L., *Therapies for Children*, San Francisco: Jossey-Bass, 1977

Silberman, C. E., *Crisis in the Classroom*, New York: Random House, 1971

Sternberg, R. J., *Beyond IQ*, Cambridge: Cambridge University Press, 1985

Stonier, T., *The Wealth of Information*, London: Methuen, 1983

Stott, D. H., *The Parent As Teacher*, London: University of London Press, 1972

Tyler, L. E., *Thinking Creatively*, San Francisco: Jossey-Bass, 1983

Vernon, P. E., *Creativity*, Harmondsworth: Penguin Books, 1970

Waddington, C. H., *Tools for Thought*, London: Jonathan Cape, 1977

Whimbey, A. and Lochhead, J., *Beyond Problem-Solving and Comprehension*, Philadelphia: Franklin Institute Press, 1984

Wonder, J. and Donovan, P., *Whole Brain Thinking*, New York: William Morrow & Co., 1984

Index

History – now available in Grafton Books

Frederick Engels
The Condition of the Working Class in England   £1.95 ☐

Field Marshal Lord Carver
The Seven Ages of the British Army (illustrated)   £4.95 ☐

Christopher Farman
The General Strike (illustrated)   £1.95 ☐

Sir Arthur Bryant
Samuel Pepys: The Man in the Making   £3.95 ☐
Samuel Pepys: The Years of Peril   £3.95 ☐
Samuel Pepys: Saviour of the Navy   £3.95 ☐

Larry Collins and Dominique Lapierre
Freedom at Midnight (illustrated)   £3.95 ☐
O Jerusalem (illustrated)   £3.95 ☐

Angus Calder
The People's War (illustrated)   £3.95 ☐

Thomas Pakenham
The Year of Liberty   £1.95 ☐

Antony Bridge
The Crusaders (illustrated)   £3.95 ☐

Joyce Marlow
The Tolpuddle Martyrs (illustrated)   £2.95 ☐

John Erickson
The Road to Stalingrad (illustrated)   £6.95 ☐
The Road to Berlin   £8.95 ☐

Robert Fisk
In Time of War (illustrated)   £4.95 ☐

To order direct from the publisher just tick the titles you want
and fill in the order form.   **GM781**

Modern society – now available in Grafton Books

Dougal Dixon
After Man (illustrated)   £4.95 ☐

Germaine Greer
The Female Eunuch   £3.95 ☐

John Howard Griffin
Black Like Me   £1.95 ☐

Peter Laurie
Beneath the City Streets   £2.50 ☐

Desmond Morris
The Pocket Guide to Manwatching (illustrated)   £5.95 ☐
Manwatching (illustrated)   £8.95 ☐
The Naked Ape   £2.95 ☐
Intimate Behaviour   £2.95 ☐
The Human Zoo   £2.50 ☐
Animal Days (autobiography)   £1.95 ☐
Gestures (illustrated)   £3.95 ☐

José Silva and Michael Miele
The Silva Mind Control Method   £2.95 ☐

Ivan Tyrell
The Survival Option (illustrated)   £2.50 ☐

Michael Binyon
Life in Russia   £2.95 ☐

To order direct from the publisher just tick the titles you want
and fill in the order form.   **GM881**

All these books are available at your local bookshop or newsagent, or can be ordered direct from the publisher.

To order direct from the publishers just tick the titles you want and fill in the form below.

Name _____

Address _____

_____

Send to:
Grafton Cash Sales
PO Box 11, Falmouth, Cornwall TR10 9EN.

Please enclose remittance to the value of the cover price plus:

UK 60p for the first book, 25p for the second book plus 15p per copy for each additional book ordered to a maximum charge of £1.90.

BFPO 60p for the first book, 25p for the second book plus 15p per copy for the next 7 books, thereafter 9p per book.

Overseas including Eire £1.25 for the first book, 75p for second book and 28p for each additional book.

_____

Grafton Books reserve the right to show new retail prices on covers, which may differ from those previously advertised in the text or elsewhere.

By the same author

David Lewis obtained his Ph.D. in Psychology from the University of Sussex. On the subject of child psychology and development he has published a number of highly successful books, including *The Secret Language of Your Child*, *How to Be a Gifted Parent* and *You Can Teach Your Child Intelligence*. With James Greene he has written *The Hidden Language of Your Handwriting*, on the scientifically based analysis of character through handwriting.